This new textbook _____ nally
clear and concise _____ ocial
science. It examine: _____ nen-
tal philosophical is _____ conceived of as systen _____ of
meanings and prac _____ as
rational behaviour, _____ ing
such questions, the r_____ upon the nature of
scientific method in social science. Is the aim to explain
the social world after a manner worked out for the natural
world, or to understand the social world from within?

This interdisciplinary text shows why philosophical thinking is vital in the social sciences. Martin Hollis illustrates the
point by connecting, for example, problems of reasons for
action, personal identity and Other Minds, with those of
Game Theory, role-playing and Other Cultures. Written
in Martin Hollis' characteristically clear and incisive prose,
it will appeal to philosophers and social scientists alike as an
outstanding introduction to the subject.

Martin Hollis is Professor of Philosophy at the School of
Economic and Social Studies at the University of East
Anglia, Norwich, and a Fellow of the British Academy.

THE PHILOSOPHY OF SOCIAL
SCIENCE

THE PHILOSOPHY OF SOCIAL SCIENCE

An introduction

MARTIN HOLLIS

Professor of Philosophy at the School of Economic and Social Studies
University of East Anglia, Norwich

CAMBRIDGE
UNIVERSITY PRESS

PUBLISHED BY THE PRESS SYNDICATE OF THE UNIVERSITY OF CAMBRIDGE
The Pitt Building, Trumpington Street, Cambridge, United Kingdom

CAMBRIDGE UNIVERSITY PRESS
The Edinburgh Building, Cambridge CB2 2RU, UK
40 West 20th Street, New York, NY 10011–4211, USA
10 Stamford Road, Oakleigh, VIC 3166, Australia
Ruiz de Alarcón 13, 28014 Madrid, Spain
Dock House, The Waterfront, Cape Town 8001, South Africa

http://www.cambridge.org

© Cambridge University Press 1994

First published 1994
Reprinted 1995, 1996, 1997, 1999, 2000

Printed in the United Kingdom at the University Press, Cambridge

A catalogue record for this book is available from the British Library

Library of Congress Cataloguing in Publication data
Hollis, Martin.
The philosophy of social science: an introduction / Martin Hollis
p.   cm.
Includes bibliographical references and index.
ISBN 0 521 44264 8. (hardback) – ISBN 0 521 44780 1 (paperback)
1. Social sciences–Philosophy.   I. Title.
H61.H665   1994
300′.1–dc20   93-47234   CIP

ISBN 0 521 44264 8 hardback
ISBN 0 521 44780 1 paperback

Contents

Preface

The sharing of ideas among philosophers and social scientists is a fertile process for all and this book seeks to spread the habit. Since it comes from a university where philosophy has its home among the social sciences and collaboration is a pleasure, I have many debts, not least to scores of students who have helped in the making of connections. The organising strategy of crossing a question about explanation and understanding with one about holism and individualism was first worked out with Steve Smith, when we were writing *Explaining and Understanding International Relations* (1990). Credit for all references to international relations in the present book goes firmly to him, along with thanks for helpful comments on an earlier draft. The forays into economics owe most to Shaun Hargreaves Heap and the articles which we have written together. He too commented helpfully on the earlier draft. My grasp of economics has also been improved by working with him and Robert Sugden on the foundations of Game Theory and on *The Theory of Choice* (1992). We have also combined in teaching the interdisciplinary Philosophy, Politics and Economics programme. Its Politics contributors include John Street, another genial provider of helpful comments. Other influences include my fellow philosophers, notably Timothy O'Hagan and Angus Ross who share my interest in several of the topics. From further afield, Bill Jordan has helped with his comments and widened my horizons by ranging across the social sciences without regard for boundaries. Other improvements are due to Geoffrey Hawthorn, John Skorupski and an anonymous American reader for the Cambridge University Press. The book's many other debts are less specific; but it would be churlish to end the list without confessing the influence of Quentin Skinner on its themes.

MARTIN HOLLIS

University of East Anglia
Norwich

CHAPTER 1

Introduction: problems of Structure and Action

The 1980s ended with the collapse of communist regimes throughout Eastern Europe. It has become hard to remember how impossible that had seemed. One great certainty of the world since 1945 was that communist and capitalist systems were both here to stay, with the Soviet Union and America as the two poles of a permanently bi-polar international order. Suddenly one pole was disintegrating. I recall switching the television on each morning with gaping disbelief, as governments fell one after another until the Soviet Union stood alone. Then the utterly impossible happened and there was no longer a Union of Soviet Socialist Republics.

Experts were as confounded as amateurs and fought unusually shy of explaining why these events were only to be expected. Brasher pundits who rushed to claim omniscience were received with amusement. The wry mood of Muscovites at the time is nicely caught by a Russian cartoon which I keep on my wall. It shows a tattered Marx, Engels and Lenin seated on a Moscow kerbstone with hats held out for kopecks. Marx is saying to the others, 'But the theory remains true!' At a lofty enough level of abstraction, of course, he could be right. There are ways of reading his work which imply that the Russian revolution in 1917 did not satisfy the conditions for the dictatorship of the proletariat, that the USSR was never socialist and that Soviet hegemony in Eastern Europe after 1945 was a further aberration. If the theory has never been tested, its truth is unimpugned. Equally, theorists who believe in bi-polarity can still contend that one pole has merely been vacated until occupied by a new power, perhaps China. But anyone open to astonishment will be more inclined

1

to suspect that, when the previous certainties exploded, some eminent structural theories went with them.

On the other hand, the fall of governments was not due simply to the action of a few heroic individuals calling the bluff of ramshackle organisations. Nor is it enough to add the massed thousands of more ordinary individuals to make up the weight which toppled the system. The story has to include social groups coming together to exert powers implicit in existing social networks. We can wonder which of the emergent pressures – nationalism? market forces? religion? – will prove to have been crucial throughout; but we cannot plausibly suppose that all previous structures were destroyed by pure action, rather as a boat is sunk by too many passengers climbing aboard. New regimes have replaced the old ones and, under the surface, old power groups have adapted and survived. So, even if some structural theories have bitten the dust, there is still a need to think about structures. Questions of structure and action have become more urgent and exciting, with the frisson felt even by philosophers, and they have only been made harder by seeing what action can do. Abrupt reminders that social order is fragile call for renewed thought about collective freedom and the cement of social life.

A spectacle of falling governments may seem too sensational an opening for a philosophical book. But I want to suggest from the start that the philosophy of social science cannot breathe in a conceptual vacuum. Although front line social science is for social scientists, they cannot advance without theorising and so, at least some of the time, without thinking philosophically. Conversely, philosophers, I shall maintain, cannot claim the ear of social scientists without being inquisitive. Boundaries are porous, more so than for the philosophy of natural science, especially when we come to discuss the understanding of social action. Meanwhile a spectacle of falling governments also serves as an image for dramatic, if slower, changes in the philosophical firmament. I was brought up with a clear idea of the proper tasks of philosophy and of its relation to an equally clear idea of what science was about. These ideas were supposed to combine without trouble, when it came to social science. In fact trouble was already brewing on all fronts, as I realised later, but its effects have been felt unevenly and they are not always evident in social science textbooks which deal with method. Even where they have permeated, one still needs to understand the old picture in order to make sense of the new or, indeed, to resist it. I shall therefore begin with an unfashionable account of human reason and the nature of science. It carries no presumption that what is unfashionable must be mistaken.

THE ENLIGHTENMENT PROJECT

The schoolroom image of modern science is one of unprejudiced Reason exploring an independent realm of nature. Nature is independent, in the sense that it is as it is, whether or not human beings observe it, bring theories to bear on it or interpret it in one way rather than another. Reason is (or can and should be) unprejudiced in the sense that science eschews superstition, traditional authority, ideology and, in a word, prejudgements and relies solely on what it has learnt from nature itself. I call it a schoolroom image because this book would not be needed, if it were simply true. But it catches a core element in the familiar idea of what marks the transition from previous eras to the modern world, modern mind and modern science. It is also a noble image which retains great influence, despite the challenge of 'post-modern' doubts.

The noble story of modernity and the progress of Reason goes something like this. Some five centuries ago scientists began to realise that traditional beliefs about the cosmos were mistaken in more than detail. New discoveries, aided by new instruments, were making nonsense of the cosmos which the church had constructed by blending the Bible with a suitable reading of ancient texts, especially Aristotle. The telescope and the microscope were starting to reveal an ordered world which, in effect, had no business to be there. By the mid-seventeenth century it was clear to open-minded philosophers and scientists that the heavens, explored by telescope, were not remotely as described in the old account which fixed the earth at their centre. It was becoming clear that, seen through the microscope, everyday matter, organic and inorganic, was composed of elements infinitely smaller and more variously structured than the Bible and Aristotelian science even hinted. This new world worked rationally but not by the principles traditionally supposed. To discern its structures and its hidden order a new scientific method was needed. The scientific revolution had a revolution in method at its core.

Call the method Reason and think of it as a light by which science can see into darkness. The light shines on nature and drives out two kinds of ignorance. One concerns matters of fact. The contemporary world had yet to be fully explored. It was rumoured to contain dragons, for instance. But were there really such creatures? If not now, then had there been any at other places and times? Such questions are empirical and to be settled by the test of experience. But human minds are finite and their direct experience extends only to a small stretch of space and time. So the light of Reason must supply a method for making inferences from what we already know to what we are justified in believing about the unknown. The other kind of ignorance concerns the idea that the inner workings of nature are hidden from the five senses. We can never see, hear, touch, taste or smell the structures, laws and forces which constitute the natural order. Newton saw apples fall with his eyes but the force and law of gravity are not to be perceived. Here the light of Reason illuminates in a deeper but more mysterious way. It lets the mind escape the confines of the senses – an idea which will give us trouble presently, especially if inferences from experience turn out to depend on knowing the principles of the hidden order, as seventeenth-century thinkers maintained.

Images of light penetrating darkness were often used by the scientific pioneers themselves. 'The Age of Enlightenment' was the eighteenth century's own name for its own progress in extending the scope of science. It refers also to a fresh direction of enquiry. If light could be cast on nature by a rational method which revealed a rational order, it could also be shed on human nature and human society. This new field of exploration offered a new kind of progress: if the human world turned out to be less well ordered than the rest of nature, science could show how to order it better. Impulses which make for conflict could be tamed and cooperative sentiments could be cultivated. With the aid of Reason, social harmony could be achieved. For, as Helvetius remarked in a memorable flush of Enlightenment optimism, 'Ethics is the agriculture of the mind'.

This whole grand attempt to discover all nature's secrets, including those of humanity, has become known as 'the Enlightenment project'. The schoolroom story opens with the progress of Reason in discovering and exploring the modern physical world. Then it adds the growth of the social sciences in the eighteenth century, as the light is turned on the enquiring mind itself and on the nature of society. The Enlightenment project is still with us and still shapes the assumptions which social scientists bring to their task. At the same time, however, it has run into serious trouble throughout the sciences and their philosophy. The trouble is especially urgent in the social sciences, where there have been special doubts about the project from the start. The broadest aim of this book is to reflect on the ambitions of Reason and to ask whether they need recasting in ways peculiar to the social sciences.

STRUCTURE AND ACTION

I have opened in this reflective vein to give warning that the realm of ideas is currently as unsettled as the map of nations. We shall return to the wider topic at the end of the chapter. Meanwhile political disturbances give rise to theoretical questions and this next section of the chapter introduces a general problem of structure and action. Political change can be analysed in two directions. One attempts to account for the action by reference to movement in an encompassing social structure and thus proceeds, so to speak, 'top down'. The other takes the actions of individuals to be the stuff of history and regards structures as the outcome of previous actions. Here the direction is 'bottom up'. We shall contrast these approaches with the aid of a robust example of each, noting that it is not obvious whether they are finally in radical conflict or can be got to complement one another. There follows a brief comment on the notion of causal explanation and what, if anything, it implies about human freedom. This will lead on to a preliminary suggestion that social action needs to be understood 'from within', rather than explained after the manner of natural science. At this stage, however, the suggestion will serve only to make sense of the plan of the book.

Do governments fall because of structural pressures or are they pushed by individuals acting in concert? More abstractly, does structure determine action or action determine structure? Or is it a bit of both? There is no sensible answer to questions as compressed as these but we must start somewhere. So, to put flesh on the idea of 'top down', here is the famous and uncompromising line taken by Karl Marx in his Preface to *A Contribution to the Critique of Political Economy* (1859):

> In the social production of their life, men enter into definite relations that are indispensable and independent of their will, relations of production which correspond to a definite stage of development of their material productive forces. The sum total of these relations of production constitutes the economic structure of society, the real foundation, on which rises a legal and political superstructure and to which correspond definite forms of social consciousness. The mode of production of material life conditions the social, political and intellectual life process in general. It is not the consciousness of men that determines their being, but, on the contrary, their social being that determines their consciousness.

Here individuals are puppets, controlled from offstage by the interplay of forces and relations of production. Societies have a 'real foundation' and a 'superstructure'. The puppets have a consciousness of what they are doing, but a false one derived from the superstructure and generated from deeper down. They may think in terms of laws made by parliaments whose members choose what they believe to be right, and of themselves as individuals who create their legal and political system. But these beliefs are distortions which serve to mask the reality and aid the working of the hidden forces.

Why, then, do governments fall? The Preface continues:

> At a certain stage of their development, the material productive forces of society come in conflict with the existing relations of production, or – what is but a legal expression for the same thing – with the property relations within which they have been at work hitherto. From forms of

development of the productive forces these relations turn into their fetters. Then begins an epoch of social revolution. With the change of the economic foundation the entire immense superstructure is more or less rapidly transformed.

Without stopping to trace the complex theory hinted at, we can note that revolutions are caused by conflict between the forces and relations of production deep in the real foundation. Structures evolve independently of actions which they generate and, since few actors are even aware of them, scientific explanations of change go deeper than the actors' own.

In considering such transformations a distinction should always be made between the material transformation of the economic conditions of production, which can be determined with the precision of natural science, and the legal, political, religious, aesthetic or philosophic – in short, ideological forms in which men become conscious of this conflict and fight it out. Just as our opinion of an individual is not based on what he thinks of himself, so can we not judge of such a period of transformation by its own consciousness; on the contrary, this consciousness must be explained rather from the contradictions of material life, from the existing conflict between the social productive forces and the relations of production.

How then does the spectator manage to see more of the game than the players? The Preface only hints at an answer to this crucial question. It hints of clues to be found by studying the 'ideological forms in which men become conscious of this conflict and fight it out', and it claims that, somehow, the ultimate causes, which lie in 'the contradictions of material life', can be identified 'with the precision of natural science'. Whatever the method involved, it cannot be an empiricist one of submitting humbly to the test of experience, since it leads to sweeping conclusions, like that in the next sentence:

No social order ever perishes before all the productive forces for which there is room in it have developed; and the new, higher relations of production never appear before the material conditions of their existence have matured in the womb of the old society itself.

The passages just cited, which are continuous, set a pithy agenda. Marx himself was not wedded to the line taken in them. Elsewhere he declared, for instance, that 'Men make their own history', although adding, 'but they do not make it just as they please; they do not make it under conditions chosen by themselves' (1852, 2nd paragraph). When his works are read together, they allow much more scope for action and actors than the Preface does. But, taken in isolation, the lapidary statements quoted will do splendidly for purposes of this chapter.

They make three different sorts of claim, which it is worth distinguishing here for future reference. The first falls under the heading of *ontology* or what there is (from the Greek word for 'being') and embodies Marx's substantive view of the world and its workings. The Preface speaks of relations and forces of production, of the economic structure of society and of its legal and political superstructure. It refers to conflicts and contradictions which bring about transformations. It identifies a causal direction, which gives 'the real foundation' priority over 'the legal, political, religious, aesthetic or philosophic – in short ideological forms' in which men become conscious of underlying conflicts. These hidden elements and relations are presented as the reality of the social world. They determine the actors' consciousness and, presumably, their actions. This reality belongs to the independent realm which science explores, external to consciousness and prior to beliefs about it. Such an ontology, which includes the social world in the natural order, is termed naturalistic.

The second sort of claim falls under the heading of *methodology*. If the social world works as described, then a scientific method is needed which can identify the reality, missed or distorted in the actors' awareness, and can lead to causal explanations. Mention of 'the precision of natural science' makes it clear that Marx, in emphasising material conditions and material productive forces, commits himself to a unitary scientific method and a single notion of explanation, which serve for all sciences. The exact method and notion are not specified here but, since they are to identify hidden structures which determine ideological forms and hence the actors' self-awareness, both will be contentious. Meanwhile, since the method is to be modelled on the natural sciences, we can dub it naturalistic too.

Thirdly, then, implicit claims are being made in *epistemology* or the theory of knowledge (for which the Greek word is *episteme*). 'It is not the consciousness of men that determines their being, but, on the contrary, their social being that determines their consciousness.' How then can Marx or anyone else know the reality of the social world? How can social scientists escape the ideological forms which distort the gaze of all human beings including social scientists? Such awkward questions fall into two groups. One group is entirely general and calls for an account of how we know anything about the world. Traditionally such an account or 'theory of knowledge' starts by defining 'knowledge', for instance as 'justified, true belief', finds a class of facts which are beyond doubt, for instance facts of observation, and shows how we can justifiably build on these foundations. But it is far from clear that knowledge of hidden structures can be had in this way; and, besides, many recent epistemologists have radical objections to the traditional approach, as we shall see. Meanwhile, there is a second group, consisting of particular questions raised in making human consciousness and human action the subject of science. Does our knowledge of ourselves, our thoughts and actions, have the same character as our knowledge of the terrain at our feet and the material world about us? The players' understanding of the games of social life may turn out to be radically unlike the knowledge involved in the natural scientist's explanations of the natural world.

Having drawn these distinctions, we can return to the initial question. Does structure determine action or does action determine structure? The Preface comes down squarely on the side of structure as the determinant. So let us next try out an equally robust but opposite answer. John Stuart Mill is best known for his essay *On Liberty* (1859), a glorious defence of individual freedom against all political and social encroachments, on the grounds that 'the only freedom which deserves the name is that of pursuing our own good in our own way'. *On Liberty* speaks for liberalism, a form of consciousness which Marx's Preface assigns to the superstructure and accounts for in structural terms. Mill will have none of that. In an open society where individuality flourishes progress comes through critical thinking and rational persuasion. This liberal vision is present in all his many works and goes with a denial that there are any such social forces as Marx alleged.

In *A System of Logic* (1843) Mill offers 'a connected view of the principles of evidence and the methods of scientific investigation', to quote the subtitle. This powerful work is divided into six books, which together still provide the best general rationale for what I shall call Positive science, especially as that term is used by social scientists. The first five books address the deductive and inductive logic of the sciences at large, with the natural sciences chiefly in mind. Book VI is titled 'On the Logic of the Moral Sciences' and turns to psychology and the social sciences, where it indeed takes 'a connected view'. Chapter 7 of Book VI opens with this ringing declaration:

The laws of the phenomena of society are, and can be, nothing but the laws of the actions and passions of human beings united together in the social state. Men, however, in a state of society, are still men; their actions and passions are obedient to the laws of individual human nature. Men are not, when brought together, converted into another kind of substance, with different properties; as hydrogen and oxygen are different from water, or as hydrogen, oxygen, carbon, and azote, are different from nerves, muscles, and tendons. Human beings in society have no properties but those which are derived from, and may be resolved into, the laws of nature of individual man.

Social science, in Mill's view, must be grounded in 'the laws of nature of individual man' because it has as subject matter only 'the actions and passions of human beings united together in the social state'. These actions and passions are 'obedient to the laws of individual human nature', however, and the logic of the moral sciences is one which lets us identify these laws. They comprise 'the laws of mind' (Chapter 4) and 'laws of the formation of character' (Chapter 5). Granted this much, Chapter 6 is in no doubt about the prospects for a social science erected on them:

All phenomena of society are phenomena of human nature, generated by the action of outward circumstances upon masses of human beings: and if, therefore, the phenomena of human thought, feeling and action are subject to fixed laws, the phenomena of society cannot but conform to fixed laws, the consequence of the preceding.

To find these laws is 'the object of the Social Science'. Once we have them we shall be able to explain and predict the whole history of society, even though we shall not know enough 'for thousands of years to come'.

Comparison with Marx's Preface is instructive. Let us use the same three headings. The *ontology* is sharply different. The whole apparatus of a real foundation of economic forces and relations is simply absent. Instead there are only individuals, their passions and actions, and, more vaguely, individual human nature governed by laws of mind and character-formation. The *methodology* is only somewhat different, however. Both thinkers hold that explanation proceeds by identifying causal laws and the conditions in which they operate. But Marx needs a way of penetrating the conscious superstructure to a deeper level in search of mechanisms which determine consciousness. Mill, untroubled by a belief in such hidden dynamics, is content to trace regularities in human behaviour to their source in human nature. This difference makes for sharp dissent about the strategy of explanation. Mill holds that the properties of human beings in society 'are derived from, and may be resolved into, the laws of nature of individual man'. Marx holds that consciousness must be explained 'from the contradictions of material life'. Such questions of strategy will concern us presently. Meanwhile the overall similarity is notable. Both thinkers espouse a naturalism implying a single logic of explanation for all sciences. Mill, although doubting whether what Marx calls 'the precision of natural science' is attainable, says clearly in Chapter 3 of Book VI that:

the science of Human Nature may be said to exist, in proportion as the approximate truths, which comprise a practical knowledge of mankind, can be exhibited as corollaries from the universal laws of human nature on which they rest.

Their different strategies of explanation – one from structure to action, the other from action to structure – are also connected to a difference in *epistemology*. As we shall see, Mill belongs squarely to an empiricist tradition which confines knowledge of the world to beliefs which observation can justify. This would make nonsense of the Preface's ambitions for social science. It is not the only rival tradition or theory of knowledge within the naturalist camp, however, although I shall leave the alternatives to the next few chapters. Any scientific theory which deals in hidden structures owes us an account of how we can know of such determinants.

DETERMINISM

The contrasts just drawn between Marx and Mill threaten to cause confusion over the vexed question of free will and determinism. It is often asked whether the social sciences increase human freedom or destroy the illusion that we have any. The Preface sounds very definite (whatever Marx may say elsewhere about men making their own history). 'It is not the consciousness of men that determines their being, but, on the contrary, their social being that determines their consciousness.' Is social science at large committed to a denial that people make choices (even if not under conditions chosen by themselves)? Well, the Preface denies it in a quite specific way by setting up an ontology of economic and social forces which shape the actors' consciousness and cause their actions. So it sounds as if Mill, by refusing any truck with such structures and forces, can readily argue that the social sciences actively help us to pursue our own good in our own way.

On the other hand Mill bases social science on the claim that 'the phenomena of human thought, feeling and action are subject to fixed laws'. How can there be freedom to pursue our own good in our own way, if all actions are the result of outward circumstances on human beings who obey universal laws of human nature? Perhaps, then, the threat of determinism arises from the idea that there are laws of any scientific kind, which govern our actions. If so, believers in human freedom may need to find a method peculiar to the social sciences, which offers more ways to explain action than by reference to causal laws. Mill, however, says exactly the opposite. It will save confusion later if we next define 'determinism' and then see how he untangles the topic.

Determinism, in the first instance and defined loosely, is the thesis that there is a complete causal order in nature: every event or state has a cause. What exactly does that mean? Answers vary, depending on whether they mention 'laws of nature' and whether they attribute 'necessity' to the relations between cause and effect. In Newtonian mechanics and physics there are absolute laws of nature, holding universally and necessarily in all places and times, and forces which drive the natural world irresistibly. Nature is a 'determined' system in a very strong sense, which sets acute problems for anyone who supposes that humans sometimes choose what will happen next.

Even so, it is not obvious that human freedom is thereby ruled out. If we think of freedom as the ability to do what we want, then, even in a complete causal order where everything happens of necessity, we can sometimes behave in ways which achieve what we want. In the words of Thomas Hobbes, whom we shall meet later, 'water hath both the liberty and the necessity of descending the channel' (1651, Ch.21). Since the will is not an act of volition but 'the last appetite in deliberating', we act freely whenever what happens next suits the last appetite which preceded it. He thus maintains that there is no conflict whatever between freedom and determinism. Another famous line tried by thorough determinists turns on the idea that freedom is, at bottom, consciousness of necessity, or an acceptance of what happens which stems from understanding why things could not be otherwise.

The topic is therefore slippery. But most thinkers who mean to leave scope for human choice have not been determinists in so strong a sense. Yet scientists seem broadly committed to some kind of determinism. This is not obvious, because many of them hold that there is either a random element in nature or an indeterminacy about what we can know of nature even in principle. That might sound like a denial of determinism which creates scope for free action. But Mill spotted that when we speak of free action we do not mean action at random or action whose explanation is beyond our ken. He was content to accept that actions may be wholly caused and wholly predictable. Yet he unswervingly maintained that free action is possible, arguing not only that freedom and determinism are compatible but also that freedom presupposes causal order.

How is this remarkable trick worked? Mill performs it in *A System of Logic* Book VI Chapter 2 titled 'Of Liberty and Necessity'.

Correctly conceived, the doctrine called Philosophical Necessity is simply this: that, given the motives which are present to an individual's mind, and given likewise the character and disposition of the individual, the manner in which he will act might be unerringly inferred: that if we know the person thoroughly, and know all the inducements which are acting upon him, we could foretell his conduct with as much certainty as we can predict any physical event.

He then points out that 'we do not feel ourselves the less free, because those to whom we are intimately known are well assured how we will act in a particular case'. Seeing nothing to fear from determinism, therefore, he goes on to argue that, although an individual always acts from a character which has been formed by circumstances, 'his own desire to mould it in a particular way is one of those circumstances, and by no means one of the least influential'. For 'we are exactly as capable of making our own character as others are of making it for us'.

Mill's hope is that, if we replace the necessity in events which is contributed by thinking in terms of structure and forces, there is nothing to fear from the idea that human action is predictable. Indeed, the more predictable the world is, and the more science helps us to predict it, the better we can know how to achieve what we value. Is this a trick? Now is not the moment to ask. For the moment, the point to notice is that determinists can disagree about the analysis of causation. Mill is not alone among determinists in denying that causes compel or necessitate their effects. He holds that laws of nature are merely regularities which allow reliable predictions. Whether he is right about that and right in his view that freedom is thereby saved are questions which will crop up again.

Marx's Preface is more strongly determinist and I am not sure that there is a consistent line to be had from all his works taken together. Nor, I think, have leading Marxist thinkers been sure. On the one hand historical materialism, construed scientifically, seems to chart an inevitable development of the economic forces and relations of production which leaves no room for conscious human initiatives. On the other hand Marx issued a manifesto and the communist party has often assigned itself a vanguard role in speeding up history or even, as in the Russian or Chinese revolutions, of inspiring great leaps forward from feudalism to socialism. Intermittently at least, Marx, like Mill, thinks of scientific knowledge as a source of power to bring about change. Meanwhile I draw attention to the Preface for a further contrast with Mill in its idea of what is involved in causality. Its causal images are often images of specific mechanisms working in particular historical conditions. 'No social order ever perishes before all the productive forces for which there is room in it have developed.' This suggests that necessities are not – or not only – those of general and universal laws but also those of particular productive forces and their working. Here is another reason why we shall need to think further about the idea of causation.

A shared, naturalistic belief in the unity of science thus leaves room for three disputes. The first is an *ontological* one about structure and action, with Marx contending that action is determined by structure and Mill insisting that all phenomena of society arise from the actions and passions of human beings. The second is *methodological*, to do with the analysis of causal explanation. Is the key idea that of necessity or merely of regularity? Is it geared to the general, for instance to general laws of nature, or to the particular, for instance to specific mechanisms? The third is *epistemological*, with Mill upholding an empiricist view that knowledge is a matter of experience and Marx needing a theory which allows knowledge of an underlying reality. We shall pursue all three disputes later.

For the moment, however, let us take stock with the help of Figure 1.1. 'Holism' refers to any approach which accounts for individual agents (human or otherwise) by appeal to some larger whole. 'Individualism' refers to any version of the contrary approach, which accounts for structures by appeal to individual agents (human or otherwise). (The reason for writing 'Systems' rather than 'Structures' in the top left box will emerge presently.) If the Preface has the right idea, then explanation proceeds 'top down' by accounting for individual actions in 'holist' terms, i.e. by reference to the working of a system. If Mill has the right idea,

Explanation   Understanding

	Explanation	Understanding
Holism	Systems	
Individualism	Agents	

Figure 1.1

then 'individualism' prevails, with explanation proceeding 'bottom up' and systems making no independent contribution or even being 'resolved into' facts about individual agents. Anyone who holds that systems and individual agents must both feature in explanations of the social world is welcome to a position which cuts the dividing line. Compromises look entirely sensible, although they do set hard questions about how to combine their elements, as we shall see. Meanwhile, notice that there is a right-hand column marked 'Understanding'. This is the topic of the next section.

UNDERSTANDING

The central dispute between 'top down' and 'bottom up', as presented so far, is not peculiar to the social sciences. Nor are the questions of ontology, methodology and epistemology which accompany it. That is because Marx and Mill were both natur-alistic thinkers, who believed that, since human beings and socie-ties belong to the natural order, a single method, broadly defined, will serve for all sciences. There is a rival tradition, however, which has a profoundly different view of society, human life and social action. 'Understanding' promises a radical alternative to 'Explanation'.

The rival tradition aims at an 'interpretative' or 'hermeneutic' social science (from the Greek word *hermeneus*, an interpreter). Its central proposition is that the social world must be understood from within, rather than explained from without. Instead of seeking the causes of behaviour, we are to seek the meaning of action. Actions derive their meaning from the shared ideas and rules of social life, and are performed by actors who mean something by them. Meanings – a nimble and ambiguous word which will give us great trouble – range from what is consciously and individually intended to what is communally and often unintendedly significant. The interplay of these elements will provide the filling for the right-hand column of Figure 1.1.

This approach stems from reflections on the character of history, especially those of Hegel, and on the writing of history. I shall take my cue from a nineteenth-century German idealist thinker, Wilhelm Dilthey (1833–1911). Dilthey identified 'meaning' as 'the category which is peculiar to life and to the historical world'. Human life, he wrote, can be understood only by means of categories which do not apply to knowledge of the physical world, like 'purpose', 'value', 'development' and 'ideal' – aspects of 'meaning'. In contrast to individualists in this same tradition, Dilthey held that the connectedness of a life can be understood only through the meaning that individual parts have for understanding the whole. But 'the whole' is not external to humanity. 'Life does not mean anything other than itself. There is nothing in it which points to a meaning beyond it' (1926, vol. vii, p.224).

Although a proper introduction to 'Understanding' will be left to Chapter 7, I shall say just enough now to fill in Figure 1.1. In glossing 'Structure' as 'Systems' in the top left quadrant, I picked a term which applies readily to the natural world. Images of mechanical systems, like the sun and planets, electro-motors or clockwork spring to mind, as do organic images of beehives, termite colonies and the human body. In more abstract vein one also thinks of computer systems, information systems and number systems. Holists often draw such analogies in explaining how social systems work, and individualists refuse to believe them. For the corresponding dispute in the right-hand column we need to gloss 'Structure' in a different way. What analytical concept best catches the idea of social life as a fabric of meanings? Recall Marx's remark about 'the legal, political, religious, aesthetic or philosophic – in short ideological forms' in which men become conscious of underlying conflicts. These forms can all be thought of as structures of rules. There are legal rules in the sense both of laws and of legal practices. There are political rules – constitutions and political conventions. Religious rules define and regulate organised religions. Aesthetic rules delineate culture; and 'philosophic' rules could be said to encompass people's ethical beliefs and their shared ways of thinking generally about themselves, their world and their place in it.

Rules are not to be thought of only as entries in rule books. They are also embodied in social institutions and practices, thus more palpably forming a 'structure' than if considered abstractly. For the notion which best captures this thought, we shall borrow from recent philosophy. Ludwig Wittgenstein's *Philosophical Investigations* (1953) makes fertile use of the notion of a 'game' in discussing human action. The rules of a game not only regulate how it is played but, more importantly, define or constitute the game itself. People could have gone fishing before there were rules to regulate this activity; but they could not have played chess without rules. Moves in a game have meaning only within the rules, as, for instance, words have meaning only within a language and within practices of communication. Although the idea of social activities as 'games' will not become clear until later chapters, it carries just the intuitive suggestion wanted for the top right box. Part of what it suggests is that games are a human and social peculiarity and hence that Understanding may turn out to involve a denial of naturalism.

How do the institutions and practices of social life relate to the human actors who participate in them? A holistic answer would be to have the games absorb the players. If actors, at least in their social capacities, desire, believe and therefore do only what is socially expected of them, then they need no separate understanding. If, for instance, they are solely the bearers of social roles, which derive entirely from determinate social positions and dictate all that role-players do, then understanding can proceed as wholly 'top down' as a pure systems-theory would have explanation proceed. The presence of meaning would not make structures less constraining on this side of the house than on the other, even if meaning does not generate action as cause generates effect.

Conversely, however, a fully individualist approach would re-verse the direction and proceed 'bottom up'. If meanings are subjective first and intersubjective only by mutual accord, an opposite account of understanding is needed. The players con-struct the games of social life, perhaps in the spirit of the social contract often postulated to account for moral and political order. In the words of Jon Elster, a staunch individualist:

The elementary unit of social life is the individual human action. To explain social institutions and social change is to show how they arise as the result of the action and interaction of individuals. (1989(a), p.13)

More pithily still: 'There are no societies, only individuals who interact with one another' (1989(b), p.248). Accordingly let us write 'Actors' in the bottom right quadrant.

As when offered a stark choice between 'Systems' and 'Agents' earlier, readers will no doubt suggest a compromise. The rules of the game constrain the players but also enable them to pursue their own ends. The players make their own history, in part by creating their own rules, but they do not do it in conditions entirely of their own choosing. Action may presuppose structure and yet also shape it. As in the 'Explanation' column, there are options which straddle the dividing line, now bidding us furnish the social world with both games and actors so as to understand it from within with the aid of both. That seems entirely sensible and I remark only that we shall nonetheless find hard problems in the blending.

Completing the matrix gives Figure 1.2.

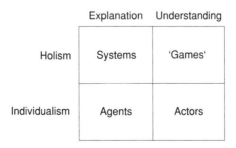

	Explanation	Understanding
Holism	Systems	'Games'
Individualism	Agents	Actors

Figure 1.2

If positions which straddle the horizontal dividing line are allowed, thus mixing 'top down' and 'bottom up', how about the vertical divide? The difference between 'Agents' and 'Actors' invites probing and that between 'Systems' and 'Games' does not look compelling either. Even if Explanation and Understanding turn out to be radically distinct, how about a bit of both? Well, for the moment, think of 'Agents' as individuals and 'Systems' as structures seen from a naturalistic perspective, and think of 'Actors' as individuals and 'Games' as structures seen from an interpretative one. When we have worked these perspectives out separately, we shall be ready to think about combining them. Meanwhile treat Figure 1.2 as a suggestive device for setting problems of structure and action, not as a direct source of answers.

THE PLAN OF THE BOOK

The book is organised accordingly, with Explanation and Understanding as its major theme and Holism and Individualism as its minor one. The next three chapters examine some leading accounts of Explanation and apply them to the social world. Chapter 2 opens in the seventeenth century with a classic question about the parts to be played by reason and experience in discovering how the world works. It explores rationalist hopes of detecting the causal order of nature, conceived as wheels and springs driving a mechanical system. Chapter 3 retorts with a classic empiricism and goes on to issue a manifesto for Positive science. Discussion then focuses on Milton Friedman's rubric for Positive economics. This makes good sense of 'the hypothetico-deductive method' but raises acute problems about the role of theory in science. Chapter 4 traces the trouble to a misplaced belief that knowledge needs 'foundations'. The suggestion that *all* claims to knowledge involve the interpretation of experience leads us, by way of Karl Popper, to pragmatism and then to fashionable thoughts about 'paradigms'. But, although several accounts of Explanation are by now on offer, none is so commanding that the social sciences can safely adopt it.

We next pause to factor in the 'vertical' dispute between Holism and Individualism. Chapter 5 tries out the 'Systems' of the top left box in Figure 1.2. It starts with an ambitious claim that social facts have 'functional' explanations, which reduce human agents to cyphers. But it presently falls back on the more modest idea that society is not a mere sum of individuals. Even this is disputed in Chapter 6, where the example picked to represent Individualism – the 'Agents' of the bottom left box – is the analysis of action proposed by Rational Choice theory and Game Theory. Since the latter has become almost a compulsory tool for social scientists, the bones of it are introduced in some detail and from scratch. But a deep problem about the analysis of social norms remains unresolved.

The 'vertical' dispute now shifts to the 'Understanding' column of Figure 1.2. Chapter 7 takes up the theme that Meaning is 'the category peculiar to life and to the historical world'. To focus it, however, we are soon attracted by Max Weber's approach to understanding social action and, in particular, his analysis of rationality. When this is contrasted with Wittgensteinian ideas about social actors as followers of rules and of action as a move in a game, we find ourselves in the top right box of Figure 1.2, with 'Games' radically unlike those played by the rational agents of Game Theory. Chapter 8 holds out for the individual 'Actors' of the bottom right box, who play the games of social life without being wholly absorbed. They can be glimpsed in the playing of social roles or, invoking an instructive analogy, in theatrical roles. Or can they? Hard questions about social identity become harder when we consider the philosophical problem of personal identity.

Chapter 9 resumes the main theme in the light of what has been learnt. Perhaps the earlier question about social norms can now be answered by combining a reworked *homo economicus* with a reworked *homo sociologicus*. That suggests a general reconciliation between Explanation and Understanding. But a happy ending is delayed by the suggestion that the social world is *constructed* from within in a way quite alien to the natural world. In that case the social sciences must rely on intersubjectivity, whereas the natural sciences have always aspired to objective knowledge.

Is Understanding then committed to some form of relativism, for good or ill? Chapter 10 makes this question the occasion for asking whether value-neutrality in the social sciences is possible or desirable. Weber is again pressed into service, this time to present the official view that, although the social sciences are bound to be 'value-relevant', they can and should be conducted in a way which is 'value-free'. But, the more we think about this line, the harder it becomes to keep to it. Chapter 11 therefore broadens the discussion. The Problem of Other Minds involves other forms of relativism, as becomes plain when we consider anthropologists seeking to understand other cultures. Possible limits to relativism are examined, in search of an escape from the notorious 'hermeneutic circle'.

The concluding chapter reflects on what we have found on this journey, which it is now time to begin.

CHAPTER 2

Discovering truth: the rationalist way

Sir Francis Bacon, often hailed as the father of modern scientific method, distinguished two ways of discovering truth. In his *First Book of Aphorisms*, published in 1620, he declared:

There are and can be only two ways of searching into and discovering truth. The one flies from the senses and particulars to the most general axioms, and from these principles, the truth of which it takes for settled and immovable, proceeds to judgement and the discovery of middle axioms. And this way is now in fashion. The other derives axioms from the senses and particulars, rising by a gradual and unbroken ascent, so that it arrives at the most general axioms last of all. This is the true way, but as yet untried.

The truth to be searched into was truth about nature, meaning the universe as God had created and furnished it. Both ways were ways of discovering the true order in nature by applying Reason scientifically. They differed sharply in their analysis of Reason and how to apply it, but they agreed on the project, that of constructing a new science based on absolutely certain truths. New ideas of Reason were accompanied by new ideas of nature and led to new ideas about human nature and society.

I start in the seventeenth century because that is when our modern intellectual world coalesced. The scientific revolution was already in full progress. In astronomy, for instance, telescopes wielded by Kepler and Galileo had long since smashed the crystal spheres, once believed to rotate around the earth. But it took some time for thinkers to realise that the new science was so systematically at odds with the old that nothing could be taken for granted. In the old story of heaven and earth everything had been found a meaning, purpose, reason, function and cause, so

23

that the story made sense on many levels together. In the new, as it gradually emerged, the universe was a mechanically ordered system, like a perfect watch. Science could discover the causes and functions of its parts without being concerned about the purpose or meaning of the whole. Admittedly the divorce between causes and meaning was not immediate. After all, a perfect watch is designed by a perfect watchmaker for a purpose. But the new notion of Reason did presently lead to this modern divorce.

The symbolic moment (with hindsight) was when René Descartes (1596–1650) marked 'the first knowledge' or certain starting point for his new philosophy, with the famous words *cogito ergo sum*, usually translated 'I think, therefore I am'. They come from his *Meditations on First Philosophy* published in 1641, where he set out to ground all knowledge in basic truths and principles accessible to a rational mind. If he cleared his mind of all preconceived ideas and of everything which he had come to accept on authority, could he be sure of anything? Yes, pure reflection guaranteed that at least one reflective mind existed, namely himself. It also guaranteed a self-evident principle – that anything self-evident is thereby true. Since 'first philosophy' included knowledge that God exists, no conflict between science and religion was intended. But, all the same, by removing the imprimatur of Reason from all traditional authorities and giving it to every reflective individual with an open mind, Descartes laid the ground for a secular science, which would be neutral on questions of meaning and value.

The 'moral' and social sciences did not take shape in earnest until the mid-eighteenth century. But, when they did, it was against a background of revolutionary scientific thinking about nature, crucial for how they have developed. In particular, naturalism is compelling, if, as La Mettrie put it in his instructively titled book *L'Homme Machine* (1747):

Man is not fashioned out of a more precious clay; Nature has used only one and the same dough, in which she has merely varied the leaven.

The mood was caught by this memorable question from Condorcet's (1795) *Sketch for a Historical Picture of Progress of the Human Mind*:

The sole foundation for belief in the natural sciences is this idea, that the general laws dictating the phenomena of the universe are necessary and constant. Why should this principle be any the less true for the development of the intellectual and moral faculties of man than for the other operations of nature? (1795, Xth Stage)

As Bacon suggests, however, there have long been deep disputes about the character of Reason and the proper method of science. The one which Bacon mentions is between those who start from 'the most general axioms', now known as rationalists, and those who start from 'the senses and particulars', now known as empiricists. Rationalism is no longer much in favour, but it remains important for its attempt to give theoretical reasoning the task of identifying hidden structures and laws, as this chapter will show. Empiricism has fared better of late and will be examined under the heading of Positive science in the next chapter. Crucially for both chapters, Bacon's two ways of searching into truth both presume that scientific knowledge can be found a settled and unmovable foundation of truths to build on. Both become vulnerable if there is no such foundation to be had – a more recent thought whose implications will occupy Chapter 4.

REASON IN SEARCH OF HIDDEN ORDER

Bacon's first way 'flies from the senses and particulars' and searches for 'the most general axioms'. This may seem perverse. Why not start in the obvious place, with perception and the experience of particular things given by the senses? The broadest answer is that the first way set out to reveal secrets of the natural order which lay beyond all powers of human observation. The scientific revolution brought with it a new vision of nature as a system of mass in motion driven by mechanical forces and governed by eternal laws. Sir Isaac Newton could see apples fall but he could not observe the force of gravity which he claimed to identify as the cause of their falling. Descartes claimed that space conforms to the analytical geometry now called Cartesian in his honour. He denied, however, that we know space to have these mathematical properties by sense experience. Instead, we know it because rational intuition guarantees the truth of some basic

axioms and whatever they entail. That calls for a theory of knowledge where the mind need not rely solely on the senses, since it
could not grasp the realities of the natural order if it did. This
remains one way for anyone who believes in unobservable forces
and structures to justify their claim to know of them. To bring it
alive, let us start with the new vision of nature at large, before
turning to social or psychological structures and forces.

In a popular seventeenth-century image the world is like a
watch. We tell the time by observing the face and hands but
that gives no clue to how it works. To discover why the hands
go round, we must prise the back off the watch and study the
springs and wheels. The springs harness forces to drive the wheels
which drive the hands in their turn. In this analogy, our five senses
are confined to the face of the watch and observation can do no
more than describe the movements of the hands. The springs and
wheels are hidden from the senses and we need another way of
knowing, if we are to learn about them.

This image turns up in, among other places, *The Plurality of
Worlds* (1686), a delightful book by Bernard de Fontenelle
(1657–1757) written to introduce general readers to those parts
of the new astronomy which were 'most Probable, Uniform and
Diverting'. Astronomy was chosen partly because it was the
source of amazing discoveries and partly because it lent itself to
novel mathematical ideas, like Descartes' analytical geometry,
and so illustrated the new philosophy. (The seventeenth century
drew no distinction between philosophy and science.) De
Fontenelle fervently admired Descartes and the book sets out to
show the merits of Cartesian ideas. It takes the form of a dialogue,
spread over five evenings, between a Philosopher and a Countess
who seeks enlightenment. The passages which follow are from the
'First Evening' in John Glanvill's enchanting (1688) translation.
They start with another popular analogy for scientific enquiry at
the time, that of going behind the scenes at the opera to discover
how the special effects are worked.

The Philosopher has just remarked that 'your true Philosopher
will not believe what he doth see and is always conjecturing at
what he doth not, which is a Life I think not much to be envied'.
He continues:

Upon this I fancy to myself that Nature very much resembleth an Opera, where you stand, you do not see the Stage as really it is; but it is plac'd with advantage, and all the Wheels and Movements are hid, to make the Representation the more agreeable. Nor do you trouble yourself how, or by what means the Machines are moved, though certainly an Engineer in the Pit is affected with what doth not touch you; he is pleas'd with the motion, and is demonstrating to himself on what it depends, and how it comes to pass. This Engineer then is like a Philosopher, though the difficulty is greater on the Philosopher's part, the Machines of the Theatre being nothing so curious as those of Nature, which disposeth her Wheels and Springs so out of sight, that we have been long a-guessing at the movement of the Universe.

The comparison with an opera was topical, because a new and splendid opera house had just been built at Versailles and was famed for its ingenuity backstage. This prompts the Philosopher to picture 'the Old Sages' sitting in the audience and trying to explain the mechanics of a scene where Phaeton, mounted in a chariot, is lifted high in the air by the winds. The Old Sages have various explanations. Some say that he is drawn up by 'a hidden Magnetick Vertue', others that he has 'a secret love for the top of the theatre' and a hundred such extravagant fancies. 'But then comes Monsieur Descartes with some of the moderns', who reveal that Phaeton rises on wires with the aid of a hidden counter-weight. Hence 'whoever will see Nature as really she is must stand behind the Scenes at the Opera'.

I perceive, said the Countess, Philosophy is now become very Mechanical.

So mechanical, said I, that I fear we shall quickly be asham'd of it; they will have the World to be in great, what a Watch is in little; which is very regular, and depends only upon the just disposing of the several parts of the movement. But pray tell me, Madam, had you not formerly a more sublime Idea of the Universe? Do you not think you did then honour it more than it deserv'd? For most have the less esteem of it since they have pretended to know it.

I am not of their opinion, said she, I value it more since I know it resembles a Watch, and the whole order of Nature the more plain and easy it is, to me it appears the more admirable.

These exchanges mark a definite break between an older scientific scheme which dealt in, for instance, 'Magnetic Vertues' and a modern one which 'has become very mechanical'. A key difference is that 'Vertue' involves ideas of purpose, meaning and proper function which belong to an older cosmology where everything had a part to play in the moral order of the cosmos. This is the blend of Aristotelian and Christian teaching which the scientific revolution was in process of destroying. Accordingly to become 'very mechanical' was to dispense with all but causal order, at any rate for purposes of science, so that scientific explanation could be cast wholly in terms of causes, effects and objective laws of nature connecting them. In particular the new scientific method required no direct reference to God's purpose in explaining how one state of the natural world leads to another.

This radical shift did not emerge all at once. Descartes himself maintained that an atheist could not be a successful scientist, because scientific knowledge depended on understanding nature as the creation of a God who decreed the kind of order displayed in it. The image of the watch is nicely poised between old and new. The movement of the hands is caused by the mechanism hidden behind the face and can be explained by prising the back off and tracing the wheels and springs. That is indeed 'very mechanical'. But the explanation is curiously blind if it fails to include the fact that a watch is intended to tell the time. The Countess finds the new order of nature 'the more admirable' because it shows how very elegantly the machinery of nature serves its purpose. A watch works by 'efficient causes' so as to serve its 'final cause', the purpose for which the watchmaker made it. This duality made for peace between the new science and religion and remained part of scientific thinking for at least another century.

All the same the decisive break had been made. The more detailed and complete the explanation of how a machine works, the less it matters why it exists. Each state of a perfect clockwork is the effect of the previous state and the cause of the next, given causal laws of its operation which can be formulated without mentioning purposes. If nature is a perfect clockwork then it runs forever in this utterly predetermined way and science can forget that God no doubt created it and wound it up in the beginning. It is as if God had said 'I declare this universe open' and then left it to itself. Questions of why the world exists increasingly became separate from questions of how it works, until atheists were no longer at an intellectual disadvantage in science.

Bacon's first way is thus a search for universal laws which hold with necessity. The vision is strongly determinist, with Reason set the task of reproducing an order of things where each event *must* occur as it does, given its cause and the inexorable laws of nature. A sharp challenge to belief in human free will is looming. Descartes himself hoped to avoid it by treating the mind or soul as an immaterial substance separate from the material world and so not governed by natural laws. The human body behaves mechanically; the mind remains free. But this famous dualism of mind and body was always precarious. Even if philosophically defensible, it is threatened as soon as the methods of natural science are turned on human nature. If 'man is not fashioned out of a more precious clay' and the social sciences are to be guided by the principle that 'the general laws dictating the phenomena of the universe are necessary and constant', the challenge is unmistakable. Yet, as hinted in the last chapter, it may be possible to reconcile freedom with determinism. For the moment let us postpone the challenge, and go deeper into the idea of science as discovery of structure hidden behind the scenes, prompted because 'your true Philosopher will not believe what he doth see'.

APPEARANCE AND REALITY

In saying that 'Nature . . . disposeth her Wheels and Springs so out of sight', de Fontenelle did not mean merely that we need telescopes and microscopes to see them. He was invoking an ancient distinction between appearance and reality. Whatever our five senses tell us is classed as 'phenomena' (from the Greek word for 'appearances') and, in Descartes' version, phenomena belong in the mind of the observer. 'Reality', by contrast, refers to whatever in the universe itself causes the phenomena. Thus, when we report seeing a red rose, we are reporting an effect in our consciousness brought about by a

particular wavelength of light (or, in a rival theory, arrangement
of corpuscles). The effect may vary in different observers and
could be very different in animals. Descartes held that objects in
nature have the properties identified in mathematical physics,
properties like shape, number, mass and motion, whereas the
data supplied by the senses have properties dependent on the
mind aware of them, like the perceived colour or smell of the
rose.

Whether this distinction can be coherently fleshed out is a
vexed question in the philosophy of perception. But it is a familiar way of talking and leads readily to thinking in terms of two
worlds, one 'inner', mental and somehow private to the perceiver,
the other 'outer', physical and independent of the perceiver.
Descartes certainly writes in this way, clearly regarding the new
science of optics as a source of discoveries about the process by
which objects in nature cause our perceptions. The reason that
your true Philosopher will not believe what he doth see is that
your true Philosopher comes to regard the data of sight as distinct
from what causes them. This dualism of two worlds sounds, in
general, very helpful to anyone who wants to speak of unobservable forces and structures, as many scientists do. The world as it
appears to us is the effect of a distinct reality, allegedly furnished
as theory claims.

But there is an obvious snag, as soon as we ask how we can
know of these unobservable structures and forces. If observation
were our only way of knowing about the world, as empiricists
maintain, the snag would be decisive. But Descartes, like many
rationalists who have taken Bacon's first way, held that we have a
second faculty which gives an access to reality denied to the
senses. He called it 'intellectual intuition' and cited mathematics, especially geometry, as a leading example of its use.
Euclidean geometry rests on five axioms, from which it derives
all its theorems with the help of logic. The resulting system, in
Descartes' view, is a linked set of truths about the properties of
space and serves as a model of how we can know more about the
universe than the senses could possibly tell us.

In his *Discourse on the Method* (1637, Part II), Descartes made this
ambitious claim:

These long chains of perfectly simple and easy reasonings by means of which geometers are accustomed to carry out their most difficult demonstrations had led me to fancy that everything that can fall under human knowledge forms a similar sequence, and that so long as we avoid accepting as true what is not so, and always preserve the right order for deduction of one thing from another, there can be nothing too remote to be reached in the end, or too well hidden to be discovered.

I cannot resist adding de Fontenelle's more playful version:

Madam, said I, since we are in the humour of mixing amorous follies with our most serious Discourses, I must tell you that in Love and the Mathematics People reason alike. Allow never so little to a Lover, yet presently you must grant him more, nay more and more, which will at last go a great way. In like manner, grant but a Mathematician one little Principle, he immediately draws a consequence from it, to which you must necessarily assent; and from this consequence another, till he leads you so far (whether you will or no) that you have much ado to believe him.

Cartesian scientific method thus relied on logical deduction to get from axioms to theorems. But deduction could not do all the work. To prove that a theorem follows is not to prove the theorem true, unless one already knows that the premises of the proof are true. How, then, do we know that Euclid's axioms, along with the basic principles of logic and mathematics, are indeed true? Descartes held that we know it by a mental faculty of intuition, which leads us to 'see' that the axioms of Euclidean geometry capture the essential properties of space. Similarly, intuition told him that he was a *res cogitans*, a thing which thinks, and guaranteed the truth of his famous *cogito ergo sum*.

Bacon elsewhere described rationalists who took his first way and tried to make mathematics the model for all knowledge as 'men of dogmas', adding that they 'resemble spiders, who make cobwebs out of their own substance'. Certainly the method seems suspect on several counts. Take Euclidean geometry, whose axioms Descartes held to be definitive. Since his time, Riemann and Lobachevsky have proposed rival geometries with alternatives to Euclid's fifth axiom (which says, roughly, that parallel lines never meet). If they are coherent, and if, as has also been claimed, space conforms to either of them, rather than to Euclid, Descartes' 'intuition' misled him. More generally, where there is more than one internally coherent system, coherence ceases to be a guarantee of how the world is. Suspicion soon falls on the very idea of intuition as a faculty of mind which sheds the light of Reason on a reality underlying appearances. It then seems that Bacon's first way indeed relies on dogmas which give rise to cobwebs spun from subjective assumptions masquerading as intuitions.

'MIDDLE AXIOMS'

Although the first way is now largely out of fashion, it was never foolish and it still haunts the philosophy of science. This is not because ghosts, once acquired, are hard to shed. The philosophy of nature remains 'very mechanical' and inclined to believe in a hidden order of unobservables beyond the reach of our five senses. As soon as science tries to deal in unobservables, it has to be able to justify such claims. If, strictly speaking, we cannot observe electrons, social institutions or the unconscious mind, then why believe claims that they exist? If explanations are offered in terms of magnetic attraction, market forces or psychic processes like Freudian repression, what warrants such causal claims? The rationalist answer was to introduce 'middle axioms' and it remains instructive, not least in making us see that it is idle to propose an ontology and explanatory method, unless one also tackles the resulting problem of knowledge.

Descartes hoped that the method which yielded the 'first knowledge' could encompass the whole of philosophy or science and lead to a single, integrated account of a single, integrated natural order. As he declared in *The Principles of Philosophy* (1644):

the whole of philosophy is like a tree, whose roots are metaphysics, whose trunk is physics and whose branches are the other sciences, which can be reduced to three principal ones, namely medicine, mechanics and morals.

Middle axioms are the nodes on the tree, the points of departure for particular sciences and then for sub-branches. Thus, having established a potent mathematical physics (the trunk), we are to identify the essential properties of human nature which make for a general science of 'morals', and then subdivide that branch into axiomatic theories of economics, politics and so on. The whole tree will consist of theories which match the natural order and which we know to be true because we have derived them from the self-evident first knowledge with the aid of middle axioms.

This is visionary stuff and alarmingly speculative, except perhaps for mathematical physics and mechanics. There, in seventeenth-century spirit, one can readily envisage real but unobservable particulars, like electrons, or forces, like gravity, and can even suppose that organised theoretical intuition gives knowledge of them. For the social sciences, however, a rationalist approach is far less perspicuous. Consider the proposition that economic behaviour is governed by market forces and the laws of supply and demand. To render it scientific, one will need a basic ontology, for instance the forces and relations of production referred to in Marx's Preface, and a methodology which lets dependent variables, like rates of profit, be explained as effects of the productive forces and relations in particular conditions. When asked how one knows all this, one will reply by laying out an economic theory which makes sense of states of the economy and add that it rests on true middle axioms introducing the basic economic concepts. When asked how one knows that the middle axioms are true, one will reply either that they are self-evident or that, although they are axioms for economics, they can be derived as theorems from more general axioms further down the tree.

Stated so bluntly, this all sounds very dogmatic. That is partly, no doubt, because it does not even hint at the complexity and sophistication achieved by Marxist economic theories. Also it is misleading, if it suggests that rationalism favours Marxist theories over others. As to that, however, neo-Classical microeconomics too can be envisaged as an axiomatic theory which sets out to capture the essence of economic behaviour by defining it as rationally self-interested choice by individuals, and then goes on to derive a crop of theorems. In some versions, moreover, the theorems purport to extend into macroeconomics, thus promising a general theory ambitious enough to please any rationalist. But, however sophisticated the analysis, critics are still likely to jib at

the whole idea of transcending the limits of observation by theoretical reflection and then claiming that such reflection carries
with it knowledge of reality. Indeed, the very fact that rival
economic theories can be given similar axiomatic treatment
seems to debar a claim to knowledge on behalf of one of them,
while another is in the field. Theorists who argue that their
favoured theory is true on the grounds that it is coherent do
indeed sound much like spiders who make cobwebs out of their
own substance.

NECESSITY

Yet rationalism offers a solution to some awkward puzzles about
necessity and at least serves to show why necessity is problematic.
Why exactly does economics, or any other science, need a theory?
Why can it not be content to observe the world and generalise
what it observes? Rationalism gives two answers, both connected
with the thought that, in the words of an old apothegm, 'the
senses reveal no necessities'.

One is that theory is needed because science is a search for
causes, whereas observation cannot get beyond mere correlations.
When a bomb explodes, it does so because energy is suddenly
released by the unbalancing of a set of forces. When prices rise,
they are responding to the pressure of market forces, governed by
the laws of supply and demand. To explain an event is to identify
its cause, thus placing it in a series of events each of which gives
rise to the next. The series is not a mere sequence but one
connected by the powers of the particulars involved to produce
the next state in conformity with the laws of nature. To think
causally is to think in terms of powerful particulars and compelling laws. The Countess had both ideas in mind when noting that
'Philosophy is now become very mechanical' and that the universe 'resembles a Watch'.

Causes are thus being ascribed some kind of necessity. When
the bough breaks, the cradle *must* fall; when prices rise and other
things are equal, demand *must* fall. When science turns 'very
mechanical', these 'musts' are not idle. We observe only that
the cradle does fall but we explain the event by showing why it

had to. If the senses reveal no necessities, what does? Here seventeenth-century rationalists made what looks like a mistake. They were deeply impressed by the luminous qualities of mathematics, which they regarded as a model for all scientific knowledge, in the spirit of Descartes' comment about 'these long chains of perfectly simple and easy reasonings'. Mathematical truths have the interesting feature that they not only *are* true but *could not possibly* be false. A mathematical proof proves that a set of axioms (A) entails a theorem (T) in the sense that it yields a statement, which can be summarised as

$$\textit{Necessarily } (A \rightarrow T)$$

Granted that the axioms are necessarily true, which we know by intuition, the proof demonstrates that T is necessarily true too. Since intuition and proof are methods of discovering that T is true, as opposed to conferring truth on T, theory can give us knowledge of necessities.

The other reason why we need theory stems from this view of logic and mathematics as a voyage of discovery into an eternal realm of numbers and relations. Facts about numbers are objective and necessary facts of a universe which, at least in these ways, could not be otherwise. The truths of mathematics are, in a seventeenth-century phrase, 'true in all possible worlds'. Pigs might fly but triangles whose sides are in the proportions 3:4:5 *must* be right-angled. Since geometry, in Descartes' view, reveals the essential properties of space, it provides an ideal model for identifying ways in which the world must be as it is. Equally, if it is true that bodies attract one another in inverse proportion to the square of their distance apart, then this too is necessarily true, and explanations which invoke this fact will be able to show why collisions must occur at the velocities involved in them.

The two answers, taken together, thus identify the puzzling necessity attaching to causal connections with the luminous necessities of logic and mathematics. That certainly sounds like a mistake. Philosophers today do not equate the force of a bullet, propelled by the force of exploding gunpowder, with the 'force' of a mathematical deduction which prevents one reaching any conclusion but the one entailed. If there is a real necessity in causal powers and mechanisms, it calls for a different sort of elucidation. In general necessities of thought, ideas or language (*de dicto*) are not to be confused with those of natural properties, powers and processes (*de re*).

That sounds only sensible, and I shall not labour the rationalist case for denying it. But, in distinguishing necessity *de dicto* from necessity *de re*, we are setting puzzles about both. The social sciences are rich in pure theories, which resemble mathematics in starting from axioms or postulates and deducing theorems from them. The most elaborate examples are in economics but there are plenty of others, for instance those of coalitions in politics, of power in sociology, of kinship in anthropology or of grammatical transformation in linguistics. Also the use of statistics involves abstract, highly structured theories involving logical deductions. We need to be clear about the purpose of such theoretical activity. Perhaps it serves only to organise empirical material, as will be suggested in the next chapter. But, even so, there is still a question of what guarantees the logical relations involved. Rationalism maintains that there are immutable laws of thought, whose necessity cannot be proved because all proof presupposes them. Whether there are any such laws will not concern us directly until the chapter on rationality and relativism, but is worth pondering in the interim.

Meanwhile, abstract theories of, for instance, rational choice, power or language look as if they were intended to offer definitive, if abstract, accounts of their subject. That is how rationalism would regard them. It is plainly contentious to hold that the purpose of a theory of, say, power is to isolate the essence of power by defining the concept of power in the way which captures that essence. On the other hand, if this is not the purpose, then what is?

Necessity *de re* is no less puzzling. In what sense, if any, *must* the cradle fall, when the bough breaks? The question recalls an obvious difficulty about Marx's Preface. Its philosophy was, as the Countess would say, 'very Mechanical', being couched in a language of hidden forces and mechanisms. Even if we think we grasp the idea of causation here and the relation envisaged be-

tween causes and their effects, there is still a palpable epistemological problem of how we can know that reality is a system of
forces, hidden from our everyday ways of knowing by experience.
If we reject the rationalist equation between logical necessity and
causal necessity but want to remain realists about social structures
and forces, we shall need a suitable account of causation. This will
be made harder in the next chapter, when empiricism has sharpened the objections to dealing in such unobservables.

CONCLUSION

Bacon's 'first way' remains influential as well as instructive. The
seventeenth-century vision of nature as an integrated system, a
complete causal order veiled from the senses, has not died out.
Nor has the hope of a unified system of scientific knowledge. But
both have become more remote and speculative as science advances, for reasons which will serve to summarise the chapter.

The rationalist *ontology* of 'Wheels and Springs', of structures
and forces operating with necessity, has become even more me-
taphorical. Progress reveals new areas of ignorance, as well as of
knowledge. Today's scientists have different, more tentative, in-
ventories of the ultimate furniture of the universe. Work on the
human genome, for instance, cannot be conducted in seventeenth-century categories. Nor is there the old confidence that a
complete causal determinism holds throughout an integrated
natural order. On the other hand, since Descartes set the roots
of his tree in metaphysics and we are not directly concerned with
the ontology of the natural sciences, metaphors may suffice. The
relevant point is that rationalism gave the human sciences a strong
invitation to search for hidden structures and forces. Whether
psychological or social, they would turn out to be the determinants of human behaviour. Acceptance of the metaphors of a
philosophy 'now become very Mechanical', as the Countess put
it, has had powerful effects on ideas of explanation in the social
sciences, as we shall find in Chapter 5.

Rationalist *methodology* was disposed to assimilate the 'necessity'
with which a cause generates its effect to the 'necessity' which
distinguishes a causal law from a mere correlation, and then to

assimilate both to the 'necessity' which marks the truths of logic and mathematics. This plainly sets more questions than it begins to answer. Here are two which will need tackling, if we are to reach a coherent view of the proper tasks of theory in the social sciences. Firstly, theories include 'long chains of perfectly simple and easy reasonings' like those 'by means of which geometers are accustomed to carry out their most difficult demonstrations'. So is one of their tasks to establish theoretical truths which are necessarily true of a realm defined by 'middle axioms'? If not, what warrantable purpose do theoretical abstractions serve? Secondly, if there are 'natural necessities' and they are *de re* rather than *de dicto*, what account of causation should we favour?

Rationalist ambitions were much helped by a distinction between appearance and reality, which relegated sense experience to an effect of external causes. That let theory, certified by 'intuition', trump observation in the search for order in nature. Even if we are wary of such a distinction, we cannot refuse the questions thus raised about the relation of theory to experience. A neat answer would be that observation in fact always trumps theory. But, as the next two chapters will show, the truth is not so neat.

Epistemologically, a manifest problem of knowledge has been posed. Do we really have a faculty of reflective reason, which lets us know what the senses cannot possibly tell us? If not, we shall need another way to justify some claims to knowledge, which extends beyond the immediate reach of the senses to what has not been observed and perhaps to what is unobservable. A still deeper epistemological problem is set if we also reject the rationalist assumption that science casts the light of Reason on a world existing independently of human exploration. The image is hard to resist, not least because it makes the external world the test of whether we have the correct concepts, theories and hypotheses. But it presupposes the standpoint of the Engineer in the Pit who can 'see the Stage as really it is'. What follows, if there is no such standpoint to be had, will be considered in Chapter 4.

Finally, it is worth noting some signs that a philosophy of science geared to the natural sciences may cause peculiar trouble for the social sciences. A warning was given by Descartes' assurance that human freedom is not threatened by modern science, because the human mind is not subject to the laws of nature. In that case, however, psychology and other human sciences seem either impossible from the start or certain to destroy our illusions of free will and moral responsibility. When we unpick this dilemma, we still have to think twice about Descartes' insistence that 'there is nothing easier for me to know than my own mind' (closing paragraph of the Second Meditation). One implication of his *Cogito* is that self-knowledge is a sure foundation for all other knowledge. Granting for the moment that there is or even can be any sure foundation at all, the social sciences might be especially tempted by self-knowledge which casts light on action from within. But they cannot allow that the actors are always the best authority on themselves and their actions. Yet a stubborn element of self-reference will obtrude when we consider the difference between Understanding and Explanation.

But we are not yet ready to question a naturalism which maintains that 'Nature has used only one and the same dough' and that a single scientific method will suffice. To start us on Bacon's second way here is an overarching question for all science. It comes from J. S. Mill's *A System of Logic* and is very much a rationalist question except that his 'uniformities' do not indicate hidden necessities:

What are the fewest and simplest assumptions, which being granted, the whole existing order of nature would result? . . . What are the fewest general propositions from which all the uniformities which exist in the universe might be deductively inferred? (1843, Book III, Chapter 4)

In search of an answer, let us turn to the senses and particulars.

CHAPTER 3

Positive science: the empiricist way

Bacon's first way of discovering truth scorned sense experience
and started from 'the most general axioms'. That may have
seemed perverse all along and it has certainly led us into difficulties. The second way beckons invitingly. Setting off from 'the
senses and particulars' and 'rising by a gradual and unbroken
ascent', it 'arrives at the most general axioms last of all'. Bacon
speaks of it as 'the true way, but as yet untried'. It has been well
tried since then, especially under the title of Positive science, and
the aim of this chapter is to discover whether it is indeed the true
way.

To show where we are heading, here is an example of the kind
of explanation which lies along it. It comes from a 1970 textbook
on scientific method for social scientists by A. Przeworski and H.
Teune. Most of the book is a technical guide to the use of
statistical models and inferences; but the authors helpfully distil
the essence of their idea of explanation in an illustrative question
and answer (1970, pp. 18–20 and 74–76). The question is: 'Why
does Monsieur Rouget, age twenty four, blond hair, brown eyes,
a worker in a large factory, vote Communist?' The answer is
broadly that 'to explain the vote of M. Rouget, one must rely
upon general probabilistic statements that are relevant for voting
behaviour and have been sufficiently confirmed against various
sets of evidence'. When such statements have been duly as-
sembled, one arrives at an explanation which looks like this:

(1) M. Rouget is a young male worker employed in a large
    factory in a social system where the church plays an impor-
    tant role, and

40

(2) young workers in large factories vote Left with a probability of
.60 to .70, and in those systems in which the role of the church
is strong, men vote Left more often than women; therefore it is
highly likely (probability of .80) that

(3) M. Rouget votes for a party of the Left.

In this style of explanation the aim is to assign the particular,
M. Rouget, to various groups for which there is a known frequency, and then to combine the frequencies so as to arrive at
an overall probability high enough to predict from. The statistical
techniques needed may be highly complex but the strategy is very
simple: show why M. Rouget is predictable. If the strategy is
sound, it simply by-passes the difficulties of Bacon's first way
and offers a form of explanation as neat and economical as one
could wish.

The chapter will start with a brief note about Positivism to save
confusion, and then explore the idea of 'a gradual and unbroken
ascent' from the senses and particulars to the most general axioms. The steps will be to introduce a basic empiricism which rests
on observation and inductive generalisations, to remove all manner of real-world necessity from the relation between cause and
effect, to present a potent idea of Positive economics with the help
of Milton Friedman and to draw a very sharp distinction between
empirical and theoretical statements, so that the latter can be
made firmly subordinate. Then we shall ask how convincing it
is to put all the work on probability and prediction, as with M.
Rouget.

POSITIVISM

Positivism is a term with many uses in social science and philosophy. At the broad end, it embraces any approach which applies
scientific method to human affairs conceived as belonging to a
natural order open to objective enquiry. That lets Comte,
Durkheim, Weber and Marx all count as Positivists and it is not
uncommon to hear them grouped together under this general
label. They do, I suppose, share an overall naturalism. But they
are strange bedfellows, when one considers their differences.

Comte's 'Positive Philosophy' was too restrictive for the others. Weber's naturalism lurked behind a methodology which gave a vital place to actors' subjective meanings and he had an empiricist's scepticism about social structures as real entities with causal powers. Durkheim, in bidding us treat social facts as things, had no such inhibitions. Marx contemplated a dialectical process in history working through class struggles. To suggest an '-ism' which groups such deep differences together is to sow confusion.

At the narrow end, I have found Positivism used, especially in international relations, to mean a behaviourism so fierce that it rejects all psychological data and qualitative methods. This is clear enough, but, since it is a specialised usage, I suggest regarding it as a tendentious one, due to a disputable belief that, because only behaviour is observable, science should set limits accordingly.

A broader term, still definite enough to be interesting, is 'Positive science'. As we shall see presently, it goes with an empiricism about scientific knowledge, which rests on observation as the moment of truth when hypotheses are tested against the facts of the world. It rejects the rationalism of the previous chapter, while remaining naturalistic. Although the stress on observation makes it suspicious of Durkheim's injunction to treat social facts as things, it does not flatly rule social facts out. Nor does it flatly disallow the psychological observation of mental states, on which we found Mill relying in Chapter 1. Nevertheless, those who advocate Positive science are more often individualists than holists and tend to distinguish between 'hard' (quantitative) and 'soft' (qualitative) data, for reasons which will emerge.

Philosophers of natural science think of Positivism as the philosophy of Positive science. But philosophers at large have come to use it as shorthand for Logical Positivism, the ferocious version of empiricism which emerged from the Vienna Circle in the 1930s and, for a time, almost swept the board. The driving idea of Logical Positivism was that, because claims to knowledge of the world can be justified only by experience, we are never entitled to assert the existence of anything beyond all possible experience. It can never be probable, let alone certain, that there are, for instance, unobservable structures, forces, instincts or dialectical processes. Indeed it cannot even be possible, since to speak of them is technically meaningless, except as shorthand for observable regularities in experience. Knowledge is grounded in particular observations and can extend to general beliefs only in so far as experience can confirm them. An ambitious programme was mounted to show how all branches of science would progress faster if cleared of non-experiential lumber. To go with it, a rumbustious bonfire was started, designed to consume traditional ethics, aesthetics, theology and metaphysics, since they too made claims which experience could not possibly confirm.

In what follows, we shall focus on the idea of a Positive science and the form of empiricism which makes best sense of it.

'A GRADUAL AND UNBROKEN ASCENT'

With this preamble, M. Rouget will serve nicely to introduce the basic idea of scientific explanation on Bacon's second way and to give warning of doubts to come. Why does he vote communist? The nub of the answer suggested is that he belongs to a group, 80 per cent of whose members vote for the Left. This might seem no explanation at all. Why do young, male factory workers in systems where the church is strong vote for the Left? How did the church get into the explanation and why did M. Rouget's blond hair and brown eyes drop out of it? What is the social mechanism which makes this group a group and pushes it Leftwards? What does a vote for the Left mean to M. Rouget and others and mean for a society with a strong church? As the questions proliferate, it becomes clear that no answers are offered beyond a bank of statistics, from which M. Rouget's vote is predictable with .80 probability. But, one might well protest, predicting is not explaining.

These doubts sound formidable but I shall next make a case for deeming them entirely misplaced, because prediction and explanation are two sides of the only coin which science can have or could need. Return to the original question, 'Why does Monsieur Rouget, age twenty four, blond hair, brown eyes, a worker in a large factory, vote Communist?'. The answer makes no mention of hair and eyes but retains age, gender and occupation, while adding a reference to the role of the church. There is no reason *a priori* why his youth should matter and his blond hair not. Indeed in some social systems, like the Third Reich, blond hair might be a relevant variable. It is simply an empirical fact that correlations between age and voting are statistically significant. It is an empirical fact too that probabilities rise for some sets of variables, like age and gender together, and not for others, like age and colour of eyes together. Church influence too happens to be significant but might not have been. If one asks why the investigator should have thought of the church unless wise to its potential importance in advance, then let it be granted that investigators do not arrive with blank minds. But any ideas they bring with them have been learnt from experience or from the work of others guided by experience. How else could we know about the world?

A supporting theory of knowledge which rests solely on the senses and particulars might go like this. Science consists of a body of beliefs some of which we know to be true and others of which we are rationally entitled to hold, given what we know. The basic beliefs are those warranted by perception, which is our only source of direct acquaintance with the world and hence our only warrant for basic statements about it. In perception the mind registers data provided by the senses and so comes to know of 'particulars' – individual items, present here and now, with whatever properties and relations we can observe them to have. These are the brute facts of experience, the features of the world we know without interpretation. Admittedly there is ambiguity about even this much, because 'experience' sometimes refers to the experiencing and sometimes to what is experienced, which, in turn, is regarded sometimes as private to consciousness and sometimes as belonging to the furniture of the world. But, either way, knowledge starts with the senses and particulars.

So construed, perception gives us a foundation for knowledge of the world but a narrow foundation. It shows us particulars here and now but tells us nothing directly of what was, or will be, or even what now exists unperceived. Nor does it tell us what is universally or, still less, necessarily the case. 'The senses conclude nothing universally,' says one old tag. 'The senses reveal no necessities,' says another. Yet, even if we can do without 'necessities', we shall get nowhere without some universal conclusions. So perception needs supplementing with a principle to justify further inferences. The traditional empiricist principle is induction. It lets us infer that what has been found true in known cases so far also holds in other cases where the same conditions obtain. Broadly, if all known ravens are black, then all ravens whatever are black. Granted such a licence to generalise, we can chart more of the world than we have experienced.

The principle of induction needs to be more carefully stated, however. That is partly because it ushers in a vast technical discussion, which I shall avoid. But also we need it to underwrite statements of probability. So let us word it as a principle of inference from known cases to a probability for the next case, as with M. Rouget. Loosely, if x per cent of workers sampled vote communist, then there is an x per cent chance that the next such worker votes communist. Schematically:

if $x\%$ of known As have the property B, then the probability that in the same conditions the next A will have the property B is $x\%$.

How do we know that the principle of induction (in this or any other version) is true? The question sets the notorious 'riddle of induction'. Presumably we do not know it by previous observation, because it claims to hold more widely than previous observation. Yet we cannot go beyond previous observation without assuming it to be true. This horrid snag threatens to put a stop to the gradual and unbroken ascent almost before it starts. But, since that would spoil the story, I shall leave the riddle of induction to another day. To make our ascent, we need something more than perception and the principle just stated will serve nicely. It extends the way in the spirit required. Perception gives us the start of Bacon's second way and induction allows an ascent which is gradual and unbroken, since every generalising step can be confirmed by experience.

Although so sublimely simple a version of empiricism is no longer in fashion, it still offers a doughty challenge to anyone claiming to know more than it allows. Its plausible starting point is that the world exists independently of us, that perception gives knowledge of some particular items of its furniture and that there is no way of knowing *a priori* (i.e. independently of experience) what else it contains. To extend our knowledge to more distant parts of time and space, we need a principle like induction. Any such principle needs to keep faith with the starting point. It must tell us what we would (probably) experience in other times and places, given such evidence as we have. But it cannot introduce into science anything of a kind beyond all possible experience. Hence its general form can only be that similar events or experiences occur in similar relations in similar conditions. Yet why ask for more?

Well, most of us do certainly ask for more. The rationalists of the previous chapter asked for an ontology of forces and structures, and a 'rational faculty' which detected them by tracing out formal theories *a priori*. Theoretical knowledge involved necessities beyond the reach of the senses and true 'in all possible worlds'. It was grounded in logic and mathematics and extended through other formal systems. Even if we reject this view of theoretical knowledge as necessities *de dicto* which reveal necessities *de re*, we may still want to take theoretical truths seriously. We might still hold that they express necessities of thought, for instance, and, as such, re-enter the story at a different place, unless we can be talked out of it in what follows.

Nor does an attack on rationalism dispose of all 'necessities' in the world. One can distinguish between formal or logical necessities, known *a priori*, and physical or natural necessities known in some other way, without abandoning the latter. We have a whole causal vocabulary erected on a firm difference between real connections and mere correlations. We speak of causes compelling effects, of forces pulling and pushing, and of the workings of a world which is, in the Countess' phrase, 'very Mechanical'. Whatever quite is involved, it goes beyond what the senses and induction could let us know.

Also, lest we forget, one aim of the Enlightenment was moral knowledge. As Condorcet declared in the work cited before, 'Truth, virtue and happiness are bound together with an indissoluble chain' (1795, Xth Stage). Whether science, and social science in particular, can tell us how we should live will be discussed in a later chapter. But, although science may turn out to be neutral about ethics, or even destructive of all claims to moral objectivity, we may still have hopes. Talk of natural rights has proved very resilient, despite waves of scepticism about moral knowledge. Many people lay claim to rights, not created by human decree, existing even where they go unrecognised and inalienable. There seems to be no warrant for such moral thinking in a theory of knowledge which starts with the senses and advances by induction.

HUME AND CAUSATION

We may want more than perception and induction allow; but can we have it and do we need it? Bacon's second way has no room for surplus baggage on its gradual and unbroken ascent. The obstacle to it which looms largest nowadays, I suspect, is our deeply embedded assumption that causal connections are not mere correlations but involve causal laws, powers or forces, and thus some kind of natural necessity. Can it be circumvented by relying on a modest inductive principle that similar sequences occur in similar conditions?

This question became critical in the eighteenth century, when a thoroughly systematic empiricism took shape and set about expelling all unempirical elements from scientific knowledge. It received a brilliant answer from David Hume (1711–76), author of, among other works, *A Treatise of Human Nature* (1739) and *Enquiries Concerning the Human Understanding* (1748). Since his answer remains as incomparable as it is classic, we shall pause to savour it.

Hume wrote the *Treatise* as a foundation for 'a complete system of the sciences'. It is evident, he remarked in his Introduction, that all the sciences have a relation, greater or less, to human nature. 'Even Mathematics, Natural Philosophy and Natural Religion are in some measure dependent on the science of MAN; since they lie under the cognisance of men, and are judged by their powers and faculties.' Hume's idea was to attempt a science of human powers and faculties, a scientific study of human reason and passion, grounded in an empirical study of 'Logic, Morals, Criticism and Politics'. This 'science of MAN' would 'comprehend almost everything which can tend to the improvement of the human mind'. Its method was to be 'experience and observation' applied to 'men's behaviour in company, in affairs and in their pleasures' with the aim of 'explaining all effects from the simplest and fewest causes'.

Having set off along Bacon's second way, Hume reached the topic of causation in Part 3 of Book I, under the general heading 'Of Knowledge and Probability'. We may hold the opinion that there is some kind of necessity involved in the relation between cause and effect, but the trivial point that the idea of an 'effect' presupposes that of a cause 'does not prove that every being must be preceded by a cause; no more than it follows, because every husband must have a wife, that therefore every man must be married' (Section 3). Any opinion that every event must have a cause or that a cause compels, produces or in any way necessitates its effect can only arise and be justified by 'observation and experiment'. Yet, when Hume reached 'The idea of necessary connection' (Section 14), he found that observation and experiment can supply only an 'experienced union', a 'constant conjunction' or regular correlation between one event and another. He concluded that nothing more was needed: we may define a *cause* to be 'An object precedent and contiguous to another and where all objects resembling the former are placed in like relations of precedency and contiguity to those objects that resemble the latter'.

Taking it more slowly with one of Hume's examples, we might ask what in experience underlies our belief that one billiard ball, striking another, causes it to move. The components are a prior event (the movement of the first ball to the point of impact) and a later event (the movement of the second ball) occurring at the same place. That is all we can observe in any particular case – something 'precedent' and 'contiguous'. What then warrants our deeming it a case of cause and effect, rather than a coincidence? It is only that a similar sequence can be observed in like conditions. A cause is simply an instance of a regularity and a causal law or law of nature simply a regularity made up of instances. If this seems too scandalous a debunking of more robust ideas of causation, then we can add a psychological element to the effect that we regard as causal those regularities which we have acquired the habit of expecting to hold. The cause of an event is thus a prior event in a regular sequence which we have come to expect to hold.

Since causation has already been declared the only relation 'that can be traced beyond our senses, and informs us of existences and objects which we do not see or feel' (Section 2), it is disconcerting to have it pared down in this way. But, if the aim is a gradual and unbroken ascent, then causality cannot involve a departure from the kind of claims to knowledge which 'observation and experiment' can justify. The best candidate for a knowable relation that can be traced beyond our senses is a general correlation. Indeed this is the only candidate, if unobservables of all kinds are ruled out as beyond possible knowledge. In similar vein, there can be no warrant for judging the existence of unobservables even probable. Hidden forces which drive the springs and wheels of a watch are no more probable than would be tiny imperceptible gremlins, postulated to perform this service. The epistemological core of probability can only be the frequency with which a correlation has been found to hold.

M. Rouget is now plain sailing. Why does he vote communist? The only warranted kind of answer is one which assigns him to categories of voters with a high frequency of voting for the Left. As we combine the categories, for instance by putting young voters and working class voters together as young, working class voters, frequencies rise. In a complex world we may never reach a 100 per cent frequency but high probabilities are enough. Recall Przeworski and Teune's remark that, 'to explain the vote of M. Rouget, one must rely on general probabilistic statements that are relevant for voting behaviour and have been sufficiently confirmed against various sets of evidence'. Why must one? It is directly because this fiercely empiricist theory of knowledge offers nothing else. General probabilistic statements are the only coin which buys more than observation certifies in full. Explanation and prediction therefore have to be two sides of this one coin. Both rely on generalisations, which are projected forwards for purposes of prediction and backwards for purposes of explanation. The explanation of particular historical actions is no exception:

The goal of science is to explain and predict why certain events occur when and where they do. Why was the Kowalski marriage not successful? Why did Smith commit a crime? Why did Napoleon attack Russia? Science is concerned with the explanation of specific events by means of statements that are invariably true from one set of circumstances to another. (1970, p.18)

It needs repeating that there need be nothing in the least simplistic about the use of statistics on Bacon's second way. The rest of Przeworski and Teune's book is firmly technical and growingly complex as they guide the reader into the refinements of modelling and measurement. But the sophistication is not meant to spoil the inspired simplicity of the basic approach. Why did Napoleon invade Russia? Well, there must be some true general statement of which the invasion is an instance warranting prediction *ex ante* and explanation *ex post*. All historical actors in similar conditions act as Napoleon did; and explanation in history thus works in the same way as any other.

POSITIVE ECONOMICS

We have now deployed a basic empiricism suited to the second way and proposed an analysis of causation which avoids any demand for natural necessities. The approach has run into a great deal of trouble since its heyday and even its advocates are losing their nerve. Yet it can still claim to embody the spirit of Positive science and, witness the durability of Positive economics in particular, the claim is still respected. Critics are asked to be patient, therefore, while I reinforce the case with the help of Milton Friedman, whose (1953) essay on 'The Methodology of Positive Economics' remains a force to be reckoned with. Although it makes even neo-Classical economists uncomfortable, it is a sharp, memorable statement of a very tempting line.

The task of Positive economics, Friedman begins, 'is to provide a system of generalisations that can be used to make correct predictions about the consequences of any change in circumstances' (p.4). This is to be done by developing 'a 'theory' or 'hypothesis' that yields valid and meaningful (i.e. not truistic) predictions about phenomena not yet observed' (p.7). The theory is to be a blend of two elements, a 'language' and 'a body of substantive hypotheses designed to abstract essential features of a complex reality' (p.7). In its role as a language, 'theory has no substantive content; it is a set of tautologies. Its function is to act as a filing system' (p.7). In its substantive role, 'theory is to be judged by its predictive power for the class of phenomena which it is intended to "explain" . . . the only test of the *validity* of a hypothesis is comparison of its predictions with experience' (p.8, his italics).

Notice that 'explain' occurs in quotation marks, whereas 'predict' does not. The aim is prediction, the means is comparison of predictions with experience. That is exactly right for a gradual and unbroken ascent where 'explanation' can only be by appeal to generalisations with known predictive power. Notice too the very sharp distinction between a 'language' or 'filing system' and 'a body of substantive hypotheses'. Since this distinction will offer critics a crucial point of entry later, it is worth pausing to back it up with the help of Logical Positivism.

THE ANALYTIC–SYNTHETIC DISTINCTION

Hume distinguished sharply between 'matters of fact' and 'relations of ideas'. The world consists of all matters of fact and, for reasons given when describing his analysis of causation, there is no necessity about any of them. The world just happens to be as it is. We know that some of it is regular; anything beyond regularity, like underlying natural necessity, is beyond our ken. Hence all true statements about the world are true 'contingently', being contingent on matters of fact and so not necessarily true in any sense (unless psychological). Conversely any statements which are necessarily true are not about the world but about relations of ideas. They depend for their truth on logical relations and the meaning of ideas in the mind.

This is clear up to a point. But it leaves one wondering how the psychology of what we expect and are in the habit of inferring relates to the logic of ideas. The ambiguity stems from the remark quoted above that 'Even Mathematics, Natural Philosophy and Natural Religion are in some measure dependent on the science of MAN'. The Logical Positivists allowed no such puzzlement, thanks to their very sharp-edged 'analytic–synthetic distinction', crisply put in A. J. Ayer's *Language, Truth and Logic* (1936, Chapter 4). All statements fit for scientific use can be divided into two exclusive kinds, analytic and synthetic. If a statement is analytic, its truth or falsity depends solely on the meanings of its terms. True analytic statements are tautologies, as, for example, 'all bachelors are unmarried' or '2 + 2 = 4'. If a statement is synthetic, its truth or falsity depends on matters of fact, as, for example, with 'all bachelors are carefree'. Thus whether all bachelors are unmarried depends on what 'bachelor' means; whether bachelors are carefree depends on how flesh-and-blood bachelors respond to life. One must never confuse words with things, for instance by thinking it a fact of the world that all bachelors are unmarried. This sort of confusion spawns many errors, like the rationalist belief that geometrical statements describe the necessary properties of space.

Someone might protest that all flesh-and-blood bachelors are indeed unmarried. Is that not a fact of the world? The Logical Positivist replies by pointing out that this 'fact' arises solely from a convention of language. 'All bachelors are unmarried' records our determination to use the word 'bachelor' as we do. It is, in a famous Logical Positivist phrase, true by convention. We could change the convention but, while it stands, married persons are not to be counted as bachelors; whereas bachelors are bachelors, whether they are carefree or not. The same goes for all truths of logic, mathematics and other formal systems. They result from rules which we have constructed and thus depend solely on human decisions. We may seem to find them amply confirmed by experience but this is only because we never allow experience to refute them. Anyone who claimed to find a circle whose circumference was not equal to its diameter x *pi* would thereby be misapplying the term 'circle'; hence it is a matter of convention, not of experience, that circles have this property.

This line makes complete sense of Friedman's distinction between substantive hypotheses (synthetic) and theoretical statements (analytic). Pure theory can only be a set of tautologies or 'language', whose function is to act as a filing system for data and hypotheses. To describe pure theory as a filing system is not to make it trivial. The growth of mathematics, for instance, has been a great intellectual labour rich in surprising theorems and the Logical Positivists did not deny that a process of discovery was involved. Their point was that those discoveries do not increase our knowledge of the world, since mathematics is a tautology. God would see all the implications of the axioms at a glance. We, being finite, have to discover them gradually and, apparently, by trial and error. But they still state relations of ideas, not matters of fact. A good filing system is a genuine achievement, not least because it can suggest new empirical hypotheses, as when a computer search for patterns among statistics throws up enlightening new correlations to investigate empirically. The crux remains, however, that no truth about the world can be established just by appeal to the filing system.

We now have a basic empiricism, which relies only on perception and induction; an analysis of causation which purges causal explanation of natural necessities; a sketch for a Positive economics or any other Positive science; and an epistemologically guided distinction between language and fact. Each step conceals long, complex philosophical argument, even before critics go to work, since empiricists are far from agreed about the most defensible theories of perception, induction and causation. Also it would be misleading to suggest that empiricism stands or falls on the merits of Logical Positivism. But I hope that the four steps present the idea of a gradual and unbroken ascent in a manner which captures the spirit of a pure empiricism and fairly invokes Friedman as a sign that Bacon's second way remains hugely influential.

If that is granted, our next task is to make the way less schematic and, at the same time, thornier. I shall comment on two questions directly raised by Friedman's essay, and then seek some practical Positive guidance on scientific method.

REALISTIC ASSUMPTIONS VS. SUCCESSFUL PREDICTIONS

Both questions concern Friedman's distinction between substantive hypotheses and theoretical language. The first arises because of a surprising twist which he himself gives to the character of a substantive hypothesis in a Positive scheme where 'theory is to be judged by its predictive power' and 'the only test of the *validity* of a hypothesis is comparison of its predictions with experience' (1953, p.8). This twist has provoked a fierce debate, which is too instructive to miss.

The distinction between language and fact, he maintains, rules out any presumption that 'hypotheses have not only "implications" but also "assumptions" and that the conformity of these "assumptions" to "reality" is a test of the validity of the hypothesis *different from* and *additional to* the test by implications' (1953, p.14, his italics). Hence it is no weakness of perfect competition models, he argues, and no strength of models of imperfect competition, that the former have less 'realistic' assumptions than the latter. Perfect competition models assume markets to consist of informed and rational buyers and sellers, many in number, each too small to affect prices, and so on. Since real markets manifestly do not fit this description, one might expect a Positive economics, with its devotion to observed facts, to prefer models which assume imperfect markets. Indeed advocates of such models commonly propose them on grounds of realism. No, says Friedman, that begs the question and breaks faith with Positive economics. The *only* question is which sort of model results in more successful predictions. *All* models involve abstraction, and the only test of the merit of an abstraction is comparison of the resulting predictions with experience. As it turns out, the predictions implied by perfect competition models fare better.

This startling twist has outraged other champions of Positive economics, like Paul Samuelson (1963, 1964), and stirred up a running controversy. I introduce it not because I pretend to be an economist but because it shows why economic theorists cannot proceed in philosophical innocence. A common retort has been that, since Positive economics is a descriptive science in the empiricist tradition, there can be no call for its assuming what everyone knows to be false. For instance, why assume that single buyers or sellers cannot influence prices, when we all know that they often can in real markets? But this retort is double-edged. Standard imperfect competition models also assume much that one might well think plainly false, for example that supply curves always rise or that outputs and costs are continuously variable. Also, to signal a later topic, all economic theories, neo-Classical, Keynesian and Marxian alike, assume that economic agents are rational in ways which experience seems plainly to contradict. So it cannot be merely obvious whether, to put it a shade paradoxically, abstractions are realistic. A test is needed and, on Bacon's second way, Friedman has a strong case for making it the success of prediction.

Critics will not easily be headed off by this manoeuvre, since there still seems to be a difference between description and prediction. Whether the oil market is competitive (or whether French industrial workers like M. Rouget have been observed to vote communist), is surely a matter of fact and prior to any predictions? Friedman's answer is to undermine this distinction by a further manoeuvre. In a section headed 'Can a hypothesis be tested by the realism of its assumptions?' he introduces the idea that scientific statements are often 'as if' true. Take, for instance, the accepted hypothesis that the acceleration of a body dropped in a vacuum is a constant, g (about 32 feet per second per second on earth), implying that the distance (s) travelled after t seconds is given by the formula $s = \frac{1}{2}gt^2$. When the formula is applied to various objects dropped from various heights in the earth's atmosphere, it is found to hold, more or less, in usefully many but not all cases.

It can therefore be stated: under a wide range of circumstances, bodies that fall in the actual atmosphere behave *as if* they were falling in a vacuum. In the language so common in economics this would be rapidly translated into: the formula assumes a vacuum. Yet it clearly does no such thing . . . The formula is accepted because it works, not because we live in an approximate vacuum – whatever that means. (1953, p.18)

His point is that the so-called 'assumptions' of every useful theory are always false, if treated as descriptions; but may still be 'as if' true, a matter to be established in the same way as for any other hypothesis. Thus the leaves round a tree may usefully be said to be positioned 'as if' each leaf deliberately tried to maximise the amount of sunlight it receives, given the position of its neighbours; a skilled billiard player makes his shots 'as if' he knew complex mathematical formulae; firms behave 'as if' they were seeking to maximise their returns aided by perfect information and simultaneous equations. It is no objection that, taken literally without 'as if', leaves, billiard players and firms do no such thing. It matters only whether predictions so derived prove successful.

The significance of this 'as if' is that it lets Positive science dabble in unobservables, provided that they are not thought more than useful fictions. Theory can be given the useful task of constructing or exploring idealisations or models which abstract from features of the actual world to a limiting case. Friedman likens perfect competition to frictionless motion, where it is 'as if' pure forces acted without interference. I call this dabbling because there is no concession to the idea of unobservables existing in nature, as opposed to the model. They have only the standing of objects in a 'virtual reality' but are none the less useful for that. Consequently Positive science need not be nervous of unobservables or of theories which refer to them. Since prediction remains the only test, there is no risk of introducing features of reality beyond all possible experience.

THE ROLE OF THEORY

Yet, on reflection, that raises more of a puzzle about the role of theory than has emerged. The second question raised by Friedman's line is whether there is, after all, more to theory than a language and filing system. One large contrast between Bacon's two ways is that 'the most general axioms' come at the start of the first and at the end of the second. That should mean that, for Positive science, theory has *none* of the ambitious tasks assigned to it in the previous chapter. At any rate, that is how I have presented the second way, with the help of Friedman and the analytic–synthetic distinction.

Let us take a fresh example of an assumption which sounds false but might be 'as if' true. Microeconomic theory is commonly presented as a formal system resting on rationality assumptions, defining a rational agent as an individual with complete and consistent preferences, all relevant information and perfect ability to calculate, and then declaring that every economic agent is rational in this sense. In a familiar shorthand, economic agents are assumed to be utility-maximisers, who calculate what will best serve their interests and act accordingly. The broad assumption was memorably stated by F. Y. Edgeworth in a book engagingly titled *Mathematical Psychics*: 'The first principle of economics is that every agent is actuated solely by self-interest' (1881, p.16). Is this statement, with its apparent air of being one of Bacon's 'most general axioms', analytic or synthetic? Does it state a principle of the filing system or a substantive hypothesis about economic behaviour?

Neither option is altogether comfortable. Edgeworth himself took it to be a useful empirical generalisation, pretty much true of the realm of finance and commerce which he was studying, although less true outside it. But that depends on taking 'self-interest' to mean something akin to 'selfishness' and presuming that we can distinguish in practice between self-regarding and other-regarding behaviour. When microeconomists invoke 'self-interest' as the propellant of economic behaviour, they usually mean it in the broader sense that agents are always motivated to satisfy whatever preferences they have. Since this will be the crucial theme used to illustrate explanatory individualism (the bottom left quadrant of the 'window' in Figure 1.2) and a topic of Chapter 6, I shall not say much here. But it is fair to point out now that, taken so broadly, it is not a hypothesis which experience might squarely refute. Any behaviour whatever *can* be squared with it, by ascribing suitable preferences to agents or by making their aims suitably long-term or by allowing for a subjective element in their beliefs about how best to achieve them. In that case, however, 'All economic agents are rational' becomes like 'All bachelors are unmarried', analytic, a tautology, which, if true at all, is 'true by convention' in the idiom of Logical Positivism.

Yet many economic theorists want microeconomic theory to be more than a set of tautologies spelling out the implications of defining 'rational agent' in the standard way; and yet they do regard the axioms as definitional. The picture of us as separate individuals each seeking to maximise our individual utility is often presented as if it had the warrant both of pure theory and of experience. But that cannot be so, if the analytic–synthetic distinction is right. Every statement belongs to one category or the other, and apparent hybrids are really two statements, one of each kind. Those of pure theory form a language or filing system: what, if anything, they apply to is always an empirical matter. Hence the assumptions of microeconomics cannot do the unitary job of guaranteeing their own truth as an analysis of the ultimate components of actual economic behaviour. Positive science rejects any such amalgam.

Friedman might be expected to respond by repeating that the rationality assumptions are 'as if' true. But he presently lets it emerge that his attitude to theory is less simple than is suggested by the passages quoted above. His famous article is a long one and only its better known first half is unequivocal about the role of the theorist as filing clerk. But, as the text progresses, the distinction between theory and fact starts to blur. Theory emerges as a source of surprising connections, fertile idealisations and new possibilities. Then comes this striking statement:

If a class of 'economic phenomena' appears varied and complex, it is, we must suppose, because we have no adequate theory to explain them. Known facts cannot be set on one side; a theory to apply 'closely to reality' on the other. A theory is the way we perceive 'facts' and we cannot perceive 'facts' without a theory. (1953, p.34)

In that case, however, the facts of the economic world are no longer independent of the language used to describe them and a central tenet of Positive science has slipped. In its place we have the idea that the assumptions of a general theory set the terms in which reality is to be classified and the criteria by which we are to judge whether a particular theory applies to it. It seems that a severely empiricist approach to social science, which tries to confine its epistemological warrants to perception, induction and the success of prediction, has discovered a need for some 'general axioms' long before reaching the end of its way. At this stage these are only cryptic hints at a new way of thinking about the relation of theory to experience but they will be pursued in the next chapter.

Meanwhile Friedman's critics will doubtless complain that it is not even 'as if' markets are perfectly competitive. I leave that debate to economists. But there is also a philosophical issue. The first question just discussed was whether Positive economics needs realistic assumptions, as distinct from successful predictions. Here I suggest that Friedman's 'as if' manoeuvre is to be commended, once we have separated two of its uses. To say that bodies in earth's atmosphere fall as if in a vacuum is presumably to claim that air usually offers too little resistance to worry about. That is straightforwardly an empirical claim. To say that a kingfisher angles its dive as if it has mastered advanced mathematics is not to conjecture that it has reached roughly this standard. It is to propose an imaginative theoretical leap, warranted by its elegance and simplicity, although only if fertile predictions result. The second question was about the role of theory, however, and here I suggest that the role just assigned has much to be said for it but threatens to subvert Bacon's second way very near the start.

DISCOVERY AND VALIDATION

How damaging to a basic empiricism is it to give theory an active role? The neatest defence is to divorce psychology from epistemology by pursuing the earlier thought that tautologies can be surprising. There is an intellectual process of discovery which gives us new ideas. Part of it consists in exploring or constructing formal systems but this is not to say that it is all a rational exercise in deductive logic, as rationalists might fancy. The starting points of formal systems are a matter of choice, imagination or psychological chance. Admittedly starting points can be revised, if they lead the theorist into difficulty, as with the progressive refinement of the axioms of number theory or mathematical logic over many years. But there is still an intellectual leap of the 'as if' variety. This reopens Bacon's second way, provided that we are firm in distinguishing the psychological process of discovering hypotheses from the epistemological process of validating them. The test of truth on Bacon's second way can only be that of experiment and observation, 'the comparison of predictions with experience'. Its rationale is firmly epistemological and there is no alternative.

With that fixed, there is then welcome scope for psychologists and sociologists of science to enquire how scientific imagination works and in what institutional settings.

This removes one large obstacle. The objection was that no science does or could confine itself to generalising from observations. Every promising scientific theory needs richer 'assumptions' from which it can spin complex webs remote from the ordinary facts of experience. If the demand for empirical realism made theory brutally subservient to experience, a way which started with the senses and rose by a gradual and unbroken ascent could achieve nothing like the present state of science. But if the empiricist demand is addressed firmly to the logic of validation, leaving discovery to dabble in whatever it fancies, then the way might still lead to the most general axioms, as Bacon hoped.

To bring this out and, at the same time, to offer the promised practical guidance on how to apply scientific method, let us next compare two diagrams from basic textbooks for social science students. The first, Figure 3.1, comes from Walter Wallace's

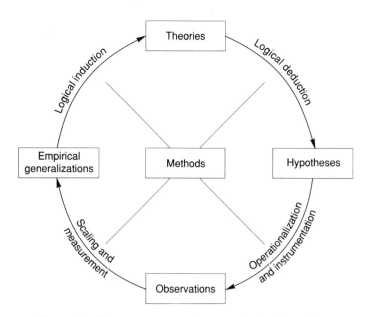

Figure 3.1   The components and process of scientific sociology

introduction to *Sociological Theory* (1969) and is labelled 'The components and process of scientific sociology'. The components are, effectively, only observations and inductive generalisations, with 'Theories' taken to be empirical generalisations generalised, and 'Hypotheses' its logical implications. Wallace gives Durkheim's theory of suicide as an illustration. We are to start by 'making direct observations on several persons who have committed suicide'. Having classified the victims into categories and computed the various rates, we arrive at an empirical generalisation like 'Protestants have a higher suicide rate than Catholics'. To advance to 'Theories' we ask 'of what can the suicide differential be taken as a special case?', and suggest, for instance, that 'suicide varies inversely with the degree of social integration' or 'acts of personal disorganisation vary inversely with the degree of social organisation'. Then we deduce further hypotheses, for instance that unmarried persons, being less socially integrated than marrieds, have a higher suicide rate. Such hypotheses, operationalised, are put to the test of further observation. If they are validated, the theory is confirmed.

Wallace's process embodies both discovery and validation. We advance by broadening generalisations, which we validate by testing their implications. We explain particular suicides by assigning them to categories with confirmed rates related to degrees of social integration. The process is like that recommended earlier for explaining M. Rouget's vote, except that, whereas he had a .80 probability of voting communist, Protestants or unmarried persons, taken at random, have a very low probability of committing suicide. Nevertheless the strategy is the same, even if the task of explaining why John Smith in particular committed suicide is not finally one for a scientific sociology which deals only in statistics and occupants of social positions.

Yet the scientific process cannot be as mechanical as this suggests. Why pick out Protestants as worth examining, rather than, say, left-handers? What prompted the idea of 'social integration', especially seeing that Durkheim himself was thinking in terms of social structures and how they maintain their equilibrium? Indeed it is high time similar questions were raised about M. Rouget too. What prompted interest in his age rather than his taste in socks and how did the church get into the story? Even if the explanations offered are suitably tailored to the method of validation *ex post*, they do not commit us to a corresponding method of discovery *ex ante*.

The second diagram recognises the difference. Figure 3.2 comes from Richard Lipsey's *Introduction to Positive Economics* (1963) whose introductory chapter lays out the bones of Positive science and scientific method. Here the process of validation is similar, in that 'Predictions' are implications derived from 'assumptions', which have been adjusted in response to the failure of previous predictions. But the diagrams are significantly different. The 'Definitions' in the top box signal something not provided by 'newly acquired facts' and, as the text of Lipsey's Introduction makes clear, 'theory' is a source of the 'hypotheses' rather than an inductive generalisation of successful ones. Otherwise the rest of Lipsey's large and increasingly theoretical guide to Positive economics would make no sense at all. But he is not afraid that he has betrayed the empirical character of Positive science. The single test of the validity of a theory remains whether its implications are consistent with the facts.

There are other differences, connected with the topic of testing, which I postpone to the next chapter. Meanwhile I shall close by stating the simplest idea of Positive science which seems to me defensible and then indicate the sorts of objection which later chapters will pursue.

CONCLUSION

The Positive notion of explanation deployed in this chapter is often called 'the covering law model': to explain is to identify the relevant generalisations which cover the case to be explained. Its blend of hypotheses and deductive inference also gives it the names of 'Deductive-Nomological (D-N) model' or 'Hypothetico-Deductive (H-D) Method'. The basic idea is very simple, however, and we can readily see the sort of explanation it proposes for M. Rouget's vote. All is a matter of observation and of inductive empirical generalisations from which his vote can be predicted.

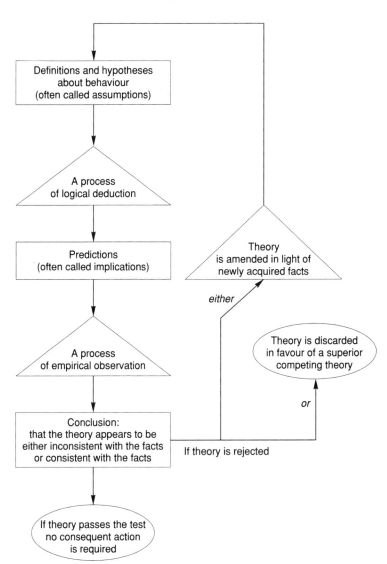

Figure 3.2

The *ontology* is of particulars, existing independently of theory and awaiting observation. These particulars are most readily taken as individual objects (including humans). But M. Rouget is an individual with parts and we should remain open-minded about whether there are other more complex individuals, like firms, nations or classes. Perhaps a Positive science which relies on observation has a view about the maximum complexity of a particular; but, if so, we have not tried to elicit it. The *methodology* is aimed at identifying regularities in the behaviour of particulars. It does not seek to detect underlying structures, forces or causal necessities, for the good reason that there are none. In involves theoretical abstraction and deductive reasoning but only for the sake of arriving at improved predictions. Inductive generalisations do the crucial work, being the bridge between known cases and the next case. They are the key to both prediction and explanation. The *epistemology* is as basic and simple a version of empiricism as will warrant the governing precept that only perception and the testing of prediction can justify claims to knowledge of the world.

So M. Rouget does vote communist 'because' he belongs to the intersection of various groups and his vote can be predicted on that basis. I stress again that the strength of so simple an answer is that it transfers the hard work to empirical research and statistical techniques which are not in the least simple. Also there is nothing simple about the lumber-clearing operations of empiricists and methodologists in keeping the ascent along Bacon's second way gradual and unbroken. But, finally, as Friedman puts it, 'the only test of the *validity* of a hypothesis is comparison of its predictions with experience'. Any explanation of M. Rouget's vote has to keep this faith.

If readers remain stubbornly unconvinced, they are in good company. The rationalism presented in Chapter 2 ran into great trouble but not of a sort which can simply be by-passed. There are urgent matters which this chapter has not resolved. Even if prediction is finally what counts, the line proposed so far cannot rely on a clear separation between matters of fact and relations of ideas, with facts independent of theory and 'ideas' regarded as components of a language which we construct. This is too simple-minded, as Friedman in effect granted when he deemed theory 'the way we perceive "facts" '. The point will be pursued in the next chapter.

Moreover, it is far from plain that prediction and explanation are two sides of the only coin. Anyone who holds that there are structures, forces and other furniture of the world which are beyond all powers of observation will certainly deny it. But so will anyone else who is not yet satisfied that Lipsey's diagram lets us distinguish accidental regularities which merely happen to have held so far from 'law-like' regularities suited to causal explanations. In that case Hume's account of causation will have omitted something crucial, since, as critics will have been itching to complain, mere constant conjunction *explains* nothing.

The next chapter therefore starts with basic doubts about our simple-minded version of empiricism. Can empiricists be more ingenious or does Bacon's second way depend on a mistake?

CHAPTER 4

Ants, Spiders and Bees: a third way?

Later in the *First Book of Aphorisms* Bacon tempers his claim that a gradual and unbroken ascent from the senses and particulars is 'the true way':

> Those who have handled sciences have been either men of experiment or men of dogmas. The men of experiment are like the ant, they only collect and use: the reasoners resemble spiders, who make cobwebs out of their own substance. But the bee takes a middle course: it gathers its material from the flowers of the garden and of the field, but transforms and digests it by a power of its own. Not unlike this is the true business of philosophy: for it neither relies solely or chiefly on the powers of the mind, nor does it take the matter which it gathers from natural history and mechanical experiments and lay it up in the memory whole, as it finds it, but lays it up in the understanding altered and digested. Therefore from a closer and purer league between these two faculties, the experimental and the rational (such as has never yet been made), much may be hoped.

These graphic similes highlight our previous two chapters. Formal systems and abstract theories are too like cobwebs to serve rationalist hopes that they correspond to the real, necessary order of the world. Pure empiricists who merely collect and use cannot do justice to the role of theory in guiding our steps. Admittedly this last point might not matter, if the process of discovery can be cleanly separated from the process of validation. But we shall be raising doubts about that in a moment. Meanwhile Bacon suggests that 'a closer and purer league between these two faculties, the experimental and the rational' will do what is needed. We are to be like the bee which 'takes a middle course: it gathers its material from the flowers of the garden and of the field, but transforms and digests it by a power of its own'. This attractive thought certainly captures a general belief that knowledge is, somehow, a blend of theory and experience, to which each contributes something beyond the scope of the other.

Here lie a host of puzzles, which are the stuff of current debate. Bacon's idea of 'a closer and purer league' is somehow to combine 'axioms' derived from the senses with 'axioms' revealed to the intellect. That sounds like a shrewd move. Traditionally there are two firm constraints on what we can rationally come to believe about the world. One is that our beliefs must be consistent with any facts known to us by observation. The other is that they must be logically coherent. Within these bounds, beliefs will be more or less probable, depending on degrees of proof or evidence. The bounds themselves, however, seem to be given without further proof or evidence. Thus Bacon calls them axioms and many philosophers have held that, without some kind of 'foundations' there could be no knowledge.

The chapter will start by propounding this view; and will then challenge it by suggesting that there can be no facts prior to all interpretation. This will raise further questions about discovery and validation, to be tackled with the help of Karl Popper. But radical thoughts will have been stirred and we shall next consider Quine's Pragmatist image of science as a web of belief. When that reminds us of the spiders who make cobwebs out of their own substance, we shall turn to Thomas Kuhn's thesis that science depends on 'paradigms'. Having then caught up with the present, untidy state of the philosophy of science, we shall be ready for two chapters of dispute between holists and individualists.

FOUNDATIONS OF KNOWLEDGE?

The idea that knowledge needs to rest on 'foundations' is crucial for understanding much of modern philosophy. The claim is that nothing can be known by proof or evidence, unless something can be known without either. Relatedly, nothing can be probable, unless something is certain. We need to see why this thesis is intensely plausible, before turning to recent developments which nevertheless deny it.

The case for 'foundations' is most easily made by reflecting that much of our knowledge depends on inference. Suppose I were to list all the propositions which I fancy that I know to be true, and then set myself the task of overhauling the list in order to winnow out any which, on reflection, I cannot warrantably claim to know. Many of the entries depend on inferences. For example, my knowledge that there were once dodos on the island of Mauritius is inferential. An inferred entry is conditional, in the sense that it is warranted only if other entries are warranted. So I shall put a star against all conditional entries on the list. Am I justified in retaining a starred entry? That depends on whether premises from which it can be inferred are also on the list and on whether at least some of them are unstarred. For, however sound an inference is, its conclusion is not a known truth, unless its premises are known truths. This applies as much to a conclusion that there *probably* were once dodos on Mauritius as to a stronger conclusion that there were once dodos there.

Now suppose I find a subset of entries which is self-contained, in that all are starred and each depends solely on the others. A subset dealing with the existence and habits of fairies might be an example. To anticipate a later chapter, so might a conceptual scheme spinning together witchcraft, oracles and magic; or a set of religious beliefs, complete with a theology. I would have to conclude that I knew the truth of none of these entries. For, if I know the truth of P only if I know the truth of Q, and if, moreover, my warrant for claiming to know Q is P itself (or else R, S etc., whose warrant is P), then I know the truth of neither P nor Q. The diameter of the circle is irrelevant and, if my whole list turns out to form such a complete subset of itself, then I know nothing at all. Hence there will have to be some unstarred entries. For knowledge to be possible, there must be some propositions which can be known without proof or evidence. These are my foundations of knowledge.

This neat and powerful argument has traditionally impressed rationalists and empiricists alike, ever since Descartes used a version of it in his *Meditations*. It covers both the experimental and the rational faculties, and holds as well for basics of logic or mathematics as for givens in perception. When empiricists rejected the pretensions of rationalism, they did not reject the argument. The data supplied to and by the senses were claimed to be 'self-evident', in the sense of known without proof or evidence, and so suited to serve as foundations. The Logical Positivists were as committed to the need for foundations as any rationalist or any other empiricist before them. All justification has to end with truths which need no further justification.

It is worth stressing that some principles of inference need to be included in the foundations. Otherwise nothing can be built on the foundations. To infer that Q is true, we need to know not only that P is true but also that if P then Q. Inferences can be challenged, and the challenge can often be met by showing that a conditional statement like 'if P then Q' is true. But this cannot be done in every case, because every demonstration itself relies on inference. Hence some basic principles have to be self-evident. The point emerges readily, when we pose the riddle of induction from the previous chapter (p. 45) by asking what reason there is to accept that, if x per cent of known As are B, there is an x per cent probability that the next A will be B. If, for every reason, one had to offer a reason why it was a reason, the regress would make the riddle unanswerable. Perhaps it does! Similarly, there is also a riddle of deduction, because any proof of a principle of logic would require a principle of logic to certify it. So, if one asks what justifies the basic principles of logic, the only answer which might avoid begging the question seems to be that they are self-evident. Any embarrassment about self-evidence is peculiar neither to empiricists nor to rationalists. All foundational systems need ultimately to assume the soundness of their 'axioms' and method of construction.

Bacon presents the bee as simply combining the 'axioms' known to our rational and experimental faculties and using whatever proof and evidence is available to either. But his remark about the mind transforming and digesting its given material 'by a power of its own' raises a deep problem about objectivity. The aim of the first way was, in de Fontenelle's image, to go behind the scenes at the opera and see how reality causes appearances. The aim of the second way was to identify the regularities in phenomena (appearances) without having to speculate on hidden causes. For both ways the mind was active in seeking truth but could be finally self-effacing, since the truths discovered were objective and untainted by any peculiarity of human involvement in the search. For both, one might say, the mind is finally a camera which records things as they are, however ingenious its operations. The current fashion is to deny that the mind can ever be a neutral recorder. Perhaps, indeed, not even a photograph is a neutral representation, because we interpret photographs, just as we interpret scenes photographed. Traditionally both ants and spiders have maintained that there are indeed moments of pure observation or intuition, when truth is revealed without interpretation. But the bee, Bacon suggests, lays nothing up in the understanding until it has been altered and digested. If he is right, then a closer and purer league between the experimental and rational faculties will not do the trick, and we shall need to find a third way.

INTERPRETATION

Empiricists are especially vulnerable to the idea that truth is never prior to all interpretation. The traditional core of their case against rationalists has always been that the 'experimental faculty' is pure, whereas the 'rational faculty' depends on the construction of the mind. Perception alone gives us unvarnished news, in the form of brute, uninterpreted facts, and, by the previous argument, without this foundation, we could know nothing of the world. The mind itself contributes nothing of substance. It is a *tabula rasa* or blank paper, on which experience writes the first knowledge. This doctrine remains crucial. For instance the hopes of a pure, Positive science discussed in the previous chapter depend squarely on it. The ingenious separation of the process of discovery from the process of validation was partly designed to preserve it. By letting the scientist import unobservables into theories and models for purposes of discovery, it took pressure off the moment of pure, neutral truth when prediction meets experience.

Yet the doctrine has been under fire from the start. A basic trouble, hinted at on p. 44, is that the idea of 'experience' is ambiguous. It is used to refer both to what is presented to us, and to the experiencing; and it leaves the relation of subjective to objective elements unclear even for a 'given' like a perceived patch of colour. Although this is not the place for a tour of the philosophy of perception, it is easy to see that the ambiguity may be endemic. To describe what we experience we must apply concepts and the suggestion is that concepts are never merely dictated by phenomena, since they are involved in classifying even phenomena. In that case there is nothing more basic than an experiencing, where concept and object are inextricable. One sees the point of Immanuel Kant's famous remark in *The Critique of Pure Reason* (1781) that 'concepts without percepts are empty; percepts without concepts are blind'. To observe is not merely to register but to judge what concepts apply. Concepts are, some-how, supplied by the mind and, since they govern what we make of the world, are not the mere servants of experience.

Empiricists do not take this lying down, of course, and I shall not try to prove that they must concede it. But I can show what difficulties it causes for the idea of a Positive science. What follows is a brief outline of three recent contributions to the philosophy of science, each exploiting the idea that experience cannot play the role in scientific knowledge which was suggested in the previous chapter. Their authors are Karl Popper, W.v.O. Quine and Thomas Kuhn.

SCIENCE AS CONJECTURES AND REFUTATIONS

Popper has influenced social thinking directly with two books in particular. *The Open Society and its Enemies* (1945) reviews the history of political thought, condemns those, like Plato, Hegel and Marx, who have sought to entrench the power of the state and com-mends the openness to critical enquiry enshrined in a tolerant, liberal society. *The Poverty of Historicism* (1960) denies Marxist and Hegelian claims that there are laws of history and dialectical processes peculiar to the social world and hence to social science. It upholds the naturalist view that the natural and social worlds are all of a piece and are amenable to the same scientific method. The method is one of 'conjectures and refutations', an

enormously influential idea in the philosophy of science at large
and one whose impact on social scientists has been no less for
entering social science by that route.

His best known essay is probably 'Science: Conjectures and
Refutations' (in Popper (1969)), the text of a 1953 lecture in
which he reflected on his work in the philosophy of science
since 1919. The question addressed is 'When should a theory
be ranked as scientific?' Its most widely accepted answer,
Popper remarks, is 'that science is distinguished from pseudo-
science – or from metaphysics – by its *empirical method*, which is
essentially *inductive*, proceeding from observation and experiment. This did not satisfy me' (p.33). For, if what counted were
the amount of evidence confirming a theory, then many pseudo-
scientific theories would have to be deemed scientific. Examples
which had long troubled and infuriated him were Marx's theory
of history, Freud's psychoanalytic theories and Adler's psychology. These theories were awash with confirming evidence but for
the unsatisfactory reason that their adherents could square them
with whatever happened. 'A Marxist could not open a newspaper
without finding on every page confirming evidence for his interpretation of history' (p.35). They were, in a word, irrefutable. But,
since this was because they ran no risk of refutation, it was no
virtue. Hence '*the criterion of the scientific status of a theory is its falsifiability, or refutability or testability*' (p.37, his italics).

For a theory to be falsifiable there must be possible conditions
in which it would be shown to be false. These conditions need to
be specified in advance of testing and stood by, if the test goes
against the theory. There must be no 'conventionalist stratagem'
of conjuring up special reasons in the form of *ad hoc* extra assumptions or reinterpretations of results to save the theory. Scientific
theories take genuine risks: pseudo-scientific or metaphysical theories do not. Correspondingly, this is the difference between
critical thinking and dogmatic thinking (and, one might add,
between open and closed societies). Critical thinking adapts to
refutation by experience; dogmatic thinking rejects the counter-
examples.

Popper presents his account of falsifiability in science as a
rejection of Hume's analysis of knowledge and of the ideas

about Positive science which stem from it, especially those propounded by the Logical Positivists. It is not immediately obvious why. The difference between empiricists and others seems to be precisely that empiricists seek humbly to respect the findings of experience, whereas Bacon's 'men of dogmas' spin cobwebs out of their own substance. The diagram of scientific method on p.63 taken from Lipsey and the sketch of a Positive economics given by Friedman appear to embody a clear sense that falsifiability is crucial. What, then, is novel and disconcerting about Popper?

Popper himself makes it partly a matter of the psychology of science and partly of the logic of science, with Hume as a target for both. Hume, as we saw, took the relation of cause and effect as central to knowledge of the world, because it was the only one which went beyond mere impressions and ideas, but then reduced causation to regularities or 'constant conjunctions' in nature, coupled with a psychological expectation that they would continue. In effect this made science an exercise in induction, as on Bacon's second way, but with the sharp proviso that 'all our reasonings concerning matters of fact rest in the end on custom'. Custom here refers to 'the association of ideas', the standard eighteenth-century account of how we come by concepts and learn language. Ideas are prompted in us by 'impressions' or simple experiences. Frequent impressions give rise to concepts, and regular conjunctions of impressions lead us to associate ideas, thus producing a conceptual scheme which reflects the world as we find it, provided that we attend to experience. The crucial relation in the forming of concepts is 'resemblance': we simply recognise that two red patches resemble one another in both being red. The edifice of knowledge thus depends on regularities in nature obtruding themselves on the mind.

Let me say at once that a careful reading of Hume finds that imagination is involved in the association of ideas and the expectations aroused by constant conjunctions. That makes for a less passive mind than I have just suggested. But it is not altogether easy to integrate these active elements with the rest of Hume's science of mind, where associations occur passively in the main, and Popper certainly takes Hume to rest everything on the givenness of resemblances. His criticism of Hume is therefore radical and uncompromising: there is no process of merely registering impressions and patterns of impressions, and hence no psychological process of induction. Hence 'the belief that we can start with pure observations alone, without anything in the nature of a theory is absurd' (p.35).

Popper contends that 'we are born with expectations: with knowledge which, although not valid *a priori*, is psychologically or genetically *a priori* i.e. prior to all observational experience' and that 'one of the most important of these expectations is that of finding a regularity' (p.47). We might usefully regard this as a gloss on Bacon's idea that the mind alters and digests experience with a power of its own and so as one reason why the scientist cannot merely collect and use observations. It thus encourages the separation between the process of discovery and the process of validation which we have already made on behalf of Positive science. Whereas Wallace's wheel (p.60) pictured a single process of mechanical generalisation for both purposes, Lipsey's apparatus (p.63) was more complex – more like a percolator – and had a box where conjectures could be introduced, provided that the work of validation was done by empirical testing. Since Lipsey admires Popper, this is no surprise; but it leaves us still asking why Popper denounces Positivism.

The answer lies in the implications for the logic of science. In inductive reasoning, broadly speaking, the more *A*s are found to be *B*s the better confirmed is the hypothesis that all *A*s are *B*s. Popper has no patience with a scientific method which relies on this logic. He flatly denies that if a hypothesis (H) implies an observation statement (O) and if O is true, then H is thereby confirmed. In formal logic there is no valid inference:

(1) $H \rightarrow O$
(2) O
therefore (3) H

Nor is there merit in making the conclusion expressly probabilistic:

therefore (3) H is more probable

That is merely the same inference in thin disguise. On the other hand there is no similar objection to a logic of falsification. There is a valid inference:

(1) $H \rightarrow O$
(2) $not\text{-}O$
therefore (3) $not\text{-}H$

and this is precisely the inference which dogmatists try to shrug off. That is the crucial difference between confirmation and falsification and the final reason why

Induction, i.e. inference based on many observations, is a myth. It is neither a psychological fact, nor a fact of ordinary life, nor one of scientific procedure. (1969, p.53)

In upshot, science is always open-ended, offering no certainties and no rest for the enquiring mind. The process of testing does not tend to eliminate all hypotheses other than the true one. Whenever a genuinely risky conjecture survives refutation, there are always plenty of other conflicting conjectures which would have survived too. The logic of validation establishes only that some theories are false. Although science eliminates theories and passes on only survivors, it passes them on 'not as dogmas but rather with the challenge to discuss them and improve on them' (p.50). The image of science which emerges is no longer one of making a uniquely correct map of a partially known landscape. Nor is it one of erecting a building on sure foundations in the traditional way. As Popper declares in *The Logic of Scientific Discovery* (1959):

The empirical basis of objective science has thus nothing 'absolute' about it. Science does not rest upon solid bedrock. The bold structure of its theories rises, as it were above a swamp. It is like a building erected on piles. The piles are driven down from above into the swamp, but not down to any natural or 'given' base; and if we stop driving the piles deeper, it is not because we have reached firm ground. We simply stop when we are satisfied that the piles are firm enough to carry the structure, as least for the time being. (p.111)

Popper's ideas are exciting and he writes splendidly. But they are not as radical as he makes out. He presents refutations as decisive moments when a theory falls foul of observation and is eliminated. These are meant to be unmistakable moments of truth, even if the truth is the negative one that a theory is false. Yet there cannot possibly be such decisive moments, unless we are sure that the same would always occur if the test were repeated. But that depends on an inductive inference from the present occasion to the next. Otherwise why not simply try it again? Deny the soundness of induction, and we have no reason to eliminate a theory just because its predictions have not been upheld on particular occasions. If Popper has indeed shown that induction is a myth, we cannot rest content with the logic of falsification. For, if he means just what he says, there will be no reason to prefer unfalsified theories and we have been led into a general scepticism. Yet, as soon as falsification is seen to rely on induction for its claim to be decisive, the riddle of induction resurfaces and Popper can no longer declare, 'Thus the problem of induction is solved' (1969, p.55).

Furthermore the moment of truth is one where theory is tested against pure observation or brute fact. Or so Popper implies. Yet 'the belief that we can start with pure observations alone, without anything in the nature of a theory is absurd' (1969, p.35). In that case theory is involved in defining the test situation and in identifying what is observed in it. When refutation is deemed to occur, the tester must, in effect, be weighing the merits of the theory which yielded the prediction against the merits of the theory which yielded the description of what experience showed. Experiments are a complex business and there is always scope for contending that they are somehow defective or do not show exactly what is supposed. Interpretation, in short, is never absent, and there is no neutral standpoint when judging which theories it is rational to accept.

These are serious objections, which show, I think, that vintage Popper is closer to a classic empiricism than he supposed. That might sound good news for Bacon's ant-like 'men of experiment', since it leaves the process by which the bee transforms and digests its material finally subject to experience. But the trouble goes deeper, as witnessed by changes in Popper's own views, for example *Objective Knowledge* (1972). We are left trying to maintain both that there are moments of pure truth when facts test theories, and that observation is never innocent of theory. The bee is not just the ant turned ruminative. Pragmatism beckons.

SCIENCE AS A WEB OF BELIEF

Pragmatism insists that the mind is always active in deciding what counts as knowledge. Yet, although that makes all our concepts and beliefs revisable, revisions are to be made in the light of experience. To put it paradoxically, theory governs experience and experience governs theory. This interplay may cause trouble in the end but is immensely fertile in the meantime. The readiest introduction to recent developments is Quine's electrifying and prescient (1953) essay 'Two Dogmas of Empiricism', whose theme I shall now sketch. The two dogmas are the twin pillars of Logical Positivism, which we treated as a rationale for Positive science in the previous chapter. They are, firstly, the analytic–synthetic distinction and, secondly, the given, uninterpreted character of basic facts of observation. Quine's article seeks to demolish both, thus also subverting the broader empiricism which Logical Positivists had intended to render precise.

As noted in the previous chapter, the analytic–synthetic distinction is a neat device for keeping what Hume called 'relations of ideas' distinct from 'matters of fact and existence', thus heading off rationalist hopes that we can have *a priori* knowledge of reality. Analytic truths are 'true by convention' and so harmless to empiricism, once one realises that they result solely from how we decide to use words. Quine endorses the part played by human convention in giving some statements a privileged position in our knowledge. But he denies that even the truths of logic and mathematics are as utterly distinct from empirical statements as the analytic–synthetic distinction makes them. His argument defies compression; but the nub of it is that 'true by convention' cannot be construed as Logical Positivism hopes. What exactly is it that marks off analytic statements from others? The question can be answered only by appeal to notions like 'necessity', 'logical

equivalence' or 'sameness of meaning', which the notion of ana-
lyticity is alleged to account for. But to make it somehow ultimately self-evident that a truth like 'All bachelors are unmarried'
is analytic is to license the kind of *a priori* intuition which empiricists must reject.

To avoid playing into the hands of the opposition, we need to
think of analytic statements as held in place by conventions which
experience can bring us to revise. They may be more deeply
entrenched in our conceptual scheme or web of belief than are
synthetic statements; but they cannot be immune to revision
altogether. When we do revise them, it has to be for the same
sort of reason too, namely that experience is resisting our attempts
to describe and order it with their help. For example, astronomers
long worked with a geometry derived from Euclidean axioms.
But, when the pressure of experience led them to wonder
whether space is best described in Euclidean terms, they revised
Euclid. Some revisions are less far-reaching than others and we
try the less radical revisions first. But priorities are a matter of
degree of entrenchment in our thinking. No statement is finally
immune to revision, not even the most elementary parts of logic
and mathematics. The threads of our intellectual fabric are none
of them pure black or white (purely analytic or purely synthetic)
but various shades of grey.

By disputing the first dogma of empiricism, Quine gives scope
for experience to influence all forms of theory. Conversely, by
disputing the second, he involves theory in every moment of
empirical truth. Synthetic or empirical statements are never directly at the mercy of experience. Even very particular ones, like
'the cat is on the mat', are connected to others as part of a web
whose inner strands and nodes are remote from the experiential
perimeter. A whole section of the web is thus at stake, when we
look to see whether the cat is on the mat. The greater the stakes,
the greater becomes our resistance to letting experience surprise
us. The connections supply us with defences, since we can invoke
them to show that we have misinterpreted experience. When
experience seems to conflict with our beliefs, we always have a
choice of what to revise; and, since we interpret whenever we
describe, one choice is to reinterpret the experience. Our beliefs

do face the tribunal of experience; but they face it as a single body and there is always room for manoeuvre. In the web of belief no statement ever has to be given up, just as no statement is immune to revision.

This takes the idea that observation without theory is absurd far further than Popper does. Observation has become so bound up with interpretation and hence with theory that, in deciding what the facts of observation are, we may be deciding between rival theories. I shall not trace the theme deeper into pragmatism at large, since its history and ramifications are too complex for this book. To strengthen our feel for it, however, here are three glorious paragraphs from Quine's 'Two Dogmas', which bring pragmatism vividly to life. Notice how even physical objects would be unobservables, were they not treated as 'convenient intermediaries', and are assigned the same epistemological status as Homeric gods.

The totality of our so-called knowledge or beliefs, from the most casual matters of geography and history to the profoundest laws of atomic physics or even of pure mathematics and logic, is a man-made fabric which impinges on experience only along the edges. Or, to change the figure, total science is like a field of force whose boundary conditions are experience. A conflict with experience at the periphery occasions readjustments in the interior of the field. Truth values have to be redistributed over some of our statements. Reevaluation of some statements entails reevaluation of others, because of their logical interconnections – the logical laws being in turn simply certain further statements of the system, certain further elements of the field. Having reevaluated one statement we must reevaluate some others, which may be statements logically connected with the first or may be the statements of logical connections themselves. But the total field is so under-determined by its boundary conditions, experience, that there is much latitude of choice as to what statements to reevaluate in the light of any single contrary experience. No particular experiences are linked with any particular statements of the interior of the field, except indirectly through considerations of equilibrium affecting the field as a whole.

If this view is right, it is misleading to speak of the empirical content of an individual statement – especially if it is a statement at all remote from the experiential periphery of the field. Furthermore it becomes folly to seek a boundary between synthetic statements, which hold contingently on experience, and analytic statements, which hold come

what may. Any statement can be held true come what may, if we make drastic enough adjustments elsewhere in the system. Even a statement very close to the periphery can be held true in the face of recalcitrant experience by pleading hallucination or by amending certain statements of the kind called logical laws. Conversely, by the same token, no statement is immune to revision. Revision even of the logical law of the excluded middle has been proposed as a means of simplifying quantum mechanics; and what difference is there in principle between such a shift and the shift whereby Kepler superseded Ptolemy, or Einstein Newton, or Darwin Aristotle?
. . .

As an empiricist I continue to think of the conceptual scheme of science as a tool, ultimately, for predicting future experience in the light of past experience. Physical objects are conceptually imported into the situation as convenient intermediaries – not by definition in terms of experience, but simply as irreducible posits comparable, epistemologically, to the gods of Homer. For my part I do, qua lay physicist, believe in physical objects and not in Homer's gods; and I consider it a scientific error to believe otherwise. But in point of epistemological footing the physical objects and the gods differ only in degree and not in kind. Both sorts of entities enter our conception only as cultural posits. The myth of physical objects is epistemologically superior to most in that it has proved more efficacious than other myths as a device for working a manageable structure into the flux of experience. (1953, section 6, paras 1,2,4)

Cashing in Quine's riotous metaphors, we are being invited to recognise both that no single hypothesis can be tested in isolation and that every observation is linked theoretically to other observations. There is no longer a simple logic of falsification. Instead, there are always irreducible options:

(1) $(H_1$ and H_2 and H_3 . . . etc.$) \rightarrow (O_1$ and O_2 and O_3 . . . etc.$)$
(2) *Not*-$(O_1$ and O_2 and O_3 . . . etc.$)$
therefore (3) *Not*-H_1 or *not*-H_2 or *not*-H_3 . . . etc.

Choice of where exactly to point the accusing finger of refutation is ours, not nature's, because there is nowhere for the mind to stand prior to all interpretation.

Thus prompted, we can now usefully ask whether Lipsey's percolator (p.63) truly embodies the idea of a Positive science after all. The percolator is meant to depict a definite process of adapting scientific hypotheses to independent facts of experience, thus serving to advance Positive economics. It is more sophisticated than Wallace's wheel (p. 60) on two counts. By recognising a distinction between processes of discovery and validation, it can allow for 'assumptions' which refer to unobservables; and, by saying that confirmation calls for 'no consequent action', it signals agreement with Popper's theme that confirmation does not raise the probability of a hypothesis. These refinements are consistent with a Positive economics. But it also takes a further step. On reflection, why does Lipsey mark the moment of truth with the word 'appears' ('the theory appears to be either inconsistent with the facts or consistent with the facts')? What determines choice at the fork where the theory is to be amended (how?) or discarded? Why is it to be discarded only if there is 'a superior competing theory'? Pragmatist thoughts are at work here. Lipsey has quietly credited the mind with more of a power of its own than straight empiricism can allow. When theory *appears* at odds with fact, we decide whether it *is* so, against a background of hitherto accepted theories. The process of testing thus slides into one of 'working a manageable structure into the flux of experience'.

Similarly, we can now resume the cryptic hints in the previous chapter that Friedman's (1953) essay gives theory more to do than a Positive science can countenance. The first half, with its celebrated account of Positive economics, leads on to a second half which could fairly be called pragmatist. 'Known facts cannot be set on one side; a theory to apply "closely to reality" on the other. A theory is the way we perceive "facts", and we cannot perceive "facts" without a theory' (p.34). This remark follows a discussion of how we should choose between theories, when several predict consistently with the facts. Friedman does not merely tell us to leave it to further experience. Instead, he recommends choosing theories which involve an abstraction or 'ideal type' marked by 'economy, clarity and precision' (1953, p.33). Theory is no longer simply a recording device or 'filing system' but has become a source of selections from the mass of data. Data can even be discarded for the sake of economy and clarity. Why exactly are we to prefer these virtues? Friedman's answer is arresting.

A fundamental hypothesis of science is that appearances are deceptive and that there is a way of looking at or interpreting or organising the evidence that will reveal superficially disconnected and diverse phenomena to be manifestations of a more fundamental and relatively simple structure. (1953, p.33)

If this 'fundamental hypothesis of science' is not to be a concession to the reality of fundamental structures in reality, it will have to state a principle for filing systems or languages. Even so, the second half of the essay threatens to destabilise its better known first half. Positive economics as an empirical science whose sole task is to predict phenomena with success yields to a Pragmatist economics, whose aim is the most simple and elegant theory consistent with those 'facts' which it leads us to perceive and deem significant. Theory is no longer merely the servant of experience.

Very well; but why exactly are we to prefer theories with the Pragmatist virtues of economy, clarity, precision, elegance, simplicity or suggestiveness? If disconnected and diverse phenomena are not manifestations of a simple, fundamental reality, such criteria are not necessarily guides to truth. Why are elegant theories more likely to survive the tribunal of experience? The answer will have to be internal to the web of belief. *Everything* which the bee lays up in the understanding has been altered and digested by the mind, operating with a power of its own. Claims about the structure of reality are no exception. It is one thing to show that theory is irreducibly involved in all understanding, and quite another to connect this activity to the search after truth.

Quine says that the tribunal of experience issues verdicts which we must accept, even if we choose how to adjust the web of belief in consequence. Whose tribunal is it? It seems to me that it can only be ours. Nature has become a myth or cultural posit, like the gods of Homer or the everyday physical objects which we bump into. In a system where no statement is immune to revision, how could statements about nature be otherwise? Indeed even the claim that we can keep (or revise) any statement at a price is misleading. It suggests that prices are imposed by nature and are a fixed element in the bargains struck with experience. But prices too are finally internal to the mind's activity, even if they have to do with the most deeply entrenched features of the web of belief, the most elementary notions of consistency and coherence. No doubt it remains useful to think in terms of negotiation with nature but, epistemologically speaking, the tribunal of experience is another myth.

The last paragraph could be accused of begging a large question, however. We have so far assumed a correspondence theory of truth, in which an empirical statement is true if and only if it corresponds to the facts. This accords nicely with the image of science as exploration and suits the case for demanding foundations of knowledge. But Pragmatism accepts none of this baggage. In internalising facts to the web of belief, it is happy to dispense with a correspondence theory of truth and to replace it with some equivalence between what is 'true' and what contributes to the simplest coherent web or what it is finally useful to believe. Since these moves take us deeper into the theory of knowledge than we can go now, I shall not try to press the previous paragraph home.

But one conclusion can safely be drawn. If Quine is right and *every* statement is open to revision, there must be more ways of ordering experience than we attempt. What limits our efforts? The traditional answer given at the start of the chapter is that reason and experience confine us to theories which accord with the known facts and the rules of logic. But Pragmatism has made both these kinds of constraint revisable. Why then do we subscribe to the myth of physical objects and the general theories of nature which go with it? Quine himself has conjectured that the answer might lie in the biology of the brain and our human constitution: we are, so to speak, hard-wired to construe experience very broadly as we do. But others have been more inclined to give cultural posits a cultural explanation.

PARADIGMS AND AFTER

The leading suggestion has been made by Thomas Kuhn in *The Structure of Scientific Revolutions* (2nd edition, 1970), where he introduces the notion of a 'paradigm'. Kuhn's researches into the history of science convinced him that the schoolroom or Enlightenment story of the smooth and steady progress of reason was simply a fiction. For instance the 'Copernican revolution', by which the earth was displaced as the fixed, central body in the heavens, involved no moment of truth when the old Ptolemaic astronomy was refuted and the new theory replaced it. On the contrary, the two astronomies coexisted uneasily for several centuries. Both could claim the evidence of observation and, although the balance shifted as telescopes improved, the Ptolemaic still had eminent defenders as late as the eighteenth century. Nor is this surprising, given that the relative motion of bodies can always be described in several ways by taking each in turn as the fixed reference point. Meanwhile the revolution which finally occurred was, at heart, a conceptual one, a growing willingness to think of the cosmos and its moral order in new ways, which presently coalesced into the modern world view. As concepts changed, historians started to view the old order through the eyes of the new and were thus led to construct the schoolroom story of reasoned discoveries.

Reflecting on this and other episodes, Kuhn was led to distinguish between normal and revolutionary science. 'Normal' science is the organised, progressive, everyday work of gathering evidence and testing hypotheses. It goes on within a framework of intellectual assumptions and established practices, which it takes for granted. This framework or 'paradigm' is not immutable, however. When normal science starts to throw up consistently unexpected results, it comes under strain. When a radically fresh way of viewing the wayward results emerges and is widely deemed to make convincing sense of them, it is overthrown. This is a 'scientific revolution' of the sort that occurred in the shift to a modern astronomy or when Einstein's theory of relativity replaced the creaking Newtonian paradigm which had served since the seventeenth century. As a paradigm shift makes its way through into a new way of conducting normal science, the scientist comes to work 'in a different world'.

The history of Kuhn's book illustrates its own thesis. The project was originally conceived in the 1940s as part of the *International Encyclopedia of Unified Science*. This was a series started by the Logical Positivists in the 1930s with the aim of overtaking and completing *L'Encyclopédie*, the project of charting all knowledge begun by 'Les Philosophes' at the acme of Enlightenment optimism. *The Structure of Scientific Revolutions* set out to convey some factual information about the history of science, thus filling a gap with, presumably, true synthetic statements. The first edition (1962) attracted little attention. But its thesis in fact threatened to put paid to the whole Positivist programme by showing that science depended on elements which had no possible place in the Logical Positivists' scheme. The second edition, with its new introduction, detonated this time-bomb and the book has become compulsory reading. To grant its thesis is to think of science, and indeed knowledge in general, in a new way, since the unavoidable paradigms which regulate normal science are not open to direct refutation, are not mere filing systems or tautologies and are too mutable to be attributed to universal and external Reason. The thesis is, in short, revolutionary.

A paradigm has two principal aspects, one intellectual and the other institutional. Intellectually it consists of a set of guiding 'axioms', to use Bacon's term, or basic tenets about the broad character of nature and how it is to be studied. Descartes' intellectual system is a good example with its bold, simple ideas about the unified system in nature, its new mathematical physics and its account of knowledge and how to achieve it. Whereas Descartes himself claimed to have discovered this new system by rational intuition, as we saw earlier, Kuhnians regard it as resting on presuppositions, for which there can be no warrant: since they comprise a framework within which all reasoning and interpretation then proceeds, they are beyond the reach of reason and experience. Yet they are not empty or idle, since they regulate the permissible uses of reason and interpretations of experience. In short they have the air of those irrefutable tenets which Popper condemned as pseudo-scientific.

On the other hand, presuppositions can shift, despite their apparent immunity to revision. The Cartesian system presently yielded to the rival Newtonian system. The Newtonian system was generalised by Immanuel Kant in *The Critique of Pure Reason* (1781) as the embodiment of the only complete and consistent set of categories capable of making sense of experience. But Kant spoke too soon, if Einstein can be credited with a better alternative – a matter which I shall not try to assess. Nor presumably will that be the end of the story in a hundred years' time. As Kuhn himself points out, these shifts emerge in the course of reasoned debate, even if each framework also sets the canon of reasoned debate. So we have a puzzle in accounting for the intellectual dynamics of systems which are equipped to rule out challenges to their stability. Perhaps some of the impetus comes from internal contradictions, which force intellectual choices when they work their way up to the surface. But Kuhn's clear message is that reason alone cannot account for everything done in the name of reason.

Accordingly, the other principal aspect of a paradigm is institutional. Normal science is also kept on track by social mechanisms. It is highly organised activity, usually with a hierarchic power structure. Young scientists serve apprenticeships, in which they learn to think and practise as required by the prevailing paradigm, and are promoted for learning the lesson well. The heroic saga of the isolated individual genius is purely a myth. Real scientists work in hierarchical communities, subject to a discipline which reinforces the paradigm. Also they need funds. Science is an industry with investors to satisfy as well as an exercise in curiosity. That usually means pleasing the government, whose aims are not disinterested. Those who pay the piper call the tune. Thus the knowledge industry is enmeshed in a wider social and political system, which helps further to explain why a particular paradigm persists and how it regulates the practice of science. Equally, a paradigm shift is likely to go with deep shifts in the distribution of power in the wider society. Even if epistemology remains important, the sociology of knowledge moves in to fill the gap which opens when paradigms are found to be beyond the epistemic reach of reason and experience.

The challenge to Enlightenment ideas of scientific knowledge is radical. I have stated it more starkly than Kuhn does, but a stark version helps to show why the notion of a paradigm has had such impact. There have been broadly two reactions, which I shall outline very briefly to show the sheer range of current discords.

Firstly, the invitation to make Reason the subject of a sociology of knowledge has been widely accepted and has encouraged many revealing studies in the sociology of science. The history of medicine, for instance, is illuminated by recognising that the acceptance of medical theories is related to the power of the church, the rise of a medical profession, the fact that doctors are mostly male and midwives female or the influence of giant pharmaceutical companies. Such applied sociology of knowledge is not subversive of Reason, if it presumes medicine to be a largely rational activity and seeks only to explain sociologically what is irrational or non-rational about it. But the very existence of paradigms suggests that what is regarded as rational activity is itself as much a social as an intellectual matter.

This suggestion invites a general and subversive relativism, where all beliefs are related to features of their social context, whatever their intellectual rationale. This is the line taken by the 'Strong Programme' in the sociology of knowledge, robustly articulated by Barry Barnes and David Bloor (1982), among others. Bloor has remarked that 'Knowledge for the sociologist is whatever men take to be knowledge. It consists of those beliefs which men confidently hold to and live by' (1976, p.2). If there is no more to knowledge than belief confidently adhered to, then even the internal connections within a web of belief depend on rules of reasoning whose local authority is a sociological matter. This is explicit in the Strong Programme and it applies equally to rules of scientific method.

Secondly, however, defenders of the Enlightenment project have not taken Kuhn lying down. Popperians especially have tried to uphold the idea that falsification is an objective process which advances knowledge, despite both the theory-dependence of observation and the apparent invulnerability of paradigms. Imre Lakatos (1978), in particular, has suggested that a scientific theory should be viewed as a core of key propositions crucial for the theory, protected by a belt or penumbra of auxiliary hypotheses many of which could be rejected without having to abandon the core. When prediction conflicts with experience, the scientist has a choice of whether to let an auxiliary hypothesis fall prey to the counter-example or to suspend judgement in the face of the anomaly to see whether the theory gets into wider trouble. The choice is governed by the state of health of the larger research programme to which the theory belongs. Any theory can always be saved by patching on new auxiliary hypotheses to explain away the previous conflict with experience. But if the patches are many and *ad hoc*, meaning that they have no theoretical rationale and are merely sticking plaster after the event, then the programme is 'degenerating'. A 'progressive' research programme responds to trouble in ways which make for theoretical sense and new conjectures in a spirit which Popper would applaud.

A feature of this response has been a counter-attack on Kuhn's sharp distinction between normal and revolutionary science. Popperians retort that the difference is a matter of degree of entrenchment, with normal science more willing to question its core theories than Kuhn recognised and revolutionary science more continuous with what went before. A sort of rapprochement has been reached. Popperians have become more holistic, more ready to think in terms of whole sets of interrelated theories and hypotheses, including those which import theoretical interpretation into the process of experiment and observation. This may abandon the definitive moments of truth at the heart of 'Conjectures and Refutations' but it lets science progress towards 'verisimilitude'. Kuhnians, no doubt reflecting that the thesis about paradigms is supposed to be a piece of objective science, have shied away from the acute relativism apparently implied by *The Structure of Scientific Revolutions*. Once we have absorbed the lesson that reason cannot be the sole arbiter of which beliefs it is rational to accept, the road is open for an objective account of science which takes social and political contexts into account. Perhaps we can come to identify the sort of context, liberal and democratic presumably, in which science fares best.

But the dragon's teeth have been sown and there may be no honest way for the warriors to avoid destroying one another. The

distinction between 'progressive' and 'degenerating' research programmes makes no sense to me, unless it presupposes the traditional view that there is an objective truth about an independent
natural world to find. Yet it seems to have been conceded that the
penetration of fact by theory and the influence of paradigms on
the criteria of sound theory destroy all traditional access by reason
to a world independent of our concepts and theories about it. The
hope that we can restore objectivity just by recognising the intellectual and institutional role of paradigms, as a prelude to
making allowance for it, seems to presuppose the neutral scientific standpoint thus undermined. At any rate, such suspicions have
been shrewdly fuelled by Paul Feyerabend's *Against Method* (1975).
So late in a long chapter I shall not try to summarise his reasons
for declaring that all attempts at universal rules of scientific
method are not only misplaced but also pernicious. They are
well worth reading and his theme is nicely captured by his remark that 'All methodologies have their limitations and the only
"rule" that survives is "anything goes"' (p.296).

The current scene is thus turbulent, even if we confine ourselves
to the descendants of Bacon's ants, spiders and bees. It is more
turbulent still, if we include the debates going on under the
banners of Deconstruction and Critical Theory. Since these require awareness of the hermeneutic tradition, however, I postpone even a token gesture, until we have explored the idea of
Understanding. Meanwhile, the chapter can best end at a point
further back on the Enlightenment trail, with *The Critique of Pure
Reason*. Kant has had slight mention so far and I do not see how to
do him justice in an introduction to the philosophy of social
science. But the *Critique* remains the preeminent attempt to combine the experimental and rational faculties, as Bacon demanded,
to recognise that all knowledge is mediated by interpretation and
yet to retain the idea of foundations for knowledge.

Kant was cited above for his remark that concepts without
percepts are empty and percepts without concepts are blind.
This interdependence of concepts and percepts is at the core of
the troubling process by which empirical material is laid up in the
understanding altered and digested. Our problem has been to
see why recognising this process does not undermine claims to

objectivity. Kant's solution in the *Critique* was to identify the concepts fundamental to our understanding of experience as acquaintance with a world of physical objects, causally related and persisting in space and time. Since experience itself acquaints us only with phenomena, this categorial apparatus is imposed by the mind. But that does not make it merely subjective or inter-subjective. Kant argued that, if we ask what makes knowledge of the world possible, we can answer by stating unique preconditions for finding a rationally describable order in experience. Any rational understanding whatever therefore presupposes this single way of working a manageable structure into the flux of experience. The categories on which understanding relies transcend experience, thus assuring us not that reality itself conforms to them but that our thinking is objectively warranted in using them. This line anticipates Quine's Pragmatism, quoted earlier, but with steel necessities, rather than rubber ones, so to speak.

Not seeing how to say more without writing a different book, I turn now to the lessons of Chapters 2, 3 and 4.

CONCLUSION

'Reason is the pace, increase of science the way, and the benefit of mankind the end,' Hobbes declared (in *Leviathan*, 1651, Chapter 5). We set off down the Enlightenment trail in high spirits. But the rationalist and empiricist ways of discovering truth both seem to have petered out; and attempts to combine them have left us afraid that 'anything goes'. Although it is too soon to despair, it is certainly time to take stock.

The rationalist way began excitingly, with the world as a watch driven by hidden wheels and springs and Reason as a source of insight into such structures and forces. But it involved a disloca-tion between reality and appearance, which invited Bacon's scornful comparison with spiders who make cobwebs out of their own substance.

The empiricist way therefore looked more promising. The world was to consist of observable particulars; induction and prediction were to do the methodological work; and a tough-minded epistemology would dispense with necessities, causal and logical alike, as components of empirical knowledge. But it proved impossible to confine interpretation and theory to the humble role proposed, even after separating the imaginative process of discovery from the patient process of validation.

Why not combine the two ways? Our attempt soon threatened to undermine the whole idea of knowledge as a temple built on self-evident foundations, *a priori* or empirical. Indeed it threatened any idea of objectivity. Even Popper's minimal moments of objective falsification proved vulnerable to Quine's insistence that no statement is immune to revision. Human knowledge emerged as a 'man-made fabric which impinges on experience only along the edges'; and, granted the pervasiveness of interpretation, even the edges were problematic. In making the mind incurably active as an interpreter of experience, we effectively blocked both of Bacon's ways to truth.

So the axe has been well and truly laid to Descartes' tree, and anything goes? Well, there are strong grounds for holding that our claims to knowledge include more than Reason, in any of its traditional definitions, can justify.

We are by now wary of the starting picture of nature as a realm independent of the enquiring mind, which science can explore with god-like objectivity. We have acquired reason to distrust the familiar distinction between human subject and external object. The general primacy traditionally given to epistemology has been shaken by challenges to the very idea that knowledge can have or needs to have foundations. This all spells trouble for the Enlightenment project. But how deep the trouble goes and what follows for the theory of knowledge are questions too large to pursue.

Enough has emerged to allow some cautious pointers to the following chapters. Here it may be helpful to reproduce Figure 1.2.

Firstly, we have found no single and commanding analysis of causal explanation in the philosophy of the natural sciences which social scientists are bound to accept. There are strong contenders inspired by Hume, which treat causal relations as statistical and think in terms of the success or failure of falsifiable predictions. But efforts to subject M. Rouget to the covering-law model and

	Explanation	Understanding
Holism	Systems	'Games'
Individualism	Agents	Actors

Figure 1.2

hypothetico-deductive method left us still wondering why he votes communist. In general, the underlying epistemologies, empiricist and pragmatist, have enough troubles of their own to leave richer analyses of causation in play.

Secondly, therefore, an ontological realism about mechanisms, forces, laws and structures also remains in play. Even if rationalism is not the friend it first appeared, empiricism and talk of webs of belief have failed to rule realism out. This is not to say that ontologies can be merely asserted, and we shall still need ways of avoiding dogmatism. But it releases an argument, which Positive science had hoped to side-track, about the merits of holism and, with it, about whether there is a distinctive sort of explanation, where individual behaviour is explained by its place in a system. That is the topic of the next chapter. Not all realists belong in the top left box of Figure 1.2, however, and, in any case, we have yet to consider the 'Agents' of the bottom left box. That will be done in Chapter 6. We broach both chapters with an unallayed curiosity about explanation and a readiness for the promised dispute between 'top down' and 'bottom up' in the left-hand column of Figure 1.2.

Thirdly, M. Rouget invites thoughts about Understanding, which will occupy Chapter 7. The original account in terms of probabilities was curiously silent about how M. Rouget viewed his vote, his world and himself. That may have been partly because Przeworski and Teune directed us to behavioural indicators like gender and occupation and we have yet to pursue J. S. Mill's call for psychological laws (or generalisations) in the opening chapter.

But it may also be because M. Rouget's own understanding does not take the form of psychological generalisations. His own 'web of belief' seems to be strung together from meanings, reasons and values. That may make us prefer Quine to Mill; but it also gives scope for disputing the naturalism so far assumed.

Fourthly, however, to explore the 'Understanding' column of Figure 1.2 is to activate a parallel dispute between 'top down' and 'bottom up'. Here the initial presumption favours individualism, in immediate reaction against the idea that history is to be written by identifying universal laws of behaviour. Yet, whatever may be in the minds of individual actors on historical occasions, they act in a context of shared meanings and rules, which permeate the options available and give scope to holism. That too will become plain in Chapter 7.

CHAPTER 5

Systems and functions

??	

Marx's Preface, quoted in Chapter 1, declared that the sum of the relations of production 'constitutes the economic structure of society, the real foundation, on which rises a legal and political superstructure . . . It is not the consciousness of men that determines their being, but, on the contrary, their social being that determines their consciousness.' By contrast, Mill stated: 'The laws of the phenomena of society are, and can be, nothing but the laws of the actions and passions of human beings united together in the social state . . . Human beings in society have no properties but those which are derived from, and may be resolved into, the laws of nature of individual man.' In the next two chapters we shall reflect on this stark disagreement.

Their aim is to flesh out the kind of thinking suited to the top left and bottom left boxes of Figure 1.2 and to see whether either can persuade us that the other is secondary. At the same time we shall be alert for signs that the explanations proposed may depend on understanding social systems or agents from within. Holists about explanation will need to deal not only with individualists but also with holists who advocate understanding. Individualists about explanation will similarly have a flank to guard against individualists who favour understanding. The examples discussed are offered not only to focus arguments about explanation in the social sciences but also in readiness for Chapter 7 on 'Understanding social action', where argument between 'top down' and 'bottom up' will continue under a new aegis.

Matters remain complicated by lack of a single, agreed analysis of causal explanation. But that is hardly surprising. Theorists who believe firmly in an ontology of social systems are almost bound to explain social phenomena in terms of underlying laws, forces and mechanisms, whose existence we are allegedly justified in inferring somehow. Theorists who are content to work with individuals and particulars have every reason to cast causal claims in a humbler form which makes observation their arbiter. (Psychological theories, like Freud's, which postulate subconscious mental forces, are to be grouped with the former, because of their richer ontology.)

The chapter will open with a discussion of functional explanation, since that belongs unmistakably in the top left box. When its special features are isolated, however, objections surface and we shall fall back on a looser holism. Either way, 'the consciousness of men' will need to have a place in explanations of social action, thus giving openings for individualism.

FUNCTIONAL EXPLANATION

Picture a termite colony, occupying a tall mud hump on an African plain. The hump is alive with worker termites and soldier termites going about their distinct kinds of business. The colony flourishes only if the proportion of soldiers to workers remains roughly the same, so that the queen and workers can be protected by the soldiers, and the queen and soldiers can be serviced by the workers. Hungry predators often invade the colony and unsettle the balance. But its fortunes are presently restored, because the huge, immobile queen, immured well below ground level, lays eggs not only in large enough numbers but also in the varying proportions required.

How can we account for her mysterious ability to respond to events on the distant surface? One explanation which might be offered is that the colony is a *system* and, like any system, has systemic needs. Whatever meets those needs is *functional* for the system and occurs *because* it is functional. The fact that the colony cannot survive, unless workers and soldiers are replaced in proportion to haphazard losses, somehow explains the fact that eggs are laid in those proportions.

If the explanation seems too blatantly circular (the colony survives because it responds and responds because it will not otherwise survive), it can be supplemented with an evolutionary story in which queens with this ability emerge by a process of natural selection acting on small random mutations. Mutations which aid survival in a given environment persist and the species comes to have a higher proportion of better equipped members. But it would only add to the original puzzle to suggest that species evolve because they survive better, if that makes survival a goal which species have. So let us stay with the bald idea that behaviour in a system can occur because the system needs it.

The termite colony is an organic system. Each termite too is an organism, whose parts combine to make it an effective individual and, moreover, equip it for its peculiar tasks in the colony. Soldiers have jaws, which are suited to the business of attacking predators, and different from the jaws of workers in this functionally relevant way. It seems very natural to describe the differences in terms indicating what purpose the distinctive organs serve. Equally, both kinds of termite have legs and that, seemingly, is because they need to get about. The obvious fact that a termite is an organism thus beguiles us readily into identifying its parts by their contribution to the insect's success – a language which almost suggests design. Yet, although some of this talk may be merely careless, there is no reason to deny that organic parts belong to organic wholes and that they relate to one another in ways which contribute to the activity of their whole. Nor is there reason to deny that an organism has needs, in the sense that it will survive and flourish only if various conditions are met.

The next beguiling step is to suggest that the parts are as they are and behave as they do *because* they serve these needs. Then, since the function of some parts, like specialised jaws, relates to the life of the colony, it is tempting to think of the colony as a larger organism, whose needs are similarly served by its varied members. There are soldiers *because* the colony needs soldiers. This starts to sound like very careless talk. Yet the parts of an organism are not haphazard and the differentiation between soldiers and workers does help the survival of the colony from day to day and from generation to generation. The egg-laying habits of the queen entice us beyond considering how they can be functional for her – only in the trivial sense that queens are distinctively egg-layers – to considering the functioning of the colony as a whole. The colony, moreover, seems to be more than the mere sum of its termites past, present and future, just as a particular termite is more than the mere sum of its parts. There is an organisation or structure involved, invisible no doubt but none the less real for that.

In what sense might the queen be said to produce proportionally more soldiers, when there is a shortage of soldiers, *because* that is what the system needs? Schematically, we have:

(S1) *A state of the system* marked by a shortage of soldiers
(B) *The queen's behaviour*, the production of extra soldiers
(S2) *A later state of the system* marked by more soldiers
and a hypothesis, premised on the colony's being a system:
(H) *Given (S1), (S2) is the cause of (B).*

In that case, however, functional explanation threatens to include causes which follow their effects. Although it is worth pausing to contemplate the idea of reversed causation, rather than simply rejecting it out of hand, it is not to be adopted lightly. Here it leads swiftly to absurdity, since there is no guarantee that the extra soldier-eggs laid (B) will in fact result in extra soldiers (S2). A hungry anteater might always gobble up the new eggs, thus depriving today's effect of its future cause! In other words, whether behaviour can be explained by citing its contribution to a system had better not depend directly on what actually happens next.

So let us adopt a suggestion from Charles Taylor (1964), that what explains (B) is not (S2) itself but two facts:

(1) that (B) is required for (S2) to occur
(2) that the colony will not maintain itself without (S2)

This removes the reversed causation by shifting the explanatory work to the notion of a functional requirement for the maintenance of a system (or attainment of some other systemic goal). If this notion (rightly) seems obscure, notice how readily we apply a similar one to human action. When Jack goes fishing, it is not the outcome itself which causes him to cast his fly – he may catch nothing – but the fact that he cannot achieve the outcome desired without doing so. Here is one realm where talk of purposes, goals and perhaps of functional requirements gives no immediate trouble and does not need causes to follow their effects. But then there is no immediate puzzle about the purposive character of a human system like Jack, at any rate where the purposes are consciously his. Nor, for that matter, is there any immediate puzzle about systems like computers and central heating with thermostatic controls, which humans consciously design.

The idea that a termite colony is a system with goals and with parts whose function is to achieve them is more puzzling. Even if the colony is somehow more than the sum of its parts, how can the mere fact that (B) is required for (S2) possibly galvanise the queen? That sounds like mystical nonsense – feedback without a feedback mechanism. In this case, however, there is indeed a mechanism. It has to do with how she is kept fed. Her food is collected on the distant surface and passed along a chain of soldiers and workers, from jaw to jaw. Since the secretions from the jaws of soldiers and workers are chemically different, the food arrives impregnated proportionally and this varying sauce triggers eggs in the inverse proportion.

Even if this too is astonishing, it is distinctly less mystical, since it introduces an ordinary causal process. Indeed, it is so much less mystical that one wonders whether we should still be thinking functionally at all. It remains true, of course, that the colony would not survive, unless there were a process which repaired damage to its division of labour. But that by itself does nothing to license the idea that the process occurs *because* it has this effect. Suspicion arises that talk of systems as wholes which are somehow more than the sum of their parts may be spurious, perhaps an extrapolation from the intentions which feature in human action.

Before pursuing the suspicion, consider a parallel comment on mechanical systems. Here too there is an enticing suggestion that what makes the planets more than a haphazard set of bodies is their interrelation in an equilibrium system. The fact that the equilibrium will not be maintained unless each planet moves as it does, given the motions of the others, explains each orbit and can also explain the adjustments which follow if an orbit is disturbed. But this fact is merely mysterious without a causal feedback mechanism. When one is supplied, the idea that the planetary system forms a purposive whole is correspondingly weakened. Were there a divine purpose at work, that would be different. Otherwise talk of the planetary system starts to sound merely like shorthand for a straightforwardly causal story about moving bodies and gravitational forces. Picture a mobile, hanging from the ceiling. Tap a bit of it and the whole system will either adjust to the impact and return to equilibrium or it will not. If not, the mobile becomes a muddle of wire and weights. But that trite observation does not warrant serious talk of what is functional for the mobile's needs.

These initial remarks are meant to introduce the bones of systemic thinking in a way which puts us somewhat on guard. The bones are a structure which is more than the sum or consequence of its elements, and elements whose behaviour can only be explained by their function in the whole. The air of purposiveness is intriguing both because the systems found in the natural world are fascinating and because they seem to call for an ontology and style of explanation beyond the scope of the previous two chapters. On the other hand, natural systems do not work by magic and, when we ask how they do work, the process of feedback involved is unpuzzlingly causal in character. Yet the whole may still seem more than the sum of its parts and we need to pin down the exact sense, if any, in which this is true.

SOCIAL FACTS AS THINGS

This is a good moment to shift attention to social science and a classic case for thinking holistically about the workings of society. In *The Rules of Sociological Method* Emile Durkheim declared that 'The first and most fundamental rule is: *Consider social facts as things*' (1895, Chapter 2, his italics). Social phenomena present themselves to us as 'external things', not as mental representations in the mind of social actors (to which we have no direct access). The rule holds even for phenomena which 'give the strongest impression of being arbitrary arrangements', not least because it usually turns out that 'facts most arbitrary in appearance will come to present, after more attentive observation, qualities of consistency and regularity that are symptomatic of their objectivity'. Moreover, '*The voluntary character of a practice should never be assumed beforehand*' (Chapter 2, Section 1, his italics). This sets the stage for the naturalistic and realist approach to social phenomena which makes the *Rules* a sociological classic.

Functional explanation is introduced in Chapter 3, titled 'Rules for distinguishing between the normal and the pathological'. The broad analogy is between functioning societies and healthy organisms, with a focus on how to identify the contributory processes. The key rule is that:

a social fact is normal, in relation to a given social type at a given phase of its development, when it is present in the average society of that species at the corresponding phase of its evolution.

There follows a compact and surprising illustrative discussion of crime – a fact 'whose pathological character appears incontestable'. We are asked to note that crime occurs in all societies and always tends to increase. Hence crime (up to a certain level) is normal, rather than pathological, and is, indeed, 'a factor in public health, an integral part of all healthy societies'. The underlying thought here is that whatever is universal and persistent is thereby 'normal' and so must have a contribution to make to sustaining societies.

How? Crime 'consists of an act that offends very strong collective sentiments', without which social solidarity would be lost. Such sentiments cannot flourish in the abstract. They can be kept vigorous only through provocation by offenders against them and the punishment of those offenders. Hence the greater the success of the 'collective consciousness' in eliminating crime, as currently defined, the more sensitive and exacting it becomes in defining fresh activities as criminal. In a society of saints 'faults which appear venial to the layman will create the same scandal that the ordinary offence does in ordinary consciousness'.

Crime is, then, necessary; it is bound up with the fundamental conditions of all social life, and by that very fact it is useful, because these conditions of which it is a part are themselves indispensable to the normal evolution of morality and law.

Nor is this all. Today's morality is often yesterday's crime, as with Socrates' crimes of independent thinking, which 'served to prepare a new morality and faith which the Athenians needed'. Thus,

Contrary to current ideas, the criminal no longer seems a totally unsociable being, a sort of parasitic element, a strange and unassimilable body, introduced into the midst of society. On the contrary, he plays a definite role in social life.

Turning to 'Rules for the explanation of social facts' in Chapter 5, Durkheim distinguishes between causes and functions. He grants that individual sentiments and intentions play their part in any historical narrative and that a general psychology can provide a framework for a causal account suited to an individualist social science. (We cited J. S. Mill's *A System of Logic* to this effect on p.10.) But he squarely denies that individual consciousnesses are more than a necessary condition of social facts:

society is not a mere sum of individuals. Rather, the system formed by their association represents a specific reality which has its own characteristics.

Individuals are always set about with social constraints, especially with inherited obligations, which cannot be explained by reference to individuals alone. To postulate corresponding instincts in human nature, for instance religious, aesthetic or moral instincts, would do nothing to explain the variety of forms which the constraints take ('individual natures are merely the indeterminate material that the social factor moulds and transforms'). It would also invite the sort of ridicule attracted by mediaevals who explained why opium makes one sleepy by postulating a *virtus dormitiva* (dormitive power) in the nature of opium, thus creating a fatuous circularity. Social facts have social, as distinct from psychological, causes and these causes are distinct from their functions.

We arrive therefore at the following principle: *The determining cause of a social fact should be sought among the social facts preceding it and not among the states of the individual consciousness . . . The function of a social fact ought always to be sought in relation to some social end.* (1895, Chapter 5, Section 2, his italics)

This sketch is not meant to do justice to the *Rules*, and still less to Durkheim's work at large. But it gives us one familiar idea of system and function to work with. It is not a completely general idea, because Durkheim has organic systems specifically in mind and has the specific aim of establishing the autonomy of social facts ('every time that a sociological phenomenon is directly explained by a psychological phenomenon, we may be sure that the explanation is false'); so there may also be systems which do not resemble organisms, or functional explanations whose elements are psychological. Meanwhile, here are the components of Durkheim's thinking in the *Rules*:

   an ontology of 'social facts', forming an order external to individual consciousness and not explicable by reference to human nature.

   a methodology wherein social facts are explained by their function 'in relation to some social end'.

   functional mechanisms working through the medium of the 'collective consciousness' and connecting social ends to the overall level of social integration needed if a society is to flourish.

   an epistemology, so far undisclosed, which warrants our subscribing to these components.

SYSTEMS AND STRUCTURES

The sociology advocated in the *Rules* recalls de Fontenelle's image of science as a foray behind the scenes at the opera or as a search occasioned because 'Nature . . . disposeth her Wheels and Springs so out of sight, that we have been long a-guessing at the movement of the Universe'. The missing epistemology might seem to take Bacon's first way, where knowledge by-passes the senses with the aid of *a priori* reasoning and discerns hidden structures in reality. Durkheim sometimes speaks in this high-handed way, as if he had simply discovered the existence of social facts and functions. In this mood he resembles one of Bacon's spiders, 'who make cobwebs out of their own substance'. If that is the best a holist or believer in unobservable systems can do, then the case is not much strengthened by granting that the empiricists in Chapter 3 and pragmatists in Chapter 4 did not altogether suc- ceed in ruling it out.

Yet the passages from Durkheim quoted above are not meant to be merely dogmatic in claiming that there are social facts and that social systems embody ends and needs. When other works, notably *Suicide* (1897) and *The Elementary Forms of the Religious Life* (1912) are reckoned with, a different epistemology emerges. We can best lead up to it by considering some large objections to the line on causes and functions taken in the *Rules*.

Much work is assigned to a basic notion of equilibrium, the state to which a system tends and from which it does not depart, unless disturbed from outside. Durkheim sometimes speaks as if equilibrium states could be identified by observation. But the idea is too ambitious for that. Even if 'observation' is construed loosely to include crime, rates of crime and such social phenomena, it does not extend to explanatory variables like public health, social solidarity and collective consciousness. Nor does it warrant talk of social ends for which phenomena like crime are, surprisingly, functional. Two distinct transcendental moves are involved, one to the existence of hidden causes and the other to the existence of equilibrium-seeking dynamics. We have not yet found a theory of knowledge to justify talk of more than necessary conditions which each element must satisfy *if* the system is to be stable.

The 'necessity' involved in a necessary condition is a modest *sine qua non* (without which, not). It is far from the missing natural necessity demanded by ambitious causal thinking, let alone the imperative necessity which might attend the presence of hidden goals. Return to the termite colony. The functions performed by each kind of termite can be stated as necessary conditions without which the colony will not continue as usual. But why should it continue as usual? If the environment changed just enough to make the present organisation ineffective, then the colony would either adapt or die out. Why expect one rather than the other? There is no harm in speaking of adaptive processes, perhaps by analogy with the healing process which occurs in wounded animals. But this is shorthand for a story about necessary conditions, not for one in which God, nature or even the colony itself cares whether it dies out or not, unless the teller is projecting a human concern of some sort. Even if each individual termite has an essential drive to self-preservation, that does not warrant ascribing such a drive to the colony as a whole.

To reinforce the point, reflect that equilibria need not be unique. Many systems which, if slightly disturbed, return to their previous equilibrium, shift to a different equilibrium, if thrown further off balance. For instance,the arrival of a new species of fish in a pond can have this effect. Nor need equilibria be static. Dynamic systems, where progressive change is inherent, are possible, with animal evolution often said to be an example. Termites may be constantly evolving, thanks to causal processes in the environment and a selective mechanism in individual termites. There are thus all sorts of ways in which colonies might adapt, none of them random, especially when considered after the event. But nothing here warrants serious talk of evolution directed to a goal. As soon as we separate necessary conditions from functional and evolutionary 'necessities', the illusion vanishes.

Hence we should, I suggest, be very wary of full-blown functional thinking which treats the necessary conditions for the persistence of a particular equilibrium state as a causal pressure towards it. Specifically, we have found no warrant to construe termite colonies as organisms by analogy with the individual organisms which comprise them, nor for construing social systems by analogy with organisms. But that does not rule out holistic causal thinking in general, nor does it scotch all functional explanation of social phenomena. Let us pursue the latter point first.

Durkheim's intriguing example of crime gains little credence from his analogy between healthy societies and healthy organisms. If the police make large inroads into the number of burglars, society does not breed more after the manner of the queen termite. But that does not close the case. Durkheim is thinking more abstractly and, at the same time, relying on the idea that viable societies possess a 'collective consciousness'. Abstractly, social systems survive only if they embody solutions to problems of maintaining internal cohesion and of reproducing themselves. Solutions to the same problem can vary. If crime and punishment were indeed essential for a flourishing collective consciousness, then the suppression of all existing crimes would be followed either by social disintegration or by the upgrading of 'venial' offences. But a society could still survive without crime, if it had a functionally equivalent solution to the problem of social stability.

In *The Elementary Forms of the Religious Life* Durkheim argues that an essential function of religion is to institute and police a distinction between the sacred and the profane. Every society needs such a distinction, not least so that its members can be got to revere its institutions. One service commonly performed by established religions is to underwrite the legitimacy of the state. From this angle, crime and punishment need to be seen in a wider context of social integration and of functional mechanisms for reinforcing social organisation through the collective consciousness.

Epistemologically, the *Elementary Forms* differs from the *Rules* by striking a deliberately Kantian note. Kant typically sought the conceptual preconditions of any system of thought which could solve the general problem of ordering experience. Durkheim seeks the functional prerequisites for a social system which can succeed in integrating its members. Like Kant, he then argues that one is justified in interpreting phenomena as embodying a solution to the relevant problem. Since this is not the place to explore the parallel, I can only hint at the point of it, which is to suggest that Durkheim takes the bee's middle course of gathering his material from the flowers of the garden and transforming it by a theoretical power of his own, with the Kantian presumption, mentioned on p.90 above, that there is a unique set of categories for the purpose. Read in this way, he is a precursor of the grand structural-functionalism which reached its climax in Talcott Parsons' *The Social System* (1951). That would serve as a majestic way to fill in the top left box. But this too is beyond our present scope.

In the *Rules* Durkheim is thinking more simply in terms of objective social forces and often writes as if the collective consciousness were an unobservable 'thing' which dictated the consciousness of each individual agent. But at times he also suggests that the collective consciousness, while external to each social actor, is nevertheless not external to all collectively and is amenable to conscious collective decisions. In that case practices may still have a voluntary character, when considered from a collective point of view, even though they account for the behaviour of individuals. At this stage of our enquiry, when we are still dealing with notions of explanation derived from the natural sciences, it may seem merely confused to talk of social practices as external to each individual and yet internal to all. But it points ahead to a version of holism suited to the top right box and will, I hope, come to make sense presently.

It is plain by now that the very idea of unobservable systems which exert purposive pressure on their parts is highly problematic, to say the least. It is very vulnerable to the objection that it is mystical without a feedback mechanism and becomes otiose when one is supplied. But this does not put paid to all claims that there are social wholes which are somehow more than the sum of their parts. So let us next seek a more modest version of this contention.

HOLISM AND INDIVIDUALISM

For present purposes, I suggest treating the case for holism as one for proceeding 'top down' in the explanation of social phenomena. The termites can again serve as a benchmark. The termite colony consists of individuals so differentiated that they can survive only in collaboration with others, and is, in this sense, more than the mere sum of its parts. But the interdependence can be described in terms either of global features of the colony or of relational properties of the termites; and it is not plain what turns on the difference, if we are no longer pressing the case for functional explanations. On the one hand, the colony is merely a sum of soldiers, workers and a queen, and its dynamics merely a sum of their interactions in response to external events. On the other hand, the properties which differentiate the termites into kinds are arbitrary except from a collective point of view, which is therefore needed for explaining the form which interactions take. It is not plain why it matters to decide whether one angle of vision is primary.

For the social sciences it is easier to find something to bother about. Individualism has many aspects, including moral and political. If holism means accepting the line in Marx's Preface, it seems to imply that we are not morally responsible for what we do and that our most cherished forms of political organisation, like a democracy of free individuals, are themselves socially determined and hence rest on an illusion. (Thus Durkheim argues in his (1898) essay 'Individualism and the Intellectuals' that individualism is itself a social phenomenon – 'the sacred form of the modern age'.) On the other hand, it is not plain that a scientific enquiry should be bothered about such matters in advance or even at all. Nor is it plain that holism need imply the determination of consciousness by hidden structures. So let us draw the battlelines more carefully.

The final dispute is no doubt an ontological one, with an ontological individualism, which maintains that there are only particulars, ranged against an ontological holism, which holds out for the real existence of structures. But it would be a mistake to join battle without further ado, partly because this contrast is too crude and partly because ontological claims are merely dogmatic, unless connected to epistemological ones.

To illustrate these reasons for caution, consider the 'level-of-analysis' problem in international relations. This problem was famously posed by David Singer in a much cited (1961) paper at a time when talk of 'the international system' was in high fashion. The question, presented as a particular case of a central problem for the social sciences, was whether the 'system' determines the behaviour of its 'units' or *vice versa*. The units here were nation states and the problem seemed to be one of settling the direction of causation. But it is teasingly insoluble in this chicken-and-egg form and Singer suggested a lateral move. He compared the dispute to one about map projections. The globe looks strikingly different in Mercator and Polar Gnomonic projections and one might be tempted to ask which is right. But, although one of these distortions may be preferable for some purposes, they are both two-dimensional projections of the same three-dimensional solid. Hence both are in one sense right and in another sense wrong. Similarly, it is not surprising that accounts of the international world are unsatisfactory, if given solely from a system perspective or wholly from a unit perspective.

Singer's analogy is attractive. But it is misleading in its suggestion that the puzzle is simply one about how to represent a well understood globe on a flat surface. There is a real question whether the international world is, so to speak, a solid object, existing apart from perspectives which human actors furnish and are guided by. Perhaps it exists only in these perspectives and so is as it is taken to be, whereas the physical planet exists regardless. Relatedly, one can also ask whether the level-of-analysis problem has been pitched at the right level by thinking in terms of mapping the globe. It is possible to deny that nation states are autonomous without having to assert that there is such a thing as the international system. Some theorists maintain that the behaviour of a nation state results from the behaviour of its internal bureaucracies and other agencies. From this point of view the nation state is a system and the bureaucracies its units. Then there is a further dispute about whether to explain the behaviour of a bureaucracy through the behaviour of the individual men and women who play roles within it or *vice versa*. Here the bureaucracy is a system and the units are human individuals. These layers of the problem are summed up in Figure 5.1, taken

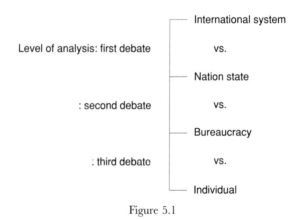

Figure 5.1

from the discussion in Hollis and Smith's *Explaining and Understanding International Relations* (1990).

The level-of-analysis problem will crop up again in Chapter 8. I introduce it now mainly to make the point that there is no simple or single opposition between holism and individualism. In particular, it is not inherently clear what counts as an individual or unit. For instance some economists treat firms as individuals, whereas others regard them as organisations. Similar remarks could be made about other social units like families, and I dare say that even undoubted individuals like Jack and Jill are, for some purposes, to be treated as organisations of their various elements. Jon Elster was quoted on p.19:

> The elementary unit of social life is the individual human action. To explain social institutions and social change is to show how they arise as the result of the action and interaction of individuals. (1989(a), p.13)

If one is being precise, the 'individuals' in the second sentence are not human actions as specified in the first. So, even at bottom, there is an ambiguity.

In complicating the dispute between holism and individualism, however, I am not trying to deny that there is a deep rivalry between 'top down' and 'bottom up'. So let us focus on what are known as *methodological individualism* and *methodological holism*. The former is nicely captured by Elster's second sentence: 'To explain social institutions and social change is to show how they arise as the result of the action and interaction of individuals'. The latter offers to explain the action and interaction of individuals, although not necessarily by reference to social institutions. Holistic psychologies are possible, as are grand holistic appeals to forces, laws and underlying historical movements which govern everything in the social world, including institutions. For our purposes, however, it will be enough to consider one typical example and Elster's reference to social institutions will serve very well.

Institutions constrain and enable individuals. They prevent some courses of action and require others. They also create opportunities, thus letting individuals do what they could not otherwise have done. The obvious opening move for holists is to contend that the constraints are far stronger than the enablements. As holists, we explain M. Rouget's communist vote by citing institutional constraints on young, male, industrial workers, which together determine it. Power resides in institutions, and individuals exercise power only in so far as they represent powerful institutions. If anyone protests that institutions are created by individuals, the reply is that the genesis of power does not matter. Frankenstein's monster soon took on a life of its own.

Conversely, the obvious individualist retort is that what constrains one individual need not constrain groups of individuals. Institutions are only rules and practices. Their power depends on acceptance by individuals or on coercion of individuals by individuals. Concerted action to change them is always possible, and that includes refusal to enforce as well as refusal to obey. Even if continuity is more usual than dramatic change, the explanation of both is to be sought in the beliefs and desires of individuals. Gradual change is common enough and is most readily explained as a sum of small individual choices tending in the same direction. For institutional or revolutionary changes we can look to concerted action, mass or elite, to account for what single individuals cannot do alone.

Holists will no doubt point out that the social world has many features, including many practices, which no one intended or approves of but which defy change. For instance economic recessions are often as beyond human control as the weather and, in general, market forces are an inescapable fact of life. Indeed, although neo-Classical economics is the most individualistic of the social sciences and the keenest to exhibit social behaviour as the product of individual choices, it yields to no one in its belief in the reality of market forces. The rational, self-interested agent is subject to the laws of supply and demand, firms which try to defy them are driven out of business and governments which sail against them are soon blown off course.

Individualists can best respond, I think, by extending the realm of choice to include the unintended consequences of separate choices. As we shall see in the next chapter, it is entirely possible for each agent to choose rationally and for their choices to sum to a result which no one wants. For instance, it may be rational for each whaler to catch every whale within reach, even though foreseeing that, if all do likewise, whales will become extinct. The famous Invisible Hand, which sometimes sees to it that self-interested choices sum to a common good, sometimes makes mischief in this way. Whatever its tendency, however, the idea that social outcomes can be the sum of individual inputs without reflecting anyone's intentions is a very useful one. For the rest, methodological individualism in the social sciences need not try to dismantle natural laws and forces. In so far as the laws of supply and demand result from natural scarcities and general features of human biology and psychology, it is not inconsistent for an individualist to appeal to them.

The holist will still want to know where people's desires come from. The standard theory of rational choice regards an action as rational if its expected utility is at least as great as that of any other available action. When calculating expected utilities, preferences are taken as given. They are more like tastes than reasoned aims. The standard theory has no interest in accounting for M. Rouget's political orientation and, more generally, no explanation of why an individual has any particular political, religious, cultural or any other preferences. Yet, if individuals are always seeking to maximise their expected utility in some automatic way, and if their choices are thus effectively determined by their preferences, holism threatens to win an easy victory. It simply offers a holistic account of preference formation, presumably by reference to the diversity of institutions. For, even if nature decides whether we prefer oranges to apples, she does not make us Hindu or Christian, socialist or conservative.

Here individualists may be inclined to appeal to a story about socialisation in which only individuals, like parents, friends, teachers, advertisers and role-models, figure. But that would invite the riposte that this makes us creatures of the social positions held by significant others in our socialisation and thus concedes the game. At best it leads to a further round of chicken-and-egg argument which I would rather not pursue now. So here instead is a more philosophical comment.

The idea of an individual agent has so far been distinctly mechanical. This applies to J. S. Mill's contention in Chapter 1 that we are dealing with 'the laws of nature of individual man' and that 'the phenomena of human thought, feeling and action are subject to fixed laws'. It applies also to the standard Rational Choice theory portrait of us as calculating utility-maximisers with given preferences. Both versions insist that actions always result from the desires and beliefs of the agent and not from any external cause, such as social institutions. But that is not very consoling, if our desires and beliefs have such external causes in their turn. Admittedly there is still the case for holding that freedom is compatible with determinism or, indeed, presupposes determinism, for which Mill was quoted as an eminent spokesman on p.14. On this account rational agents who make utility-maximising choices are acting freely by the test of whether their actions further their preferences. But the whole approach is no less mechanical for that.

So perhaps we should look for a form of individualism where individuals are more reflective and self-directed than has yet emerged. That is easier said than done, however, because of the traditional ideas of scientific explanation which have guided us so far. Being originally addressed to a natural world of objects without consciousness, these ideas allow for human complexity but cannot readily incorporate human autonomy. On the other hand, the bee, which 'transforms and digests' its material 'by a power of its own' and 'lays it up in the understanding altered and digested', is active in an unmechanical way; and, in general, pragmatist accounts of knowledge make us creative and imaginative interpreters of a world which, in effect, we construct. So it should be possible to find more room for manoeuvre than is offered by psychological laws, given preferences and rational calculation. But, since this thought is ahead of the game, I shall now sum up the case for and against methodological holism.

CONCLUSION

We have tried two ways of construing the claim that societies or institutions are 'systems' so as to find something suitably holistic and causal for the top left box. Both agree with Durkheim that 'society is not a mere sum of individuals', and that individual behaviour is to be explained by reference to irreducibly social facts. One is markedly more contestable than the other.

The more ambitious proposes a notion of functional explanation, where systems are credited with needs, purposes or goals which explain why their parts behave as they do. Analogies with termite colonies and the planetary system look plausible. But, even here, functionalism is mystical, unless we specify a feedback mechanism, which then turns out to do most or all of the explanatory work in an unpuzzlingly causal way. More abstractly, necessary conditions for a system to persist or return to an equilibrium are not to be confused with necessitating causal powers or immanent goals. For social systems, moreover, the feedback has to involve 'collective consciousness' in Durkheim's language or, as individualists will insist on putting it, the consciousness of human agents. This at once undercuts analogies with organic and mechanical systems in general; and, if it points instead to analogies with systems embodying human intentions, like central heating systems or indeed human beings themselves, that does not help advocates of theories suited to the top left box.

Less ambitiously, therefore, holism may prefer the blander claim that there are social facts and forces, which still bid us account for individual behaviour by reference to wholes with causal powers, specifically to social institutions. This is still strong stuff and nothing in the chapter rules it out. But it invites compromises, where 'system' and 'units' both contribute to outcomes by a process of mutual influence. For example, how a particular economy works may depend both on the pressures of market forces and on decisions by individual firms; how a firm behaves may depend both on its collective character as an organisation and on what its members choose to do. Whatever the level at which the level-of-analysis problem is pitched, however, the way is now open for individualists to argue that society is finally indeed a mere sum of individuals, combining to bring about what no one can do alone. Add the thought that the consequences of separate individual actions can sum to produce outcomes which no one intended or wants and individualism has the makings of a strong riposte.

The riposte is strengthened by objecting that holists have been speaking of real structures and causal powers for which they as yet have no epistemological warrant. It is also strengthened for most of us, if the kinds of causal relations which we can know to exist are integral to free action, as compatibilists like J. S. Mill maintain. But neither move is conclusive. Holists can still argue that, since they can explain phenomena by postulating unobservable causal mechanisms and there is no better explanation, they are justified in so doing. They can also argue that even a 'soft' determinism, where desires and beliefs are causes of action, is no help to free will, while beliefs and desires are externally caused and the agent is merely an efficient calculator. These counter-moves are not conclusive either, in my view, and debate remains open.

Finally, return to Durkheim's 'collective consciousness'. Here are three brief comments, pointing ahead. Firstly, if it is construed to suit the top left box, it involves false consciousness. This is especially plain in the functionalist story, where, for instance, people outraged by crime are unaware that crime is socially useful and worshippers in church are unaware that they are there to increase social solidarity and to legitimate the social system. But there is also a more general train of thought which will start in Chapter 7 by asking how institutions and consciousness are related. If institutions consist of rules, norms and practices which depend on how actors interpret them, we may have to rethink the very idea that institutions cause actions. This dark hint points to a potential break with naturalism as will be made explicit when we turn to Chapter 7.

Secondly, under the umbrella of Understanding, there is still dispute between individualism and holism. Rules, norms and practices are no doubt external to each actor but, as we shall see in Chapter 8, that need not make the actors their creatures. The claim that 'collective consciousness' is a social fact, when translated into a language of Understanding, will offer scope for a fresh version of individualism.

Thirdly, meanwhile, individualism has yet to show its mettle in the service of explanation. That is the task of the next chapter.

CHAPTER 6

Games with Rational Agents

??	

Individualism, in a general and robust form, maintains that there are only particulars, with the methodological rider that, in the final analysis, reference to particulars can account for whatever seems to involve something more. But social scientists are as inquisitive as anyone about human individuals, what makes them tick and whether they are the creators or creatures of the social world. This curiosity, I hope, warrants a focus on versions of individualism, where individuals are human agents with desires and beliefs and act in ways which account for what happens. Admittedly, there are behaviourists, who contend that a properly scientific approach neither wants nor needs to credit individuals with a subjective point of view or, indeed, any mental states. Also we have noted that, in some theories usually deemed individualist, the individuals are firms, nations or other agents lacking flesh and blood. But, indulging my own curiosity, I propose to explore the thesis that 'history is the <u>result of human action</u>, not <u>of human design</u>'. ~~Not~~ pre determined.

That quotation comes from the eighteenth-century Scottish philosopher Adam Ferguson and nudges us towards economics as the social science where a humane kind of individualism has been most thoroughly deployed. Lionel Robbins defined economics as 'the science which studies the relationship between ends and scarce means which have alternative uses', and this makes it potentially a very far-ranging science indeed (1932, p.15). Politics and sociology are only two of the social sciences which have lately become fascinated with 'economic' analyses of social interaction. The idea that we behave in all aspects of our lives as we typically do in market situations is not only intriguing in itself

115

but also prompts a potent individualist account of institutions, norms and practices, thus robbing holism of its trumps.

'Humane' is perhaps the wrong word. The economic theory of Rational Choice treats us as rational, self-interested individuals, each intent on maximising our own utility. Game Theory, which goes on to analyse interaction, rests on Rational Choice theory. This hardly sounds like humane treatment; but the approach can be made more generous than it seems at first. The chapter will start by defining a rational agent with the standard notion of rationality in economics. It will then sketch the elements of Game Theory. That will be followed by a discussion of the emergence of norms and whether we now have an analysis which can account for them.

RATIONAL AGENTS

'The first principle of economics is that every agent is actuated solely by self-interest.' Edgeworth's remark remains a good starting point, not least because his title, *Mathematical Psychics*, so well captures the spirit of what is afoot (1881, p.16). But it needs caution. Not all economists will accept it as their first principle, although neo-Classicists commonly do and although others, like Keynesians and Marxists, usually employ the stock notion of rationality when analysing individual action. Also there is still the problem, left unresolved when we introduced it on p.57, of deciding whether Edgeworth's dictum offers a falsifiable hypothesis or has some other status. For the moment, however, let us concentrate on rational agents and the sense in which they are actuated by 'self-interest'.

Rational Choice theory begins with a single, ideally rational individual, classically Robinson Crusoe alone on his desert island. He has three components: *fully ordered preferences*, *complete information* and *a perfect internal computer*. He acts rationally in as much as he chooses the action which he correctly calculates to be most instrumental in satisfying his preferences.

Suppose, for instance, that Crusoe is trying to decide whether it is worth the trouble of making a net, so as to catch more fish than he now can with a pointed stick. The consequences of making a net are not only (probably) more fish tomorrow but also the effort of making it and less fish today. Think of consequences as possible states of the world, brought about by his choice of action. If he was sure of one fish a day without a net and sure of four fish with a net after a fishless and tiring first day, his rational choice would depend simply on how he ranks these two outcomes. He simply chooses the action whose consequences he prefers.]

Where outcomes are not certain, matters are more complex. The theory assumes that he has a complete ranking of all possible outcomes, regardless of their probability. It then assumes that his information is complete, in that he knows how likely each outcome is. (To be exact, he has a 'subjective probability distribution' which is complete and consistent; and thus has a subjective view of the chances of, say, two fish or three or four and so on, which will not land him in contradictions.) Since he also has a perfect internal computer, he can now calculate the *expected utility* of making a net and compare it with that of not making one. The expected utility is the sum of the utility of each possible outcome, discounted for the probability that it will not in fact occur. (To grasp the idea, think of a £1 bet on a card drawn at random from a full pack, with generous payoffs of £5 for a Spade and £3 for any red card. Assuming that utilities are reflected in cash profits or losses, a bet on a Spade has an expected utility of 0.25 (= £5/4 − £1) and a bet on red of 0.50 (= £3/2 − £1).) A rational agent always rejects actions with lower expected utility and is indifferent between those with the same expected utility. Notice that the calculation may need to allow for varying costs as well as varying probabilities.

The complexities make it plain that the ideally rational agent is very idealised indeed. None of us ever has such a complete and consistent set of preferences over the range even of the likelier outcomes. We have nothing close to complete information and the device of working with subjective probabilities in a world of uncertainty is distinctly artificial. We are not blessed with perfect internal computers. Nevertheless, this is the ideal-type case of a simple and potent notion of rationality. We act rationally, when we know what we want, have a shrewd idea how likely each course of action is to satisfy us at what cost, and choose the action which is thus the most effective means to our ends.

Rational action is thus *instrumentally* rational action. It does not matter whether people prefer oranges to apples, guns to butter or virtue to vice. Rational agents can have any (consistent) preferences, and are rational if and only if their choices maximise their expected utility accordingly. There is no further question of the rationality of their ends. Questions of whether preferences cause actions or merely derive from what is chosen can wait.

We can now be clearer about 'self-interest'. Edgeworth took people to be so self-regarding and selfish, at least in the realm of commerce, that they were indeed 'self-interested' in the everyday sense of the term. More generally, economics has been dubbed 'the dismal science' partly because economists often take a similar view of agents in economic or even social life at large. But, strictly, the standard first principle assumes only that agents are guided by their own preferences. In this sense saints are as 'self-interested' as sinners and the theory of Rational Choice is not committed to any view about how saintly or sinful we are. Although we shall need to ask later quite what, philosophically, it is committed to, we begin by assuming only that agents seek to maximise their own expected utility.

THE THEORY OF GAMES

Rational Choice theory opens with a single agent in an independent environment. Having given a basic definition of rational choice, it then explores the implications making the agent no longer certain about the consequences of action. The environment sets *parameters*, within which choices are to be made. A static environment is not required but any dynamics are independent of the agent's decisions. It is not as if the god of the sea were trying to anticipate Crusoe's moves. Call choices made in an independent environment *parametric*. As soon as Man Friday enters the scene, however, Crusoe's rational choice may depend on what Friday will choose. Each may need a *strategy* which takes account of the other's strategy. Call choices which are interdependent in this way *strategic*. Game Theory starts here. It analyses strategic rational choices in an ideal-type setting where each rational agent knows, among other things, that other agents are rational in the sense already defined.

That sounds daunting but the basic idea is still simple. The basic scenario requires two agents, each with a choice of two actions. Since it saves confusion if we can refer to the agents as 'he' and 'she', let us replace Crusoe and Friday from now on with Jack and Jill. Suppose that Jack and Jill are motorists who meet at opposite ends of a narrow bridge with room for only one car. Each must choose whether to advance or wait. There are four possible outcomes: (Stop, Stop), (Go, Go), (Stop, Go), (Go, Stop). The situation is a 'game', with the schematic form shown in Figure 6.1.

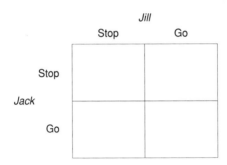

Figure 6.1

What happens depends partly on how each player ranks the four outcomes. Crucially, however, what *payoff* each receives may depend on which choice of action the other player makes. So each must also allow for how the other ranks the outcomes and also for what the other is thinking. Thus Jack may need to know what Jill expects him to do and *vice versa*. We can best deploy the idea by considering four basic games.

FOUR BASIC GAMES

(1) Coordination

Suppose initially that neither minds who waits and that there are thus two outcomes which each ranks equal best (and two inferior ones). This makes the game a *coordination game,* as shown in Figure 6.2.

The pairs of numbers in the boxes give the *payoff* to each player with the left (or row) player's first and then the top (or column) player's. Thus (1,1) in the bottom left box tells us that, if Jack goes and Jill stops, Jack receives '1' and Jill receives '1'. The payoff numbers sometimes represent specific 'goods' like sums of money (or 'bads', if prefaced by a minus sign). Sometimes they are to be thought of as 'utils', the famous units of Jeremy Bentham's 'felicific calculus' which he hoped would one day enable utilitarians to calculate 'the greater happiness of the greater number', when choosing among actions or social policies. Sometimes they merely represent each player's preferences, rather than quantities of anything, so that Figure 6.2 tells us only that both players prefer the two outcomes where they coordinate to those where they do not. I postpone any queries about whether it matters how we read the *utility numbers,* as they are usually called.

In Figure 6.2 Jack and Jill are stuck. There are, in a sense, two *solutions* to the game and hence, in another sense, none. (Stop, Go) is a solution, in the sense that if Jack stops, Jill's rational choice is

		Jill	
		Stop	Go
Jack	Stop	0, 0	1, 1
	Go	1, 1	0, 0

Figure 6.2   Coordination game I

to go; and if Jill goes, Jack's rational choice is to stop. That gives us the crucial notion of a *Nash-equilibrium*, a pair of strategies, one for each player, where each is a best reply to the other. The pair forms an equilibrium in that it is a stable outcome, since neither has a better strategy, given the other's strategy. (It is called a 'Nash-equilibrium' after the game theorist John Nash.) (Stop, Stop) is not an equilibrium, because, if Jack stops, Jill's rational choice is 'Go'.

If (Stop, Go) were the only equilibrium, we might conclude that the players would know what to do. But (Go, Stop) is another. Neither Jack nor Jill can deduce which the other will aim for. So perhaps each considers tossing a coin. This introduces a further idea, that of a *mixed strategy*, which I shall mention briefly and then set aside, because it only spoils the elegance and impact of the basic analysis. A mixed strategy is one arrived at by, so to speak, using weighted dice to decide. Here Jack might play Stop with a probability of one half; if Jill knew this, she could not improve on doing likewise; nor could Jack then do better by changing his strategy. The pair of strategies would form a *mixed strategy equilibrium*. (The example should not be read as suggesting that one half is the only suitable probability value or that there is a mixed strategy equilibrium only where the players are otherwise stuck.)

In a coordination game, then, there are two (or more) equilibria and the players must each decide which to aim for. If Figure 6.2 captures the nub of the situation, why are narrow bridges not a source of chaos? How, for that matter, do motorists manage to pass on roads, where each is, in the abstract, indifferent between both keeping left and both keeping right? How, in general, do strangers manage to coordinate a hundred times a day? One answer starts by pointing out that Figure 6.2 represents a *one-shot* game, taken in isolation. Matters would be different, if it belonged to a series or *supergame*. If Jack and Jill were regularly to arrive at the bridge at the same moment, a convention might emerge, for instance that Jill should go first. Or, even if this is their only encounter, they might be able to take advantage of conventions which have emerged in other games, like 'ladies first' or 'the driver travelling uphill has right of way'. Or they might talk it over and agree to a solution. There seem to be many possibilities. But we need to tread gingerly. If Game Theory is to be a potent tool for analysing social life, it must not simply assume the existence of conventions. In its ambitious versions, at any rate, it needs to show how rational agents can arrive at them and exactly how they can make one outcome a salient or focal point to aim at. Nor may it assume that the players can make agreements with the aid of language, if, as game theorists commonly presume, language is grounded in conventions. There are depths here, which we shall return to.

Meanwhile, not all coordination games have the symmetry of Figure 6.2, where the two equilibria are equally ranked by both players. Figure 6.3 shows a coordination game where Jack and Jill would both rather she went first.

There is still a second equilibrium, where Jack chooses 'Go', and Jill's best reply is 'Stop', in which case Jack indeed does best to choose 'Go'. But its payoff is (1, 1) which is worse for both than (2, 2). Where an outcome is superior for all players, it is natural to assume that each player is rational to play the strategy which contributes to it. (Such an outcome is dubbed 'Pareto-superior', after Vilfredo Pareto, an outcome being Pareto-superior to another if at least one player does better and no one does worse). In that case the coordination game in Figure 6.3 would have a unique solution, although even this seemingly irresistible thought will be challenged later.

Jill

		Stop	Go
Jack	Stop	0, 0	2, 2
	Go	1, 1	0, 0

Figure 6.3   Coordination game II

The key point about coordination games is that the players have a mutual interest in coordinating. Since there is no conflict of interest, it would be odd if rational agents failed to find mutually beneficial solutions, at least with repeated play. Superficially at any rate, this thought offers a simple key to the existence of a society where 'every agent is actuated solely by self-interest'. Provided that individual interests are mutually served, it is not surprising that individuals form associations. There is no puzzle about the emergence of a society which improves on the state of nature for everyone. Furthermore, conventions which benefit everyone need no enforcing among rational agents. So, if interests were never in conflict, civil society could be analysed as a set of coordination games and anarchists might be right to maintain that a society without government is as possible as it is desirable.

(2) The Prisoner's Dilemma

Since we are analysing an ideal-type world where everyone is wholly rational, it may not be an objection to this anarchist's utopia that social life is not utopian in practice. But interests can conflict, perhaps even in utopia. Where there is pure conflict, games may have no solutions short of war. Where interests overlap without coinciding, however, Game Theory becomes fascinating.

Suppose that Jack and Jill have become better acquainted and discovered a mutual penchant for crime. Soon they have committed several robberies and have graduated to murder. Sadly for them, however, they have just been arrested by a vigilant police force. The police can prove that they have done a robbery and know, but cannot prove without a confession, that they have also committed a murder. The cunning police chief has them placed in separate cells and makes each an offer. 'If you care to confess to the murder,' he assures each, 'and your partner does not, you will go entirely free. Your partner will be charged and executed but you will go free; and, of course, *vice versa*, if your partner confesses and you do not. If you both confess, you will both be charged with murder and, as a reward for being helpful, will receive a ten-year sentence. If neither confesses, you will get two years apiece for robbery. This offer is being made to each of you.' Assuming that this can all be taken at face value, and Jack and Jill know it, what is each player's rational strategy?

The game is given in Figure 6.4, with the utility numbers representing the preference orders over the possible outcomes. Thus both rank (Silent, Silent) above (Confess, Confess) but are sharply at odds for the rest. Jack will be best suited if he confesses and she sits tight and worst suited contrariwise; for Jill it is the other way about. It may seem at first that each player's rational strategy depends on what the other is likely to do. After all, silence is a better strategy for both than confession. But Game Theory bids Jack reflect that, if Jill confesses, he does better to confess (ten years beats execution), and that, if Jill stays silent, he again does better to confess (freedom beats two years in gaol). Hence confession is better for him, *whatever she does*; and, by parity of reasoning, better for her, *whatever he does*. So both confess regardless and a contented chief of police has them both sent down for a decade.

To arrive at this conclusion abstractly, look at the utility numbers first from Jack's point of view and then from Jill's. Jack notes that 'Confess' scores him 4 and 'Silent' scores him 3, if Jill chooses the left-hand column; and 'Confess' scores him 2 and 'Silent' scores him 1, if she chooses the right hand column. Thus 'Confess' is his *dominant* strategy, in that it scores higher than 'Silent' (the *dominated* strategy), whatever Jill does. Similarly, for Jill's payoffs, 4 beats 3 in the top row and 2 beats 1 in the bottom

| | | Jill | |
		Silent	Confess
Jack	Silent	3, 3	1, 4
	Confess	4, 1	2, 2

Figure 6.4   The Prisoner's Dilemma

row, making 'Confess' her dominant strategy. A rational agent never chooses a dominated strategy.

Is there no honour among thieves? Not if, as in Figure 6.4, there is an unique Nash-equilibrium, however disastrous. Confession is the best reply to confession; silence is not the best reply to silence. How exactly has the chief of police trapped them? An obvious suggestion is that the trick was to put them in separate cells, where they could not communicate. Very well, give them a few minutes together to plan a joint strategy. No doubt they will agree to keep silent. But will they keep their agreement? Each must now choose whether to keep it or break it; so substitute 'Keep' for 'Silent' and 'Break' for 'Confess' in Figure 6.4. That seems fair enough, since, by the measure of the resulting sentences, each presumably ranks the outcomes as in the table.

Outcome			*Ranking*
Self	+	*Other*	
Break		Keep	1st
Keep		Keep	2nd
Break		Break	3rd
Keep		Break	4th

If Other plays 'Keep', Self does better to play 'Break'; if Other plays 'Break', Self again does better to play 'Break'. As in Figure 6.4, there is a dominant strategy for both players and it sums to a Pareto-inferior outcome. In other words, utility numbers being unaffected, communication and an apparent agreement leave the game essentially as before. Jack and Jill have a mutual interest in avoiding confession by both but cannot yet escape their dilemma by agreeing to cooperate. Words are cheap talk, as game theorists are wont to say.

What happens if the game is repeated several times? Here it may seem that each player will perceive the folly of pegging away at an inferior outcome. A strategy of 'tit for tat' looks more promising: play obligingly in the first round and then keep it up, provided that the other player does likewise. If Jack and Jill both play tit for tat in a ten-round game with the payoffs as in Figure 6.4, each will emerge with a score of thirty, instead of the twenty which repeating the unsociable strategy of the one-shot game would produce.

But this thought hits a dramatic snag. In a ten-round game, there is nothing to gain from cooperative play in the final round. Since there is no further round, where uncooperative play can be punished, the final round is effectively a one-shot game with the old strategy dominant. But in that case there is nothing to gain from cooperative play in the ninth round, since rational players are going to play their dominant strategy in the tenth regardless. The same therefore goes for the eighth round, the seventh, the sixth and so on. The whole cooperative scheme unravels back to the opening round, where Jack and Jill will thus find that each is rational to play the equilibrium strategy whatever the other does. How sad!

That chain of reasoning is typical of some quirky-looking results apparently implicit in Game Theory, and presents a significant crux, to be explored later. It does not hold, if the game has infinitely many rounds or if players do not know which round is the last. But, where it does hold, it holds however many rounds the game has. The case for cooperation unravels logically as easily for one hundred rounds as for ten, even though one might suppose that the trouble starts only as the game nears its end. Intriguingly, however, when the game is played with student volunteers in the economics research laboratory at my university, the (known) length of the series does matter, with defections starting only when the end comes close and economics students defecting earlier than others. This is consistent with similar American reports (including the point about economics students) and, more loosely, with what seems to happen in everyday life. Is there more honour even among thieves than Game Theory implies? If so, is it rational or irrational to act on it?

Before we broach such questions, here are two more games. Since I cite them for what they have in common, one might have been enough. But, since they are distinct and tend to turn up in different realms of discussion, there is room for both.

(3) Chicken

When Jack and Jill emerge from prison, they are angry enough to fight a duel. Like Texas teenagers of the 1950s (whose behaviour gave the game its name), they each acquire a car and line up facing each other a distance apart on an empty lonely road. In a moment they will drive down the narrow highway at speed towards a head-on collision. Whoever swerves first will be 'Chicken'. For each, loss of face would be terrible but a crash would be worse.

Chicken differs from the Prisoner's Dilemma in having two equilibria with pure (unmixed) strategies: (Swerve, Middle) and (Middle, Swerve). Jack thus has no clear choice of strategy, since, by parity of reasoning, neither has Jill. That might seem to make for a happy outcome, at least in a Chicken supergame, since the players each lack a dominant strategy leading to collective disaster. But, whereas there may be some pressure (so far mysterious) to cooperate in the repeated Prisoner's Dilemma, players of Chicken are less disposed to be amiable. Since Jack knows that it is rational for Jill to swerve if she expects him not to, it pays him to acquire a reputation for bravado. One way to acquire it, moreover, is to play even a one-shot game by visibly setting himself on a collision course from which she knows that he cannot back down. These strategies of 'reputation-building' and 'commitment', as game theorists dub them, enrich the game in

		Jill	
		Swerve	Middle
Jack	Swerve	3, 3	2, 4
	Middle	4, 2	1, 1

Figure 6.5   Chicken

ways which do not tend to benefit both players, as they do in the Prisoner's Dilemma.

That makes it disquieting to find Chicken analysed in depth by those studying arms races. There has been much debate whether the game which reveals most about an arms race is Chicken, the Prisoner's Dilemma or some other game. The belief that it is Chicken inclines policy-makers to nuclear strategies which petrify the rest of us. But complexities soon set in. For instance, the chilling policy of Mutual Assured Destruction (MAD) recommends arming to the teeth with nuclear weapons on the grounds that no one will then dare to start the Chicken game. Even if this were to make for nuclear peace, however, it might thereby encourage Chicken games with lesser weapons, since no one will dare retaliate with a nuclear strike.

Even without pursuing the example, we can notice a further crux. The real-world games of war and peace are played not among ideally rational agents but among less abstract Jacks and Jills. Jack needs to know not whether the game truly is Chicken but whether Jill thinks it is. To complicate matters, however, there is a sense in which the game cannot fail to be what the players think it is: the game is theirs. Also, neither would quite think it a 'game' of any sort, were there not intense interaction between academic game theorists and policy-makers (who pay for much of the research). Here is a case where the ideas which social scientists put into the heads of agents shape the very world which the social scientists are trying to analyse. If the case is as typical as I suspect, it gives reason for thinking not only that the agents' understanding is relevant to the social scientists' explanations but also that, being the stuff of the social world, it sets them a profound methodological challenge.

(4) Battle of the Sexes

Having at last cooled off, Jack and Jill resume their partnership. But their problems are not over. Soon they find themselves playing Battle of the Sexes. This game gets its Thurberesque or mildly Freudian name from the following scenario. Jack and Jill have agreed to spend the evening together at an event, which is to be

Jill

	Bullfight	Concert
Bullfight	4, 3	2, 1
Concert	1, 2	3, 4

Jack

Figure 6.6   Battle of the Sexes

either a bullfight or a concert. But they have forgotten to agree which and it is too late to communicate. Each prefers an event in the other's company to going alone but Jack likes bullfights and Jill likes concerts. Each must therefore choose where to go, given the preferences shown in Figure 6.6. How should each choose?

Here (4, 3) and (3, 4) are both equilibria but, for a one-shot game, there is no pure strategy. If a convention were to emerge, for instance that women defer to the wishes of men, then the supergame might be determinate and so might even the one-shot game in a society where the convention was well known. For, as soon as Jack believes that Jill expects him to go to the bullfight and Jill knows this, the bullfight becomes the rational choice for both. In a repeated game, these expectations serve to lock Jill into a series of bullfights – a symbolic point about any society where even one-shot encounters are influenced by a presumption that the Jacks call the shots and the Jills oblige. Potentially there is a highly instructive lesson here about the nature of power and why losers are 'rational' to respect a distribution of power which works against them, when out-of-equilibrium strategies would suit them worse. It bears, for instance, on whether those who engage in free-market transactions thereby show themselves to do so freely and with consent, or, on the contrary, may merely be assisting in their own alienation.

These four games are not the only ones worth knowing about but I hope that they are enough to give a feel for game-theoretic analysis, to indicate some instructive applications and, in a moment, to raise questions about its basis. At any rate, we can now address its claim to offer a thoroughly individualist analysis of social institutions and of society at large. I shall make some general remarks about social theories which rest on a notion of contract and then raise a crux about the analysis of social norms.

THE SOCIAL CONTRACT

Ambitious claims are often made for Game Theory as a tool of social analysis, especially by those who see it as the cutting edge of a general individualism. We have had strong assurances from J. S. Mill that 'human beings in society have no properties but those which are derived from, and may be resolved into, the laws of nature of individual man' (p.10), and from Jon Elster that 'the elementary unit of social life is the individual human action' (p.19). Yet we are born into a world of institutions which socialise us, shape our goals and values, condition our options and outlast our demise. So what could render plausible Elster's claim that 'to explain social institutions and social change is to show how they arise as a result of the action and interaction of individuals'?

The broadest question is why societies exist at all and a simple answer might be that they embody a social contract, being associations of individuals who find it rational to cooperate. Coordination games illustrate this answer readily and offer the plausible suggestion that primary 'institutions' are simply the sort of conventions which emerge with repeated play as guidance where there are multiple equilibria. Wherever there is no conflict of interest, individuals have nothing to lose and plenty to gain by hitting on rules which it suits everyone to follow. Although not every institution can be analysed as a deposit resulting from previous games of coordination, it is not implausible to suggest that societies rest ultimately on mutual self-interest, so that their very existence can be analysed as a solution to a basic problem of coordination. To strengthen this ingenuous thought, it is especially plausible to think of language as a set of conventions which serve a mutual interest in coordination. It does not matter what we call a spade, provided that we all give it the same name. Different languages are different solutions to the same ultimate coordination game, and so, perhaps, are the various schemes of moral or normative concepts through which societies ensure stability in thought, word and deed.

If this were all there was to it, society could, in theory, arise through a sort of social contract which needs no enforcement and exist without government. This cheerful anarchism is not refuted by the obvious prevalence of enforcements, because the process of coordination can go wrong. One enjoyable anarchist theme is that government is indeed needed, but only to remedy the ills caused by government, without which there would be no ills to remedy. Similar thinking may inspire libertarian ideas of what a completely free market would achieve, although this is not to belittle the strenuous intellectual efforts by economists which yield the complexities of general equilibrium theory. Enforcement is needed only to correct distortions of what could be better achieved by unenforced cooperation among fully rational individuals.

A contrary view of the social contract makes the Prisoner's Dilemma the crucial game. This view has a distinguished pedigree, usually traced to *Leviathan* by Thomas Hobbes, published in 1651 in the aftermath of the English civil war. Contemplating that grim episode, Hobbes produced an individualist analysis of human nature and society intended to explain 'the art of making and maintaining commonwealths'. *Leviathan* opens with several chapters exhibiting human beings as mechanically-driven creatures, each bent on securing his own 'felicity'. 'The felicity of this life,' Hobbes remarks in Chapter 9, 'consisteth not in the repose of a mind satisfied' but in a continual progress of desire from one object to another, not 'to enjoy once only, and for one instant of time; but to assure for ever the way of his future desire'. This being the human condition, all mankind has 'a perpetual and restless desire of power after power, that ceaseth only in death'. Here is a classic statement of the idea that all rational action is aimed at maximising the agent's expected utility, with the Hobbesian rider that, 'because life itself is but motion' (Chapter 6), the aim can never remain satisfied for long.

In that case it is far from plain how society is possible and Hobbes turns a sharp eye to 'those qualities of mankind concerning their living together in peace and unity'. The mordant

Chapter 13 is titled 'Of the Natural Condition of Mankind as Concerning their Felicity, and Misery'. It takes the crux to be that 'if any two men desire the same thing, which nevertheless they cannot both enjoy, they become enemies' and opines that 'in the nature of man there are three principal causes of quarrel'. These are 'first, competition; secondly, diffidence; thirdly, glory'. Competition makes men invade one another for gain. Diffidence, or, as we would now say, distrust, makes for preemptive strikes. Glory, which equates loosely with what we now call status, makes men aggressive whenever they sense that they are undervalued. Such inbuilt causes of quarrel make mere associations fragile, to say the least. 'Hence it is manifest that during the time men live without a common power to keep them all in awe, they are in that condition which is called war; and such a war as is of everyman against everyman'. This condition is Hobbes' celebrated and bleak state of nature, where 'there is continual fear, and danger of violent death; and the life of man is solitary, poor, nasty, brutish and short'.

So how do we come to live together in peace and unity? Hobbes reasons that men are inclined to peace by 'fear of death; desire of such things as are necessary to commodious living; and a hope by their industry to obtain them'. These passions incline us to peace, but are not enough to overcome the causes of quarrel, however, unless there is 'a common power to keep all in awe'. Otherwise we shall each continue to invade one another, because that remains our dominant strategy, whatever others do. We are still 'enemies', wanting things which we cannot all have and, although each will apparently subscribe to articles of peace, each will break them if he can. Since 'the weakest has strength enough to kill the strongest, either by secret machination, or in confederacy with others, that are in the same danger as himself', no one is safe.

There is some dispute among game theorists as to which game best illuminates the theme of *Leviathan*. But there is an evident case for deeming it the Prisoner's Dilemma, although with more players than Jack and Jill – an n-person version, setting what game theorists term the *free-rider problem*. Everyone is better served by peace than by war; so we might suppose that peace will emerge spontaneously. But, even if it did, each player is still better served by being a free-rider who takes the benefits but fails to contribute. For instance, if a peaceable convention of promise-keeping emerges, the free-rider makes promises, gets something in exchange and then does not keep them. If all behave like this, society reverts, of course, to war (whose nature 'consisteth not in actual fighting; but in the known disposition thereto'). The bones of the argument were contained in the discussion of the vain agreement to keep silent which Jack and Jill made on p.125, when allowed to communicate in the Prisoner's Dilemma.

In Hobbes' words 'Covenants without the sword are but words, and of no strength to secure a man at all' (Chapter 17). Accordingly he argues that the only escape is to create 'a power to keep all in awe' and to arm this sovereign with the sword. That is the 'Leviathan' of the book's title, a sovereign authority created by a social contract to protect us from invasion, domestic and foreign, and to secure us in our covenants with one another. The Introduction describes Leviathan as 'an artificial man', shown in the original frontispiece as a crowned king armed with the weapons of church and state. This sovereign figure seems to be wearing chain mail, but look closer and it is in fact made up of tiny human individuals. That captures Hobbes' theme precisely. Society is an artifice which lets rational individuals escape the Prisoner's Dilemma.

NORMS AND COOPERATION

That gives us two individualist ways of analysing social norms, both fundamental enough to be called theories of the social contract. They are not the only such theories but they point conveniently to a broad division of social models into those premised on consensus and those premised on conflict. Broadly, consensus models start with coordination and then need to account for norms which are not merely self-enforcing; conflict models insist that our basic interests may overlap but emphatically do not coincide, and thus make the root problem how cooperation is possible. Either way, we are owed a theoretical account of the role of norms in a world where all agents are rational individuals guided by their own preferences.

The shared individualism makes the basic game in both analyses *non-cooperative* in Game Theory parlance. This may sound a perverse way to describe a coordination game, where the players have a mutual interest in cooperating. But game theorists classify a game as *cooperative* only if players can rely on any agreement being kept, and conventions arising even in coordination games do not have the strongly binding character here envisaged. Whereas cooperative games presuppose a solution to the problem of how norms arise and why they persist, coordination games seem to need make no assumption of norms and institutions and are thus deemed non-cooperative. The problem, in essence, is how and whether non-cooperative games can give rise to cooperative ones.

Hobbes' answer is that they cannot do so directly but that rational individuals can agree to create a power which they cannot then escape. With Leviathan in place and equipped with a sword, everyday contracts can be made and bargains struck in the knowledge that defections will be punished. In the state of nature everyone arms to the teeth because being armed is better than not being armed, whatever others do. But once there is a sovereign claiming the monopoly of legitimate force, the payoffs for going armed change, since peace and 'commodious living' become possible. This strongly suggests that norms, like promise-keeping, truth-telling and respect for moral obligations in general, work only in so far as there are sanctions. We are good when it pays to be good; and it pays only when we are sure of punishment for being bad.

Interestingly, however, Hobbes clearly thinks that, although there are no obligations in the state of nature ('the notions of right and wrong, justice and injustice have there no place'), the creation of Leviathan makes possible obligations which are indeed morally binding. Even prisoners of war, released upon a promise to pay a ransom, have an obligation to pay up, even though beyond reach of reprisal. This goes with his finely balanced reply to 'the fool', who 'hath said in his heart that there is no such thing as justice' (Chapter 15) and remains critical for current contractarian theories of ethics and justice, like David Gauthier's *Morals by Agreement* (1986). Whether Hobbes can maintain this, given his own analysis, is disputable and I shall not discuss *Leviathan* itself further here. But the issue is absolutely crucial for the whole attempt to analyse institutions as conventions and to regard conventions as emerging from interaction among rational agents to their mutual benefit.

No society can function without trust. Our account of games among instrumentally rational agents leaves it unclear how far ideally rational agents can be trusted. That is partly, I think, because the exact sense of 'trust' is not yet plain and partly because too little has yet been said about how rational agents are motivated.

There is a weak sense of 'trust' in which Jack can be trusted to do whatever it is predictable that he will do, rather as a reliable alarm clock can be trusted to ring at the set time. In this sense, Jack can be trusted to do what maximises his expected utility. But, to get at the problem of trust, we need to distinguish this usage from two others. To say that no society can function without trust is usually either to say that it needs social norms to do with truth-telling, promise-keeping and the honouring of agreements, which operate even on occasions when one could break them without penalty, or to say that it needs members who recognise and respect moral obligations. Whether social norms and moral obligations are finally distinct is for dispute and more will be said in Chapter 10. To bring out what they have in common, consider the game theorist's apothegm that 'words are cheap talk'. The thought behind it is that, since Jack will do only what suits his preferences, Jill does well to attend to his preferences and not to his words. For example, his offer to keep silent in a one-shot game is to be trusted only if he would keep silent without it. By contrast, for persons bound by social norms or moral principles, to give one's word creates an effective reason for keeping it.

Since strategies of reputation-building and commitment are available to rational agents, it may seem that Game Theory can incorporate binding agreements readily enough. But the motivation of a rational agent is solely forward-looking. All the game diagrams indicate clearly that actions are motivated solely by their

resulting payoffs. Jack's preferences can, of course, be influenced
by sanctions and it may be that some of these sanctions are
internal. Thus it may be that he feels rotten, if he breaks a
promise; but, if so, this shows up as a disutility in his mathematical psychics. Reasons for action are never backward-looking, in
the sense of operating solely because of a past event. To make that
possible, we would need a notion of rationality distinct from the
instrumental one governing this chapter.

There may be scope, however, for making agents more complex. Comparison with utilitarianism is instructive. Its initial version, that we should always do the *act* with the best consequences,
arguably could, if adopted by everyone, lead to a society without a
reliable institution of promise-keeping. This consequence would
be worse than what would happen if we always acted in accordance with the *rules* which would lead to the best consequences if
followed by all. Rule-utilitarianism can thus seem the better version, with its forward-looking reasons for acting on backward-
looking reasons. But critics complain that it does the job only if
so Kantian that it is no longer a version of utilitarianism.
Similarly, rational agents who were more reflective and distanced
from their own preferences might each do better for themselves.
But it is not plain that the change can be introduced without
destroying the basis of Rational Choice theory. Whether it can
will become clearer in Chapter 9.

Short of this, there remains a strong case for holding that
cooperation sometimes requires the *prior* acceptance of social
norms or moral obligations which the theory therefore cannot
account for from scratch. Yet I do not want to press too hard.
The examples offered have been ones where out-of-equilibrium
outcomes are Pareto-superior. But what might rationally prompt
honour among thieves in the Prisoner's Dilemma or mutual non-
aggression in Chicken is only a higher prudence. It has yet to be
proved that suitably prudent agents need be radically different from
the rational seekers of marginal advantage with whom we began.

Even if some conventions are proving elusive to analyse, thus
giving trouble for the individualist account of rules norms and
practices, others still seem straightforward. So let me just mention

very briefly two further problems, both arising from the existence of multiple equilibria in many games.

The more obvious one is illustrated by Battle of the Sexes, where each equilibrium distributes benefits unequally. If a convention emerges, for instance that Jills do what best pleases Jacks, it is easy to see why it may persist. But how does one particular equilibrium emerge as salient or focal? Chance is a possible answer. But, contemplating plausible examples of the game, one is more inclined to point to the distribution of power. Nothing in the chapter affords any clue to the nature and origins of power, since vague remarks about social evolution merely veil the problem and the fiction of an explicit social contract is only a fiction.

The subtler problem concerns the whole idea of convention. A convention is being analysed as a set of mutual expectations which reinforce one another to make a particular equilibrium salient. On the highway, for instance, Jack is rational to keep left if he expects Jill to keep left and *vice versa*. Yes; but he is also rational to keep right if he expects Jill to keep right and *vice versa*. Both pairs of expectations are mutually self-reinforcing. How and why exactly does an established habit of keeping left (in Britain) give Jack a sufficient reason to keep left next time? To reply that left has become salient begs the question and, surprisingly, nothing yet said offers more. Left is Jack's rational choice only if he expects that Jill expects . . . (that he expects that she expects . . .) that he will choose left. Equally, right is his rational choice if he expects that she expects . . . (that he expects that she expects . . .) that he will choose right. Each of these infinite hypotheticals is a tautology and nothing shows why previous behaviour renders one categorical and the other irrelevant.

Even more astonishingly, perhaps, the same point arises with the version in Figure 6.3, where both players prefer the same equilibrium. Stop is indeed Jack's uniquely rational choice *if* he expects that she expects . . . But, equally, 'Go' is still his uniquely rational choice, *if* he expects that she expects . . . Again something more is wanted than has yet been offered to determine which hypothetical is to guide action.

Jill

	Stop	Go
Stop	0, 0	2, 2
Go	1, 1	0, 0

Jack

Figure 6.3   Coordination game II

This may seem incredible. But the case for it is accepted by some, although not all, game theorists and stems directly from Thomas Schelling's respected *The Strategy of Conflict* (1960). If it is correct, it undermines David Lewis' *Convention* (1969), the classic statement of the view of conventions, linguistic and social, which is standard for Game Theory and has been assumed in this chapter. Incredible or not, however, it would not astonish two older philosophers. Hume would take it to reinforce his contention that all our reasonings rest in the end on custom and so cannot explain the basis of custom. Kant would take it to show that the instrumental rationality of self-interested prudence is subordinate to a higher rationality of practical reason where each person is directly motivated to do what is right by the test of fairness, justice or morality.

Since there is no room to flesh out these quick hints at deep philosophical perplexities, it is time to sum up.

CONCLUSION

Game Theory abstracts from the tangles of the social world to a pure realm peopled by ideally rational agents equipped with fully ordered preferences, complete information and a perfect internal computer. Their preferences can be completely and consistently represented by a ranking of the possible outcomes of interaction, an interaction being the sum of the consequences of separate individual actions. Their information includes 'common knowledge' that other players are rational agents, and is so complete that anything known to anyone is known to everyone. Their computers see to it that, taking probabilities into account, each can derive everyone's rational strategy, where there is one. Although we have considered only four of the games such people play, we can see the power of the theory and, at the same time, raise some awkward questions about its limitations.

Coordination games introduce the basic notion of strategic choice. Jack's rational choice depends on what Jill will choose and *vice versa*. With repeated play, it is easy to conjecture that the emergence of a convention can guide them to a mutually beneficial equilibrium. That makes an interesting suggestion about a sort of norm which needs no enforcement and, more grandly, about consensus as the basis of a theory of the social contract. On reflection, however, we can still wonder whether Game Theory itself contains enough to explain exactly how and why conventions guide choices.

The Prisoner's Dilemma makes the vital point that individually rational choices can sum to collectively inferior results. An 'Invisible Hand' often makes mischief for all. Interestingly, the kind of norm which might prevent this happening seems to need enforcement, because it is otherwise subject to free-riding. Hobbes thought so, and *Leviathan* remains crucial for theories of the social contract and much else. Meanwhile down-to-earth examples of the Dilemma are legion, if one examines the fragility of attempts to preserve rain forests, protect endangered species, save energy, achieve a voluntary incomes policy, stop the arms race, prevent global warming and more modestly, Keep Britain Tidy. Yet, if what is really needed is genuine trust and moral conduct, it is tantalisingly unclear whether one would want even a fully rational agent as one's neighbour. How far can such a rational fool ultimately be trusted?

Chicken sets the problem of what strategy is rational in a game with more than one equilibrium and an endemic conflict of interest between the players. If Jack is unsure of his rational strategy because unsure of Jill's, then her uncertainties are increased by contemplating his. This makes Chicken games dangerous, indeed lethal if played with weapons of destruction. Moreover players in real life may be uncertain whether their present game is truly Chicken and whether the other players also take it to be Chicken. Among the intriguing questions raised is what difference it makes when flesh-and-blood players, like American nuclear strategists or British Treasury mandarins, have had lessons in Game Theory and bear them in mind.

Battle of the Sexes was discussed only fleetingly but will crop up again. Jack and Jill both gain from coordination but the two ways of achieving it benefit them differentially. In a repeated game one player looks like getting locked in to an inferior equilibrium. Meanwhile the general question again arises about the limitations of Game Theory in analysing games where there are multiple equilibria.

Individualism, as purveyed by Rational Choice theory and Game Theory, deals with social norms in two ways. One is by showing how repeated interaction can generate them as solutions to problems arising in the games. But even if that works for truly consensual norms which suit everyone, it remains unclear that it does so for norms vulnerable to free-riding. The crux is trust and whether rational prudence can make us trustworthy even on occasions when we could escape reprisal. The other way is to tuck them into agents' preferences. Thus the good Samaritan had altruistic preferences which led him to rescue a stranger, while those with other preferences walked past on the other side of the road. When George Washington, as legend has it, owned up to felling a cherry tree with the words 'Father, I cannot tell a lie', he was acting on a strong ethical preference for honesty. The theory is silent about the sources of preference, which it treats as 'given', and the crux is whether, in failing to say more, it leaves individualism to be trumped by a holistic story about the social determination of preferences.

For instance, to look ahead, preferences are often aligned with roles. Parents tend to prefer outcomes which benefit their children. French industrial workers like M. Rouget tend to prefer the policies of the Left. Bureaucrats often make the interests of their bureaucracy their own. Military advisers to governments favour military solutions to political problems. This means that choices which might seem inferior, if one considered them in abstraction from social positions, can become entirely rational if one connects preferences to roles, thus embedding norms in the analysis. It is disingenuous to claim that Rational Choice theory is thereby enabled to account for role-specific behaviour. If a structure of social relations is being tucked away in agents' preference orders and is doing the effective work, then we shall want to know more about it than Rational Choice theory attempts to tell us. A similar point can be made about the enriched psychology just envisaged, where it sounds no less disingenuous to present altruists as people who happen to derive utility from raising the utility of others. But this is to anticipate Chapter 8 and I end by identifying three puzzles.

(1) Can game-theoretic analysis account for all manner of social norms or must it presuppose at least some of them?
(2) How does its abstract analysis of an ideal-type world peopled by ideally rational agents relate to our ordinary world of unidealised persons?
(3) Where it does reveal significant features of social interaction, is it an exercise in explanation or in understanding?

CHAPTER 7

Understanding social action

In trying to focus the problem of structure and action on M. Rouget's vote, we might have hoped that there is an agreed method of explanation in the natural sciences which could be imported into the social sciences. But there is not; and that is partly, no doubt, why it is hard to decide whether the holistic approaches deployed in Chapter 5 are undercut by the Rational Choice version of individualism proposed in Chapter 6. On the other hand, there have been signs that the social sciences may call for a scientific method of their own. The next two chapters will examine some ideas about the understanding of social action which suggest that the social world can only be tackled from within and by methods different from those suited to the natural sciences.

To clear the deck, let us start with a brisk reminder. M. Rouget took the stage in Chapter 3 as a case study in Positive science and the application of a universal scientific method to social phenomena. To explain his voting communist was to cite statistics from which his vote could have been predicted with high probability. The epistemic warrant was a principle of induction, and the scientific method was one for confirming or refuting inductive generalisations, as in Lipsey's 'percolator'. This approach to explanation has fared badly even for the natural world. A merely inductive warrant offers too little and claims too much. It offers too little because it cannot guide choice among rival theories which are all consistent with the observed facts. Nor can it ground a needed distinction between causal laws and accidental correlations. It claims too much by assuming that facts can be identified prior to all theory and interpretation, as pragmatism

142

pointed out sharply in Chapter 4. Meanwhile it has nothing to offer realists, whose explanations involve unobservable structures and causal mechanisms. As to that, however, the rationalism of Chapter 2, although 'very mechanical' in its way, does not satisfy today's realists and we are still owed the their epistemological warrant for inferring the structures and mechanisms which they regard as the best explanations.

The moral to be drawn is only the modest one that we can be open-minded about the analysis of social action. If the stuff and order of the social world is sufficiently unlike the natural, then causal explanation may have to yield to interpretative under-standing. Even so, there may still be room for compromise and collaboration. But that can wait.

We are now under the aegis of the hermeneutic or interpreta-tive tradition in social theory and its governing imperative that the social world must be understood from within. In its full splendour it is a very grand tradition, with as strong a sense of the underlying movement of history as rationalists or realists have ever had of the hidden order of nature. In this aspect it is often termed 'historicist' and its tutelary genius is Georg Wilhelm Friedrich Hegel (1770–1831). Hegel remains a central figure in current social theory, having survived Marx's famous claim to have stood him back on his feet by establishing dialectical materialism and Popper's at-tempted refutation of both of them as pseudoscience in *The Poverty of Historicism* (1960). But the grand ambitions of historicism cannot be conveyed briefly and they obscure some clear and simple reasons for deeming the social sciences peculiar. So, as in Chapter 1 (p.17), I open the case for an interpretative ap-proach to the social realm with Dilthey's remark that 'meaning' is 'the category which is peculiar to life and to the historical world'.

We shall begin by noting four ways in which meaning or meanings may be peculiar and by connecting the topic with the philosophical problem of Other Minds. Attention will then focus on the concept of rationality, here introduced with the help of Max Weber. A different approach to understanding will next be sought in Wittgensteinian ideas about social action as the follow-ing of rules and the playing of 'games'. Since this sense of 'game' contrasts radically with that of Game Theory, we can then play *homo economicus* off against *homo sociologicus*, using a version of the latter which, on the whole, belongs in the top right box. Attempts to give social actors more autonomy will be left to the next chapter.

FOUR KINDS OF MEANING

What might be peculiar about meaning as a category or about meanings as examples? Here are four possible preliminary answers with no obvious parallel in physics and little parallel in biology.

Firstly, human actions have meaning. They embody intentions, express emotions, are done for reasons and are influenced by ideas about value. The agent means something by them. This is (usually) possible only because there is a conscious stock of meanings to draw upon. There are conventions and symbols which others can be expected to recognise. Even if animal behaviour, being often purposive, displays feelings and is directed to goals, it does not draw on a conscious stock of conventions and symbols. Although a ring round the moon 'means' rain, it does so only in the sense that it is correlated, perhaps causally, with rain. Spontaneous tears, a natural sign of grief, are not to be confused with symbols of grief, for instance when a flag flown at half mast means that a death is being mourned.

Secondly, this distinction between the meaning of an action and what the actor means by it relates to one between what words mean and what people mean by them. Language is a prime candidate for the key to the peculiarity of social life. Indeed one recent line of thought holds that all social actions and interactions should be regarded as a 'text' and construed as if they were utterances. The connections among action, thought and language are at least intimate, and it can be argued that all private thought and individual action presuppose a shared language, thus making language more than an instrument to serve human purposes. None of this applies to the behaviour of atoms. It may perhaps apply to the squirrels in my garden warning each other that a cat is stalking them, or to the mating song of the whale, or to the bees' honey dance; and chimpanzees can apparently be taught words by humans. But, if so, this does more to show that some animals have a rudimentary social life than that the conceptual complexities of human language are at the other end of a continuum which starts with physical atoms.

Thirdly, unlike animal habits, human practices are imbued with normative expectations (to be distinguished presently from the game theorist's rational expectations). They embody ideas about what one is entitled to expect of people and are reinforced by guilt and shame in the face of reproach for failure to live up to them. Underlying the expectations specific to a particular role there is usually a broader ethics or, often, a set of religious beliefs, which extend the seen world into an unseen world of values, ideals and sacred beings. I word this carefully so that, in making it matter what meaning people find in their lives and performances, we are not committing ourselves to an unseen world and an external meaning which life has. But, even when worded neutrally, there is a moral dimension to social life which a 'moral science' will need to capture. A scientific method designed for physics and adapted to biology may be radically unsuited to deal with it.

Fourthly, although my cat may hold beliefs, for instance that there is food to be had by leading me to the cupboard where it is kept, she does not hold theories about the nature of things. We do. In particular, we hold theories about human beings which are influenced by the social sciences. Freudian psychology, for example, has shaped many people's self-understanding. Game Theory, as noted earlier, has affected the conduct of foreign policy by decision-makers convinced of the merits of Game Theory. The meaning of many actions depends on the model of the social world which is in the actors' heads. This curious feature of social theories, that they are, so to speak, tied to their own tails, will prove important later.

THE PROBLEM OF OTHER MINDS

These four suggestions involve several senses of 'meaning' and are, I confess, pretty miscellaneous. I shall try to harness them in a moment by reflecting further on the notion of rationality. But first we should identify a philosophical problem which they all raise. The core epistemological problem so far has been the problem of Knowledge: by what criterion do we know that a belief is true or at least that we are justified in holding it? This question has ramified into others about the faculties of mind, the character of the natural order, the difference between science and pseudoscience and the relation of theory to experience. But its core remains one about inference from narrow premises to wider conclusions, especially when those conclusions refer to unobservables. In so far as 'meaning' is indeed the category peculiar to the social sciences, the problem of Knowledge gets an acute twist – the problem of Other Minds.

The four suggestions distinguish, in effect, between behaviour and action, between signs and symbols, between signals and utterances, between habits and practices, between regularities and norms, in short between natural adaptive responses to a changing environment and self-conscious, theoretically-informed social interaction. The first term in each pair sets the previous epistemological puzzles of inference and interpretation. These puzzles also apply to the second term in each pair but there is then a further twist. To arrive at the meaning of actions and utterances, we need the actors' interpretations. If it takes interpretation of data to know that one sees a human body with its arm in the air, it takes a second interpretation to know that the body is someone waving goodbye. The problem, premised on the separateness of persons, is how one mind can know what is in the mind of another. This is the philosophers' problem of Other Minds. It becomes central for the social sciences as soon as one thinks of understanding action as involving an interpretation of an interpretation, a 'double hermeneutic', as it is commonly called. Among its instances is one crucial for anthropology, that of Other Cultures, which arises when we ask how members of one culture (or sub-culture) can penetrate the inwardness of another.

As a revealing gloss on the problem, think about the difference between a spectator and an agent. An astronomer is a spectator, watching what happens in the distant heavens and explaining the behaviour of this law-governed realm. Reports may start in the first person ('*I* see Venus here and now') but reference to a personal point of view soon drops out. In general, natural science aims at a spectator's view and any retreat from it, made for reasons in the earlier chapters, is reluctant. The basic presumption remains stubbornly that nature is independent of human belief: one cannot keep dry by refusing to believe that it is raining. If naturalism is right, the social scientist aims at a spectator's view too, whatever the complications arising because humans are agents and social actors: the spectator can see at least as much of the game as the players. Yes, adherents of the hermeneutic tradition reply, but only if one first reconstructs the players' point of view and that radically changes the character of the exercise; there is a fundamental difference between understanding and explaining, since what happens in the social world depends on its meaning for the agents in a way without parallel in the realm of the stars. In these terms the problem of Other Minds becomes radically peculiar to social science, instead of a mere complication within the problem of Knowledge.

RATIONALITY: A WEBERIAN APPROACH

That is only a rough gloss, however, and we need some precise way to distinguish between explaining and understanding. Even if 'meaning' is a suggestive category, I do not myself find it a helpful one. There are too many senses of meaning which might be relevant, thus making it too hard to decide what account scientific explanation can or cannot take of meanings. A better idea to work with, I find, is that of rationality. It is easier to analyse and serves better to focus disputes both between explaining and understanding and between holistic and individualistic understanding. This is not an original thought. It occurred notably to Max Weber (1864–1920) and we cannot do better than start with his analysis of social action and how to understand it.

'The science of society attempts the interpretative understanding of social action,' Weber declared in the opening pages of *Economy and Society* (published in 1922), the classic source for the Weberian distinction between explaining (*erklären*) and understanding (*verstehen*). In 'action' he includes 'all human action when and in so far as the acting individual attaches subjective meaning to it'. By 'social action' he means action 'which takes account of the behaviour of others and is thereby oriented in its course'. For example, he says, cyclists engage in social action when entering traffic, whereas people who put up umbrellas in the rain do not. For, although umbrellas are social objects and a crowd of umbrellas may indicate a social event, there is no social action involved in putting up an umbrella, at least in so far as each person takes account only of the weather.

Notice that Weber's starting point is an individualist one. He begins with individual actors who attach subjective meaning to their actions. ('Subjective meaning', in Weber's usage, covers whatever emotions, ideas, aims or values an action can embody or express.) Then he introduces social action as an interplay considered from the point of view of each individual, a move well suited to our earlier games with rational agents. This starting point will be challenged later in the chapter but, meanwhile, it conveniently lets us pick out two aspects of the meaning of action or utterance which obtruded earlier. There is its subjective meaning (what the actor meant by it) and its intersubjective meaning (what the action meant). Cyclists cannot orient their behaviour in its course unless they can rely on a shared reading of signals given and received. There is a question, analytically, of whether the individual intentions are prior to the shared reading, as Weber implies, or whether the intentions are possible only because there are public 'rules of the game'. But, either way, interpretative understanding needs to reckon with both.

Weber then specifies four pure types of action, the first two of which are to be understood by reconstructing the agent's reasons. The first is instrumentally rational (*zweckrational*) action, where the agent chooses the most effective means to an end. This is the 'economic' type of rationality implicit in the orthodox microeconomics and idealised in Expected Utility Theory, the instrumental rationality assumed throughout our previous chapter. The second is value-rational (*wertrational*) action, where the goal or value pursued is so important to the actor that it drives out all weighing of costs and consequences. Acts of sheer heroism and self-sacrifice are examples, as are, more broadly, acts done from duty or some other moral principle. The third pure type of action is 'traditional' action, typical of traditional, norm-bound societies and to be understood by identifying the relevant norms. Weber defines it as 'the expression of settled custom' and remarks dismissively that it is standardly 'simply a dull reaction to accustomed stimuli'. Fourthly there is 'affective' action, where the agent is prompted by a simple, unreflective desire, for instance to drink a glass of water because thirsty.

These are pure or ideal types of action, whereas most everyday actions, Weber says, are of mixed type. But the ideal types need to be distinguished because they require different kinds of understanding. *Zweckrational* action is to be understood by reconstructing the calculation of expected utility which went into it: why Jack's choice of apples rather than pears was rational, given his preferences, information and resources. As in the previous chapter, the type is 'ideal' not only because it abstracts from all but 'economic' considerations but also because it abstracts to an ideally rational agent. Understanding proceeds by identifying the ideally correct solution to the agent's problem of choice and then applying it as a yardstick. If Jack has indeed made the rational choice, then the reconstruction tells us how he arrived at it. If not, then the reconstruction identifies what needs further explanation, namely the agent's failure to act rationally. To understand, for instance, why a general orders a regiment to advance in a battle, we first work out whether that was his best decision. This may seem a surprising detour in what sounded like a descriptive method but Weber is definite about it and it bears on questions of whether Rational Choice and Game Theories are at fault, if social actors do not act consistently with them.

Wertrational action is to be understood by identifying its overriding goal or value, and traditional action by identifying the custom to which it conformed. Here it is harder to see what Weber has in mind and we should first take note of two stages in understanding. He says that understanding starts with empathy or *direktes Verstehen*, which is like perception. By empathy we know (without inference) that a man swinging an axe is cutting wood or that a marksman is aiming a rifle. In other words there is a basic process of social observation in which the data are actions, not physical objects and behaviour from which actions are inferred. Then there is explanatory understanding or *erklärendes Verstehen* by which we come to know that the cutter of wood is earning a living as a wood-cutter or that the marksman is out for revenge. Explanatory understanding is a matter of assigning an action to 'a complex of meanings'. It can be done 'historically', where we identify a specific motive, for instance that the marksman is aiming to kill his brother's murderer; or 'sociologically', where we identify a common phenomenon like a vendetta and understand the particular case as an example; or 'ideal-typically', where we analyse the action with the aid of an ideal type, as in the 'economic' rational-choice case above.

There are other ideal types besides the economic, however. There are also conceptual ideal types which take a concept like 'feudal', 'patrimonial', 'charismatic' or 'bureaucratic' and analyse the pure form of the social relationships involved. Best known perhaps is Weber's analysis of bureaucracy as an organisation where order is secured by the following of rules within a hierarchical structure whose effective goal is the maintenance of its own procedures. What makes this type ideal is not only its purity but also the orderliness it discerns in or imposes on apparently irrational phenomena. Then there are 'average types' of the sort found in the use of statistics where we are averaging 'differences of degree among qualitatively similar kinds of behaviour'. The idea here, I think, is that what is picked out as typical in theory needs to be shown to be empirically significant too. Thus whether we have understood why M. Rouget votes communist depends both on the theoretical sense to be made of his vote and on his being an 'average' communist voter by some statistical reckoning.

Weber's approach is a suggestive but uneasy blend of elements, each of which, taken separately, bears plausibly on the analysis of rational action, but which, taken together, leave it obscure where we are. Clearest is the claim made for an instrumental notion of rationality (*Zweckrationalität*) for purposes of understanding 'economic' action by reference to what an ideally rational agent would choose. Recent developments in Rational Choice theory and Game Theory have given this line on social action immense power, as we have seen. But Weber's 'acting individual' is not solely *homo economicus*. Even in the modern world where 'rational–legal' arrangements have replaced 'traditional' ones, *homo sociologicus* is firmly present, most typically perhaps in the role of the bureaucrat. This individual is a rule-follower in an organisation whose structure of rules gives order to his world and his place in it. In some moods Weber sees these structures as denials of reason and in others as bulwarks of rational order in a decaying civilisation. At any rate they are a major element in social action and one which makes us think further about the relation of rational action to rules. That is partly why Weber's 'explanatory understanding' becomes so complicated, we shall find. Meanwhile there is some suggestion that, whereas for *homo economicus* to be rational is to calculate, for *homo sociologicus* to be rational is to follow a rule. Let us next pursue this thought.

SOCIAL ACTION AS RULE-FOLLOWING

The hermeneutic imperative is to understand social action from within. 'From within what?' we might ask. The stock individualist reply is: 'from within the mind of each acting individual'. An alternative reply is: 'from within the rules which give it meaning'. These replies both sound right, in echo of our earlier distinction between what an action means and what an actor means by it. For instance, if one asks how winking (action) differs from blinking (reflex movement), the answer needs to refer both to social conventions which make winks a vehicle for information, hints, reservations, conspiracies, warnings or bidding at auctions, and to the actor's intention to perform one of these speech-acts rather than another. For language especially, it seems luminously plain that to understand an utterance we must know both what it means and what the utterer means by it. But different senses of meaning appear to be involved. When my German friend says '*Dieser Hund ist gefährlich*', his words mean 'This dog is dangerous' and he no doubt means to warn me to keep away from it. One is inclined to comment that what makes the utterance rational is his wish and intention to warn me, rather than the fact that it conforms to the rules of German sentence construction for applying the predicate 'dangerous' to dogs. But the connection between rationality and rule-following may be much more intimate.

This is a good moment to introduce Wittgenstein's *Philosophical Investigations* (1953) with its fertile analogy between languages and games. To say 'This dog is dangerous' is to make a move in a game of communication, rather as to play *P-K4* is to make a move in a game of chess. A visiting Martian, seeing a human being shift a small piece of wood a small distance on a squared surface, would not know that a pawn had been moved. To recognise a pawn as a pawn the visitor needs to grasp the rules and point of the activity. Without its rules, indeed, there would be no such activity as chess and no pawns to move. Similarly, 'This dog is dangerous' is mere noise, unless it is an instance of rules applied in a situation. Rules of language define a 'game' which would not exist without them.

A game like chess is not a device or instrument with an external purpose, which makes sense of how the game is played. For, even if it has some loose aim like amusement, that does not account for its particular form. Moves within a game of chess have only purposes which derive from the rules. Jill plays *P-K4* because, standardly, it is the best move, she believes, in that position, where 'best' refers to her prospects of winning, as specified in the clauses spelling out checkmate. This is not to deny that moves can sometimes be made for extraneous reasons, as when she deliberately plays badly against a beginner needing encouragement or against the vain dictator of a banana republic. But such occasions presuppose standard ones, and she will fail in her purpose if she is not convincing. Similarly, although there are non-standard games with chess pieces, like 'losing chess' where the aim is to have all one's pieces captured, there is always the question of whether these are variants of the standard game or not chess at all. The core of the game consists of rules, which set the scope and limits of what can be understood about occasions of play from within.

To be precise, the rules of chess (or any other game) are of two sorts, constitutive and regulative. Constitutive rules create the game by defining its purposes, its legitimate moves and the powers of its pieces. Without such rules there is no game, rather as one might say that there is no language without some rules of grammar. Regulative rules then govern choice among the legitimate moves. They range from rules of thumb, like 'Castle early', to rules of etiquette, like 'Don't fidget'. The distinction is not always clear but the difference is roughly that, if one breaks regulative rules, one is not playing the game well or appropriately, whereas, if one breaks the constitutive rules, one is not playing it at all. Ambiguity about borderlines is often useful to theorists and players alike and certainly does not imply that there is no vital difference.

In learning the rules of a game, one is learning 'how to go on', in Wittgenstein's pithy phrase, how to do what is required, to avoid what is forbidden and to pick one's way through what is permitted in the spirit of the game. Chess is both a good and a bad example for purposes of understanding social life by analogy with games. It illustrates well the internal and constructed character of meaningful activity and the internal nature of reasons for particular moves. But it is misleading, if it suggests that social activities have complete and consistent rules, covering all eventualities. Diplomacy, for instance, is interestingly game-like in some ways. Diplomatic manoeuvres and signals need to be interpreted with a knowledge of the conventions and an awareness that diplomats expect one another to share this knowledge. But the conventions are open-ended and the purpose of diplomacy is not served merely by passing the platitudes at cocktail parties. The aims of the diplomatic game are external to it, even if they are not external to all the games which nations play. The analogy is instructive but limited.

Similarly, the law is certainly game-like not only in its reliance on conventions but especially if one thinks of it as partly constructed through the work of courts. Courts decide whether there has been a breach of the law. Sometimes this is a straightforward matter of fact: was Jack elsewhere and therefore innocent of strangling Jill? Sometimes it turns on the interpretation of agreed facts: Jack admits killing Jill but denies that he murdered her. Sometimes the interpretation of the law is at issue: if Jill is senile and dying of cancer and Jack is her doctor, is he culpable if he fails to treat her pneumonia? These latter questions of interpretation are akin to asking whether someone has broken the rules of a game, where it is less than clear what exactly the rules imply on a particular occasion. To understand what happens in courts, we need to understand the practice of law, the rules of the legal game, in depth.

On the other hand, we may think that there is also more to it. This could be simply a matter of relating legal practice to other practices and institutions, for instance to law-making bodies, like Parliament. To understand moves in one game, we must often understand other games too. But we might also want to step back altogether. Some legal theorists argue that the process of law makes sense only as the pursuit of justice, rather as the process of science makes sense only as a search after the truth about nature. Here the meaning of the game would be external to the rules of the game, because the rules are subject to the external test of whether they are just. An unjust law is to be condemned, whatever the institutional authority for it. Theorists who believe in 'natural law' take this view, in opposition to legal positivists, who deny that there can be any such external standpoint. That raises a question of relativism, or the scope and limits of understanding from within, which will crop up later.

Meanwhile there could also be more to law than the legal game for a different sort of reason. One might argue that the process of law makes final sense only in relation to the distribution of power in a society. In echo of Marx's distinction between base and superstructure, cited in Chapter 1, one could hold that a society has the legal norms which its material conditions demand. In that case the meaning of the game could be deemed to be external not because of moral considerations but for the sort of structural and functional reasons sketched in Chapter 5. Either way, the analogy between legal processes and games would be instructive up to a point but not the whole story.

Social theorists impressed by Wittgenstein may nonetheless insist that the analogy does indicate the whole story. There is something mesmeric about his lapidary remark that 'What has to be accepted, the given, is, so to say, *forms of life*' (1953, II.226). The suggestion is that particular actions belong to particular practices, which are embedded within the wider practices which go to make up a culture. To understand a particular action or practice fully, we may need to grasp the wider context and see how broad collective ideas of what matters for the proper conduct of life contribute to the sense of how to go on particular occasions. But the story is, in the end, self-contained. It rests finally with 'forms of life', which have to be accepted as given, because there is nothing further to account for them. Notice the use of the plural. There is no single 'form of life' in terms of which lesser forms make sense, not even one for each culture and still less one universal form of all cultures. The plural is a reprise of Wittgenstein's earlier comment that there is nothing which all games have in common:

> Don't say: There *must* be something common, or they would not be called 'games' – but *look and see* whether there is anything common to all. For if you look at them you will not see something that is common to *all*, but similarities, relationships, and a whole series of them at that. (1953, I.66)

There is nothing more unitary than a complex network of similarities, overlapping and criss-crossing, but characterised as 'family resemblance'. Just try finding more of a common core, he adds, to 'board-games, card-games, Olympic games and so on'.

One philosopher inspired by this theme is Peter Winch, whose (1958) book *The Idea of a Social Science* puts it to striking use. Winch opens by denying that science can proceed by testing theories and hypotheses against the facts of an independent world so as to find causal explanations of how the world works. We must not presume that reality is independent of thought or that to understand reality is to explain its workings causally. On the contrary, 'our idea of what belongs to the realm of reality is given for us in the concepts which we use' (1958, p.15). These concepts come complete with criteria for deciding the truth of statements describing a realm of reality, for instance those employed by physicists in talking about the behaviour of particles or by witchdoctors in identifying signs of witchcraft. Groups of concepts are the cognitive aspects of institutions and each institution therefore embodies ideas of what is real and how it is to be understood. Thus, 'connected with the realisation that intelligibility takes many and varied forms is the realisation that reality has no key' (p.102). Science embodies the key to the reality of a world of particles; religion embodies the key to the reality of a spiritual world. It is scientific practice to seek causes and religious practice to seek meaning. These practices, each being peculiar to its own form of life, are not in competition, since reality has no external or universal key.

Institutions, cognitively speaking, embody ideas. But, as with Kuhn's paradigms, they are also constituted by social relationships and rules. This, however, is not to anchor them externally. 'Social relations are expressions of ideas about reality' (p.23). 'All behaviour which is meaningful is *eo ipso* rule-governed' (p.52). To understand the activities of monks, for instance, we must see the daily life of the monastery as an expression of rules which give meaning to their relationships. Thus the three knots on the end of the rope which some monks wear signify vows of poverty, chastity and obedience. The vows make sense of the knots and the ideas of a spiritual reality embodied in the monastic order make sense of the vows. What is true of monks is true of everyone else too, with due allowance for varied ideas, varied rules and varied forms of life.

The implications for method in the social sciences are striking. It is no good basing our understanding of societies on the methods of the natural sciences, Winch holds. 'The central concepts which belong to our understanding of social life are incompatible with concepts central to the activity of scientific prediction' (p.94). Prediction and causal explanation are indeed proper activities for natural sciences, since that form of life includes ideas of reality which make them appropriate rules of method. But natural science is a 'game', and only one game among others. Other social games embody other ideas; and a social scientist must understand each from within and in its own terms, by finding the varied rules which diverse groups of actors follow. Presumably the sociology of science is a higher-order game, one which involves studying the game of explanation so as to understand the activities of its players.

All this, when summarised so starkly, is very strong stuff. It seems to allow no appeal beyond forms of life, neither to an external reality which some or all forms of life seek to make sense of nor to independent criteria of what it is rational to believe or do. That makes it sternly idealistic – there are only 'games' expressing ideas – and sharply relativistic, in that diverse forms of life are self-contained and closed to external criticism. Moreover, human beings appear to feature only as social actors, players of games who do all and only what they take the rules to require of them. The monk, with his highly structured life, is all mankind's epitome. Since *The Idea of a Social Science* is a short book which sets out to apply and explore a possible reading of Wittgenstein, and since his other work, especially on action and ethics, is much more nuanced, I would not want to saddle Winch himself with these views untrammelled. Nevertheless the themes just cited are boldly stated in *The Idea of a Social Science* and will serve nicely as a way of filling in our top right box. A stark summary yields an ideal-type account of institutions as embodiments of collective meanings which readily invites holistic understanding, as Figure 7.1 points out crisply.

RULES AND RATIONALITY

We have found that meaning, Dilthey's 'category which is peculiar to life and to the historical world', can be glossed as rationality in, broadly, two ways. Both ways are prompted by the reflection that 'meaning' is an elusive term with many uses and the subject of several conflicting theories of meaning. Both therefore connect meaning to what makes action intelligible, namely the fact that it

	Explanation	Understanding
Holism		'Games' (rules, practices, forms of life)
Individualism		

Figure 7.1

is (usually) rational from the agent's point of view. They then diverge over how to analyse 'rational'.

The simpler and clearer analysis adopts Weber's ideal-type of economically rational action, where the agent is an individual *homo economicus* equipped with desires (preferences), beliefs (information) and an internal computer, who seeks the most effective means to satisfy his desires (or maximise his expected utility). Analysis proceeds by identifying those elements and reconstructing the agent's deliberations so as to display the action as instrumentally rational. That leaves a question of what to do about irrational action. But, if we follow Weber in stressing subjective meanings and are liberal with interpretative charity, most or even all actions will come out as subjectively rational from the agent's point of view.

This gloss hardly seems to help the thesis that Understanding differs from Explanation, however. Although it nods to the hermeneutic imperative to understand action from within, it does so merely by being willing to play up the subjective elements in what seems to remain the topic of the previous chapter. Most game theorists see themselves as providing tools for causal explanations of action and will be inclined to say that Weber has merely muddied the water by discussing instrumental rationality (*Zweckrationalität*) under the heading of Understanding. Although there are reasons to think this view mistaken, they have yet to emerge; and, since *homo economicus* has been a pretty mechanical agent so far, I think that he is more comfortable so far in the bottom left box of Figure 7.1.

That is not to say, however, that the previous chapter had a cogent account of social norms. Those which could plausibly be said to emerge as mutually useful solutions to problems of coordination did indeed look like conventions, in the sense of regularities which it is safe to bet on. But others, which headed off mutually self-defeating choices only by injecting obligations or other backward-looking reasons into interactions, remained stubbornly resistant. Tucking them away in the agent's given preferences did nothing to tame them. On the contrary, the need for this ruse strengthened the case for a *homo sociologicus* distinct from or even prior to *homo economicus*.

Accordingly, the other way of glossing meaning as rationality sets social action firmly within a context of norms, rules, practices and institutions. So pervasive is this context that it is at least tempting to think of the agents not only as social actors before they are individuals but also as plural before they are singular. In other words it is tempting to contrast a *homo economicus* who belongs in the bottom left box of Figure 7.1 with a *homo sociologicus* whose primary home is in the top right box, where norms, rules, practices and institutions give a notion of social structure suited to the 'Understanding' column. That threatens to conceive of social actors so as to make them creatures of this new and softer kind of structure. But that may not be the upshot, if we are no longer thinking causally about the relation of rules to actions which fall under a rule. Postponing for the moment the question of whether 'creature' is the right word, we can next usefully contrast Wittgensteinian 'games' both with the individualistic games of Game Theory and with the causal structures suited to holistic explanation.

A 'game', construed with help from Wittgenstein, is a normative structure, external to each of its players. Yet, in contrast to the external structures or systems envisaged in the top left box under the heading of 'Explanation', games are internal to the players collectively. They are external to each but internal to all – intersubjective rather than objective, one might say. Games, we might readily suppose, are historically and culturally specific, with a real enough power to set the terms in which people think and relate but only in their own place and time. If so, it would not be surprising to find only overlapping and criss-crossing resemblances among the games of social life and no universal features which all normative structures have in common. An ontology whose primary elements are intersubjective contrasts both with an ontology with objective wholes, independent of human consciousness, and with one whose primary elements are subjectively motivated, individual actions.

Methodologically, the intersubjective route to understanding is to identify the constitutive and regulative rules of the relevant 'game' (institution, practice, 'form of life'), exhibit the associated normative expectations and thus understand action as the doing of what is normatively expected in a situation structured by the rules.

Epistemologically, the crux is whether this approach embodies a solution to the problem of Other Minds. In effect, we have blended Weber's value-rational (*wertrational*) action, performed regardless of consequences, with his 'traditional' action ('the expression of settled custom'). If action is indeed made intelligible by reconstructing it in this way, we can know what is in other minds by identifying their customary rules and shared meanings. That sounds plausible. But it has been worked out in this chapter by making the rules of the game all-important and the players wholly their obedient followers. That is contestable, we shall shortly see.

CONCLUSION

We began the chapter with four peculiarities of meaning, which have no obvious parallel in physics and little in biology, and a suggestion that the problem of Other Minds is central to the social sciences. To check how clearly we have managed to contrast explaining with understanding, let us return to the opening peculiarities.

Firstly, actions have meaning. There is a contrast between natural signs, as when a ring round the moon 'means' rain, and conventional symbols, like a flag at half mast. Natural signs and their underlying causes are the stuff of scientific explanation and squarely a topic for the earlier chapters. This is not to deny that some questions about scientific ideas invite us to recognise that science, like religion, is an attempt to make sense of experience in ways involving symbolic kinds of meaning. Nor is it to deny that some human and social behaviour lends itself to scientific explanation. Hence there will be much to think about in Chapter 9, when we come to relate Explanation and Understanding. Meanwhile actions have two peculiar sorts of meaning: what they mean in so far as they are signals taken from a common stock of conventions; and what the actor means or intends by them. To understand action we need a line on Other Minds which allows the reconstruction of both. Will Wittgensteinian reflections on the playing of games suffice?

Secondly, language has meaning. This obvious truth helps to sharpen the last point, since language is often seen as the key to understanding how thought informs action. It is certainly seen in this light by Wittgensteinians, and anyone who pursues the references to *Philosophical Investigations* will find that 'language games' are the subtlest and deepest illustration of the general theme about rules. Understanding what people think and do is not only *like* understanding the uses of language but can even be equated with understanding how words mean what they do, if one construes 'language' so as to garner the insights offered by phrases like 'the language of mathematics', 'the language of art' or 'the language of politics'. Moreover the obvious truth that there are many languages carries a suggestion, which we may or may not wish to resist, that there are many games, many ways of thinking and many forms of life, each constituted by its own rules, just as languages have their own rules. It is as if all action were a text to be read by understanding the rules of the language in which it is written. How far does this take us?

Thirdly, practices have meaning. The previous paragraph stressed the meaning of words rather than what people mean by their words. This begs the question against theories of language which analyse utterance into a mutual recognition, between speaker and hearer, of what the speaker intended to convey. In that individualist kind of analysis, linguistic conventions emerge as an aid to individuals and, in general, individual thought is prior to the linguistic vehicle of its expression. Practices similarly emerge as convenient solutions to individual problems. Wittgensteinians work the other way round, with the existence of practices as a precondition for individual actions which rely on them. Practices, construed communally in this way, are not merely habitual regularities of behaviour. They embody shared values and give rise to normative expectations, couched in a moral language of praise for fulfilling them and blame for failure. By enriching the notion of a game so as to stress its normative texture, we can propose a sense of structure appropriate for the 'Understanding' column. Does that dispose of Rational Choice individualism, the presumption that action is prior to convention and hence to practices?

Fourthly, there is the complex point that social actors have models of the world and of themselves in their minds. Furthermore they credit one another with such models. Weber defined social action as action 'which takes account of the behaviour of others and is thereby oriented in its course'. The 'account' taken soon becomes very sophisticated. Even unreflective people are players of games where they constantly need to know what others want and believe and which require mutual recognition of subtle normative expectations. Among the factors influencing these 'models', consciously or unconsciously, are the models of social action put in circulation by social scientists. This suggests disconcertingly that whether an account of social action offered by social science is correct may depend partly on whether it is believed. Although it is prudent to postpone this dizzying thought, it certainly gives the social scientist one headache which natural scientists are spared.

CHAPTER 8

Self and roles

A central problem for this part of the book concerns social norms, their ontological character, our knowledge of them and its methodological implications. Chapter 5 likened them initially to laws of nature, external to us and forming a causal order. Under the heading of 'functional explanation', social structures were conceived as *systems* in static or dynamic, perhaps shifting, equilibrium, with individual actions explained as responses to the functional demands of the system. Durkheim's *Rules* and its example of crime were invoked in illustration. But, like Durkheim himself elsewhere, we were unsure how seriously to take the analogy between societies and organisms. So we fell back on a broader holism, which relied only on the autonomy of social facts. Individualism then entered a protest on behalf of neo-Classical economics by introducing Rational Choice theory and Game Theory. But, with a rational agent defined in Chapter 6 as a given bundle of ordered preferences, a stock of accurate information and an efficient computer, the protest invited a swift riposte. Holism retorted that preferences are dictated by the social structure or system, with calculations of expected utility merely a mechanism by which its demands are transmitted. Social norms can thus still be exhibited as the core of a social structure or, in so far as talk of 'systems' remains legitimate, as mechanisms in the dynamics of a social system.

We then turned to Understanding. In Chapter 7 norms were presented as the constitutive and regulative rules of institutions or practices and hence of social life. This bespoke a fresh ontology, where meaning, being the category peculiar to the historical world, is integral to the identity of institutions and where rules

163

are radically unlike laws of nature. Understanding called for a method which works 'from within' and perhaps a fresh account of the character of knowledge. While hostile to all forms of merely behavioural explanation, however, this approach is neutral between individualism and holism. If social norms cover all social situations and are complete in their guidance, then actors, provided that they are fully obedient, seem no less the creatures of norms than before. Yet this portrait of *homo sociologicus* may strike us as overdrawn and we wondered how to give the actors some autonomy.

The challenge is, in effect, to find a way of filling the bottom right box with actors who are not the creatures of norms and also not the rational agents who ran into trouble in Chapter 6. Such actors, to put the same message constructively, will have something of the rational agents' ability to negotiate and renegotiate conventions, while remaining subject to the normative demands of the games of social life. This way of expressing it embodies two contrasts. One is between conventions as solutions to games lacking a single equilibrium and conventions as rules with a Wittgensteinian character. The other is between games as interactions between rational agents where choices are strategic and games as treated in the previous chapter. A related contrast is between expectations as predictions based on common knowledge of what others will do and expectations as normative.

The present chapter sets off by pinning down these differences and then redrawing the portrait of *homo sociologicus*. It will be done by examining the concept of a role and exploring the idea that persons are the sum of their roles, first in a context of institutional roles and then by analogy with theatrical roles. This concept of role-play is, I believe, among the most powerful and fertile for a social science whose epistemology and method belong to Understanding. Contrary to first impressions, it does not belong squarely in the top right box. Are we the sum of the roles we play? Even if the answer is Yes, there are questions about the notion of *social identity*, which will favour a compromise between holism and individualism in the 'Understanding' column. If it is No, there are questions of what philosophers term *personal identity*. This hardy perennial of philosophy will leave us at the end of the chapter with a renewed individualist curiosity about rational agents.

POSITIONS AND ROLES

To deploy the notion of a role, let us envisage society as a scheme of *social positions*, each associated with an institution or organisation. Some institutions and organisations are highly structured, often hierarchically, like the US army with its strongly defined positions of colonel, corporal and private. Some are looser hierarchies, like the Church of England with its bishops, parish priests, vergers and communicant members. Some are structured without ranks, like a commune with a division of labour. This is not to suggest that all typified social behaviour goes with definite positions in an explicit structure or that all identifiable social activities belong to institutions. One might or might not wish to maintain that the positions in English society include those of burglar, friend, TV personality and mistress; or that English institutions include dog-fighting and family picnics. For the moment it is enough that there are some definite institutions, organisations and hence positions.

Now think of a social order as a sum of relations within and between institutions (and organisations). Positions are related internally by reference to the purpose of the institution and what needs to be done to carry it out. Externally, institutions are influenced by other institutions in a mobile social context. Here one might go on to postulate an overarching social structure, along with a cohesive, unitary account of stability and change, for instance in the functionalist spirit of Chapter 5 or in a more ambitious historicist spirit than we attempted in Chapter 7. But that is optional and one might prefer to regard the social order as a precarious array of fragile institutions, whose persistence is not guaranteed. Although there are deep themes here, a holist can adopt either attitude to social order, provided that any fragility is not attributed to independent actions by individuals.

In either case think of social positions as directly animated by the *roles* associated with each position and performed by incumbents – the presidents, street sweepers, bureaucrats, priests, soldiers, clerks, parents and so on, who form the social pageant. On a holistic analysis, these incumbents do just what their positions require of them, being driven 'top down' by the demands of the role. Individual incumbents are highly replaceable. Bureaucrats come and bureaucrats go; and the bureaucracy trundles on. Officers are posted or killed, but the regiment marches on with newcomers doing the old jobs. In a cabinet reshuffle, ministers often move from a spending ministry like Education, where they have been calling for more money for schools, to a tight-fisted ministry like the Treasury, where they soon set about blocking their own previous efforts. Institutions outlast those who play the roles which keep them moving and have ways of ensuring that new recruits to their offices behave as suits the institution. This is, to be sure, a very disputable view of the insignificance of particular role-players, but it serves holism nicely.

There are, however, two different ways to regard what I have just referred to as the demands of a role. A systemic theory (top left box) is inclined to treat them as forces transmitted through social positions, with a role defined merely as the dynamic aspect of a social position. This cavalier disregard for the actors was challenged by Game Theory by making it matter what actors expect other actors to do, given common knowledge of their preferences. The notion of a role can certainly be introduced into this general dispute about the explanation of social action. But, if it signals merely a set of preferences typically associated with a social position, holism wins by uncovering a social structure concealed in the pattern of preferences. In so far as roles are construed as sets of rational expectations, we are being offered a useful shorthand for what is *normal* (as distinct from normative). Thus a banker does what bankers normally do and this regularity is a useful aid to prediction by customers, as it saves effort in arriving at predictions and hence rational choices. That bankers do not always act as Rational Choice theory predicts raises a question about the relevance of ideal-type theorising; but only, so far, in a way which suits the holism of the top left box.

When we turn to Understanding, however, the demands of a role take on a different character. They consist of *normative* expectations, a set of quasi-moral duties to perform, entitlements to their performance and rights to criticise, complain and seek redress in case of failings. That roles involve 'duties' does indeed commonly give rise to 'normal' behaviour. But not all normal or regular behaviour stems from normative expectations. Normal and normative entwine intriguingly. When I was in the army, successful quartermasters were sure to have more in their stores than appeared in their ledgers. The surplus had several uses. It meant that the quartermaster could not be caught short by a snap inspection. It let him respond helpfully to sudden demands from the colonel and do favours for cronies with urgent problems of being caught short. It allowed trading on the civilian black market, sometimes but not always for the benefit of the regiment. In short this well recognised breach of the official regulations was so normal and, up to a point, so helpful to the regiment that one could wonder whether it was, in truth, normatively expected. Similarly, political systems which lay very fierce public demands of integrity on, say, Senators and members of Congress, often tacitly connive at a normal level of what would have to be denounced as corruption, if a scandal blew up. Perhaps pork-barrel politics and back-room log-rolling are a normatively permitted or even expected way of fulfilling otherwise impossible demands.

Such examples make us think of roles as rules to which an incumbent is subject and hence as involving more than predictions. But they also stop us thinking of roles as rules which are or even could be made fully explicit in rulebooks. To do them justice, we must enrich the concept of a role. They are neutral, however, between two ways of doing so. We could hold on to the idea that there is a coherent scheme of rules for the playing of roles, although not necessarily one which the actors may fully and consciously recognise. That would be consistent with a picture of institutions as each upholding its constitutive rules within an overall form of life by shaping the explicit and implicit normative expectations attached to social positions. This would promise an analysis suited to the top right box. Alternatively we could argue that roles can involve indefinite or even inconsistent normative expectations, which give the role-players room for manoeuvre in interpreting their roles or in pursuing extraneous purposes. That would suggest an analysis suited to Understanding but calling for actors who are not slavishly obedient. Since such actors do not sound like the rational individuals considered so far, curiosity is aroused.

From a structural, 'top down' point of view, the actors need to be conceived as fully obedient to the demands of their roles. The simplest line is to regard them as puppets on invisible strings, or as cultural dopes or dupes blithely unconscious of their mental conditioning. This line, while leaving room for interesting debate about the mechanics of obedience, is so strongly deterministic that the actors are finally insignificant. It might therefore seem to imply that, if the actors do matter, they must be disobedient. But this is to forget the Wittgensteinian account of rule-following in Chapter 7. The idea that actors can be obedient without being mechanical offers holism a fresh resource. At the same time it risks giving several hostages to a fresh kind of individualism. To bring this out, let us return to the level-of-analysis problem in international relations, briefly raised in Chapter 5.

THE LEVEL-OF-ANALYSIS PROBLEM

The question was one of whether the 'system' determines the behaviour of its units or *vice versa*. The units envisaged were nation states. This way of viewing the problem has given rise to a lively debate much influenced by Hobbes, since there is an appealing analogy between the initial anarchy of an international world without world government and the state of nature in *Leviathan*. Nation states can be seen as rational individuals facing the Hobbesian problem of order and groping for a solution. The crux is then whether international events and trends can be analysed game-theoretically by tracing them to an interplay of strategic choices by individual nations each pursuing its national interest. If so, the stakes are high, given Hobbesian grounds for thinking the likeliest long-term outcomes to be world government and world war.

This 'Rational Actor' model is not rejected only by believers in the reality of an international system whose pressures shape the behaviour of nations. Other critics object that nations are not unitary actors or rational individuals of the sort envisaged. They point out that within each nation state many agencies are at work, notably bureaucracies and pressure groups with a direct hand in foreign policy decisions. The actions of the state are the outcome of manoeuvres among these agencies, each acting in its own interest, rather as the actions of a firm in a market are the result of interplay among the units within its organisation. In an international relations context this approach is known as the 'Bureaucratic Politics' model.

Here advocates of a Rational Actor model find themselves defending the state, as a system or structure, against attempts to show that its behaviour arises from the interplay of units within it. Nor do 'level-of-analysis' problems end there. If a Bureaucratic Politics model were to win, there would at once be a further question about the relation of a bureaucracy to its human members. Here the bureaucracy would be the system or structure and its members the units. A Rational Actor model would then get another chance, this time with human beings, instead of nation states, as the rational actors. To make for clarity it is worth repeating the 'level of analysis' diagram, here labelled Figure 8.1.

To put flesh on these abstractions, we can usefully turn to Graham Allison's much cited *Essence of Decision* (1971), where a Bureaucratic Politics model is robustly put to work. The book makes a study of the 1962 Cuban missile crisis which could

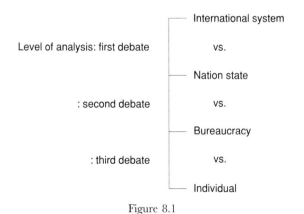

Figure 8.1

have provoked a nuclear war. The crisis arose when American intelligence sources reported Soviet ships heading for Cuba with a cargo of nuclear weapons. Faced with the prospect of an enemy nuclear base on its very doorstep, the United States responded by declaring a blockade and threatening to sink the Soviet ships, unless they turned back. The Soviet Union made it clear that it would then retaliate. The United States made it equally clear that targets in Russia were well within its ballistic range. This lethal game of Chicken was played out on television over several days, while the ships steamed relentlessly closer. (I vividly recall sitting with fellow graduate students at Harvard frozen to the television screen, like rabbits in the headlights of a car which might or might not stop.) In the event the Soviet fleet was ordered to turn back and the cold war did not escalate. The American gamble had apparently paid off.

The media portrayed the crisis as peculiarly one for President John F. Kennedy, personifying America and appointed by an unkind fortune to make the critical decisions as an individual. Although this was not to deny the presence of experts and policy advisers, it made the essence of decision the President's will. This picture is more heroic than suits the version of the Rational Actor model where the state is the unitary decision-making unit, but is not incompatible with it, if one thinks of the President as indeed personifying America as a nation state. Allison concluded, however, that American policy in the crisis owed most to the bureaucracies and other sectional interests represented at crucial meetings chaired by Kennedy as the crisis developed. Decisions followed the balance of opinion on these elite occasions. Moreover, the advice tendered by each person as his own was invariably well suited to the interests which he represented. The decisions taken were invariably those favoured by winning coalitions of these interests. An apothegm (minted by Don Price) sums up this Bureaucratic Politics model memorably: *Where you stand depends on where you sit.*

States, political agencies and actors all feature in the analysis. State behaviour is definitely a dependent variable but it is less plain how the agencies and actors are related to one another. Agencies like the State Department and Defense Department had distinct interests but how far they succeeded in advancing them depended on the skill of the players as well as the importance of the agency. These actors played their roles loyally throughout, thus illustrating the point that obedient actors need not be mechanical actors, especially in an office whose demands include ingenuity. Although a bureaucracy selects, trains and promotes officials who will serve its interests, it knows that puppets, dopes and dupes often make ineffective performers. But, while the demands of the role remain paramount, the point does more to enrich a Bureaucratic Politics model than to subvert it. Other players, like the President's advisers and the President himself, were there in something closer to a personal capacity. Since they too were clearly players of roles, they whet our curiosity about the limits of the model.

INSTITUTIONAL ROLES AND THE DRAMATURGICAL ANALOGY

The Cuban missile crisis is thus very illuminating, at least if it is safe to generalise from it. That could be doubted. It is an example of collective decision-making by a powerful elite representing well defined social positions and interests. The actors have far more latitude for interpretation and manoeuvre than do more ordinary institutional role-players sandwiched in the layers of an organisation or belonging to, so to speak, its infantry. There obedience looks more nearly automatic. Elites, one might complain, are distinctly untypical of institutional role-players at large. Besides, this particular example of elite decision-making is also peculiar in being sharply focused on an issue of the moment. The participants were there for a precise purpose and any conflict due to their having other positions and roles was muted.

Very well, let us extend the idea of institutional roles to other institutions like firms, professional bodies, churches and football clubs. Obedience still refuses to be mechanical, especially where the conflicting claims of several roles are involved. The more we stress these aspects of institutional role-play, the more human *homo sociologicus* becomes.

Institutions are not the buildings which house some of them. They are sets of positions organised to pursue a general goal with the aid of members who are not altogether theirs to command. Social positions and roles, moreover, include many where 'institution' sounds too formal a term and it is more natural to speak of organisations, groups or practices, thus stressing the fluid and overlapping character of people's commitments. For instance, Jack may be a father, Baptist and football referee as well as a career social worker; Jill may be a mother, flautist and Conservative councillor as well as a company director. Normative expectations surround them in each of these very various capacities. Their lives can hardly be so arranged that their roles are free of all conflict. Jack has the unnerving dilemmas of a harassed social worker to face. Jill, as a local councillor, has information and influence which it is tempting but forbidden to use for the sake of her business. Both must work out how their children figure among the claims on their attention. Even if some constraints are included in their portfolios, for instance that Jack is not free to referee football on Sundays, there is no possible handbook which might settle all questions of priority among conflicts.

In deciding how to go on, role-players must use their judgement, as can be brought out by considering conflict first within a role, then between role-players, then between roles. Take Jack's dilemma as a social worker, when deciding whether to put a child at risk of abuse under a Child Protection Order. Removal will probably be traumatic, perhaps more so, I have heard social workers say privately, than some abuse. But Jack is also very conscious that some abused children end up dead. He will have to use his personal judgement. Admittedly, he is not all on his own. He has colleagues and there may be a casework team, who review cases as they develop. But they will be influenced by how he describes a situation which he is best placed to observe; and, in any case, they too can only exercise their judgement. Yet judgement is not a form of disobedience; it goes with the role. If one were to insist on trying to codify the whole practice of social work, the code would simply have to be peppered with instructions to use one's judgement.

That role-playing is rarely mechanical is still plainer, if we consider conflict between role-players. Jill does not always agree with her fellow councillors on how to interpret party policy and how best to execute it. In applying policy, she is sometimes at odds with her local government officials, whose professional views and allegiances give them aims and reference groups which do not coincide with hers. Her political opponents are naturally out to increase her difficulties; and groups outside the local government arena have all manner of other interests which councillors must reckon with. Many of these factors are recurrent, so that present decisions are influenced both by a history of previous encounters and by a need to look ahead to future ones. Although she has allies and is not short of advice, she needs sometimes to distrust the former and ignore the latter. In short, the role calls for the skills of a political animal – a kind of practical reasoning which eludes codification. If she is any good at it, she brings something of herself to what, nevertheless, is a typically institutional role.

This suggestion that role-play cannot be understood without allowing for the person who plays the role is also borne out by next thinking of Jill as the player of several roles. The priorities among the claims of family, career, politics and whatever else are not automatic. There may be some rough 'do's and 'don't's, like 'sick children come first', but, in general, she has to decide her own. Nor could it be otherwise in any society where multiple roles are permitted. One can envisage a handbook which forbad some combinations, like brothel-keeper and bishop, but not one which regulated all permitted mixtures. Inevitably, people are left to sort out the shape of their lives for themselves. Although it does not follow that the self is distinct from the sum of its roles, as I shall point out presently, we can safely reject any purely mechanical analysis of how institutions secure obedience.

Institutional role-play thus defies any simple systemic analysis which seeks to translate the imperatives of social positions directly into specific courses of action required by the system. It definitely has to be understood from within. That is not a conclusive case for the bottom right box, because, on the vertical axis, compromises with holism are looming and, besides, anything revealed by understanding may yet be subject to further explanation in a wider framework. But we have certainly reached a point where it would be helpful to turn the spotlight on the actors as persons.

Spotlight is a metaphor, introduced to remind us that the study of institutions and organisations is not the only source of talk about roles in the social sciences. Another, especially popular in microsociology and social psychology, is the fertile thought that social roles are played out as if on stage in the theatre of social life. When de Fontenelle, back in Chapter 2, said that 'Nature very much resembleth an Opera', he wanted us to notice the hidden stage machinery. Now let us fancy that society very much resembleth a theatre, so as to explore what is known as 'the dramaturgical analogy'. The analogy is with the characters in a play or with the actors who play the characters or, fascinatingly, with both.

If the institutional story is less holistic than it looks, the dramaturgical analogy is less individualist. That may be surprising, if one starts with memories of the school play, where Hamlet was badly acted by the youth one sat next to in the maths class. The initial image is of an individual donning a mask and pretending to be someone else. When Jaques observes in *As You Like It*

> All the world's a stage,
> And all the men and women merely players:

he adds at once

> They have their exits and their entrances;
> And one man in his time plays many parts.

The analogy seems to bid us distinguish between man and masks and note that the real actor lives off-stage, between performances.

On reflection, however, the analogy seems better directed to the characters in the play, leading a scripted existence and doing what the plot demands. The actors are altogether more shadowy, especially if we stop thinking of theatre after the model of a school play. Good actors do not so much impersonate characters as personify them. Laurence Olivier *is* Hamlet in the classic film version, admirers hold; and whatever quite 'is' may mean, it involves more than pretence. (To add a twist, others would say that Mel Gibson *is* Hamlet in the later film version. What is the dispute about and could they all be right?) If *all* the world's a stage, then we are always on stage and our many exits are from one part into another part. Jaques' seven ages include the school-boy, lover and slipper'd pantaloon as well as the soldier bearded like the pard and the justice full of wise saws. If the bedroom is as much a stage as the boardroom, this notion of role becomes markedly less individualist.

Yet that cannot be a decisive thought. If plays like *Hamlet* reveal a truth about life, their message is not that life is a script, written by an author and transferred to the stage by a director. The author is a parasite, creative but needing material from life to work on, and the director's interpretation must appeal to the audience's prior understanding of life. Nor is it otherwise with a semi-scripted drama, where the actors are given only their char-acters, an outline and a starting point. That merely shifts some of the work to them. Theatre itself is predicated neither on the idea that we are the sum of our roles nor on its denial. This does not stop dramatists taking sides, of course. Sometimes they tell us that all the world's a stage, sometimes that life's a tale told by an idiot, full of sound and fury and signifying nothing, sometimes that we are what we freely choose. These are competing hypotheses, none of which is inherent in the dramaturgical analogy itself. There is no single or incontestable truth about social life to be had at the box office.

Both accounts of role-play are thus inherently ambiguous about the self which plays the roles. We can grant that 'where you stand depends on where you sit', without making the self a mere mouth-piece. We can also agree that 'one man in his time plays many parts', without thereby deciding whether he is the sum of the parts. The crux, presumably, is how interchangeable the actors are. Most of us, I fancy, will recognise that we often have little room for social manoeuvre, thus accepting that anyone in the same position would have the same constraints. But few will extend this story to all our roles, or even to any which we play for long enough to make them our own. I cheated, admittedly, by giving Jack and Jill a comfortable social existence, with careers where initiative goes with the job. That assigns them to a tiny minority of the world's population and suggests that the impera-tives of the public arena are looser than, in general, they are. But even small and occasional choices in a life lived at subsistence level would be enough to show that we need to include a chooser. Meanwhile, we are stubborn about our uniqueness in our personal lives. Our friends, parents, children and lovers are no more replaceable for us than, we hope, we are for them.

SOCIAL IDENTITY AND PERSONAL IDENTITY

Both when thinking about institutions and when contemplating the world as a stage, we have been led to ask about the identity of the actors. Since identity is among the hardest concepts in philosophy, it would be convenient if nothing too philosophical were at stake here. Peter Berger remarks in his *Invitation to Sociology*, 'To say "I am a man" is just as much a proclamation of role as to say "I am a colonel in the U.S.Army"' (1963, Chapter 5). He is pointing out that there are gender roles as much as military ones and that both illustrate his chapter's title, 'Society in Man'.

What can I say about myself without proclaiming a role? '*Cogito*'? 'I am a person'? Many philosophers would regard these utterances as starting points for a discussion of 'personal identity', as distinct from 'social identity'. They would be content to grant that each of us has a social identity, a sum of roles and relations which answers the question 'Who are you?' But, they would add, when we ask 'who am I?' we raise a different sort of question. Two different persons could have the same set of social attributes and thus have the same social identity. But that would not make them the very same person, philosophically speaking, since personal identity is not a matter of high degrees of similarity of any attributes. At any rate, that is the traditional approach to the philosophical problem of personal identity, inspired by a sense that each person is necessarily unique. Still influenced, perhaps, by the idea that each soul is unique in the sight of God, the question of what it is to be a person is commonly answered so as to make Jack *necessarily* a different particular person from Jill. This is not to say that all philosophers hold the identity of persons to have this strictness. But the presumption still stands, until we are offered good enough reason to reject it.

Questions about the concept of a person might seem central to the claims of individualism in the social sciences. But they do not suit the style of individualism so far considered. *Homo economicus* is very much a *type* of individual, whose particular human exemplifications are of no interest to Rational Choice and Game Theory except as embodiments of different sets of preferences. Although we labelled the players Jack and Jill in Chapter 6, this was spurious local colour and the games were between any pair of rational agents with the preferences specified. *Homo sociologicus*, even when made active rather than passive, is another type. In giving Jack and Jill some highly specific sets of roles to play, we were chiefly interested in their social identities. In general, the contrast between individuals and wholes envisaged so far has been one between atoms and molecules or between units and systems or between actions and norms. For purposes of understanding, as much as for those of explanation, we have accepted that, since science must generalise, individuals are relevant only if they are typical. Yet we have also been led to complain that *homo economicus* is, so far, too mechanical and hence too little of an individual. We have suggested that an element of highly personal judgement is involved in the playing of roles, thus hinting that *homo economicus* might need one too. So there may be a gap in individualism's usual account of individuals, and one which a philosophical analysis of personal identity could fill.

Unsurprisingly, however, philosophers disagree both about what it is to be a person and about what makes each person unique. Current debates usually take Descartes and Locke as their historical point of departure. Descartes held that each of us is an eternal, non-physical substance, a *res cogitans* or conscious being endowed with free will. Locke contended that we owe our knowledge of our continued existence through time to memory, which makes us aware of who we were yesterday and what we did then. In treating the self as an immaterial substance blessed with self knowledge, these accounts were reassuringly consistent with orthodox Christian beliefs about the soul. But they set many problems. How does this immaterial self relate to the brain, the body and the rest of the physical world? Is memory either necessary or sufficient to let me identify who I was yesterday? Even if I know intuitively that I am a *res cogitans*, can I know that there are other minds? Such questions may not be fatal but they have prompted a search for alternative views.

Three are especially relevant. The first is Hume's, speaking for all empiricists who deny that introspection can reveal the existence of a substantial self:

> When I turn my reflection on *myself*, I never can perceive this *self* without some one or more perceptions; nor can I ever perceive any thing but the perceptions. It is the composition of these, therefore, which forms the self. (1739, Appendix)

In that case persons have no peculiar sort of identity. As with other objects, their identity is always a matter of the continuity of properties and relations. What makes separate persons different is their different perceptions, due partly to the fact that their bodies have a different history in space and time. Similarly, two peas in a pod have properties in common, which make them both peas, and separate properties and relations which make them different, particular peas. Hume was finally dissatisfied with his own treatment of the identity of bodies, as he confessed gracefully in the same Appendix, but remained sure that persons were not peculiar. Recent empiricists have followed his lead. It is a lead congenial to a straightforward naturalism, which treats agents as complex natural objects, as when introducing *homo economicus* as a body with preferences, information and a computer programme.

Secondly, there is Kant's argument for a 'transcendental unity of apperception' in *The Critique of Pure Reason* ('Transcendental Analytic', Book I, Chapter 2, Section 2). The idea, in barest outline, is that, since experience presents us only with 'phenomena', our ability to unify the data of experience into enduring objects, and our warrant for doing so, must derive from elsewhere. These unities, not being available to experience, are 'transcendental' and are the work of our understanding, which groups phenomena and brings them under concepts, organised within a framework of categories. In so doing, we are referring separate phenomena to the consciousness of a single judging mind. But the unity and self-identity of the judging mind is also not presented to us by perception or introspection.

It too is a transcendental unity, now of 'apperception' or self-awareness, known to us by reflection on the presuppositions of reflection itself.

This transcendental self is active in making sense of the world and of its own part in the world. It orders experience on the assumption that everything in the world takes place solely in accordance with the laws of nature and there is no freedom. Yet to make sense of phenomena it has to assume that there is another kind of causality too, that of freedom. Kant explores this 'antinomy of pure reason' as the third of four antinomies, each consisting of a thesis and a conflicting antithesis, in search of an elusive synthesis ('Transcendental Dialectic', Book II, Chapter 2, Section 2). That the self is a free agent in a world where there is no freedom is an antinomy which well captures our difficulties in deciding how to conceptualise social action. We are agents who can never be caught in the act but must nevertheless be presupposed in understanding it.

Thirdly, however, pragmatists tend to regard this transcendental self as baggage left over from attempts to think of the self as a *res cogitans*. Although Kant was right to reject the empiricist view that experience is all we have or need, he was wrong to demand any kind of real self in order to make sense of the activity of interpretation. The web of belief is actively woven but not under the direction of a master-weaver (e.g. Rorty, 1987). The line was memorably stated much earlier on by William James in *The Principles of Psychology* (1890, Chapter 10). James insists both on the 'I' (the self as knower) and the 'Me' (the self as known). The 'empirical self or *me*' has three aspects:

the material self or body;
the social self – 'a man's social self is the recognition which he gets from his mates . . . properly speaking a man has as many social selves as there are individuals who recognise him';
the spiritual self – 'a man's inner or subjective being, his psychic faculties or dispositions, taken concretely'.

The I, which knows the Me, is no more than 'a passing, judging Thought', not a real or transcendental Thinker. But it matters nonetheless, because thinking and judging are activities, not aggregates of mental events.

All these lines retain advocates. Nor are descendants of Locke and Descartes extinct. Philosophical theories of personal identity are thus deeply and ramifyingly divergent. But that does not make them irrelevant to the question of whether we are more than the sum of our roles. On the contrary, the issues are philosophically tangled at just the points where this chapter has run into difficulty. Consequently its closing section will be an invitation to plunge deeper into the central problems of philosophy.

CONCLUSION

To insist on exploring the social world from within is not to give the game to Understanding, since Explanation may yet secure the final word. But it will have to be the *final* word. First thoughts about norms, institutions and practices are contrary both to systemic theory and to Game Theory. Such 'structures', although external to each actor, are internal to all collectively, being woven from public rules and meanings which have no place in termite colonies or planetary systems. Nor could normative structures serve as collective guides to action, if the individuals, whose acceptance sustains them, thought of themselves by analogy with termites in a colony or cogs in a machine. Yet they are not readily analysed as conventions in a sense suited to Rational Choice theory and Game Theory. The mutual expectations involved are normative rather than predictive and presuppose a quasi-moral scheme of duties and entitlements which so far eludes game-theoretic analysis.

Thus prompted, we focused attention on the idea of role as a set of normative expectations attached to a social position. The holism of the top right box would be well served if persons in the public arena always acted in accord with clear directives issuing from their social positions, and triumphantly so if there were norm-governed social positions to annex all social relationships, however apparently personal or intimate. The actors could then be absorbed by their positions, becoming the sum of their roles in the normative structure of society. We tried this line out with the help of a Bureaucratic Politics model and its pithy claim that 'where you stand depends on where you sit'. Here institutions and organisations were presented as the source of action both for fictive rational individuals, like the nation state, and for the flesh-and-blood individuals who do their bidding. A victory on both fronts at this key level of analysis promised a general victory for holism.

But, even if where you stand does depend on where you sit, there is still great latitude in interpreting roles, especially for anyone playing several. Role conflict unmasks the self caught in it. This self might be likened to an actor in a theatre, hidden behind the mask of a character in a play, as apparently suggested by the dramaturgical analogy. On reflection, however, the analogy is as ambiguous about the self as the institutional perspective is about its absence. Both bid us separate the players from their roles in one breath and include them in the next. Perhaps this is because we have been working with Wittgensteinian ideas of rules and practices, where the ambiguity is engrained. Rules tell the actor 'how to go on' and yet are constructed from the interpretations which the actors place on this guidance. Curiosity about the self is unallayed. It is further sharpened by a foray into the philosophical problem of personal identity, where a haunting belief in a Cartesian ego is offset by the failure of introspection to catch a glimpse of 'any thing but the perceptions'. But this may show only that the unity of apperception is transcendental.

Reference to Kant at least defines the difficulty. On the one hand we look to Understanding to protect the autonomy of the self as a source of initiatives which are subject to rational and moral judgement. On the other hand action is subject, like every event, to causal laws, which are the province of Explanation. This antinomy remains so far unresolved.

Anthony Giddens has written that 'the structural properties of social systems are both the medium and outcome of the reproduction of the practices which constitute those systems' (1979, p.69). That strikes just the right note for the top right box, where norms, institutions and practices feed on one another. But the actors refuse to be absorbed by the interplay of medium and outcome. They have their exits and their entrances and, crucially, their reasons for doing what they think rational and right. We have yet to do them justice.

CHAPTER 9

Explaining and understanding

Without adequacy on the level of meaning, our generalisations remain mere statements of *statistical* probability, either not intelligible at all or only imperfectly intelligible . . . On the other hand, from the point of view of sociological knowledge, even the most certain adequacy on the level of meaning signifies an acceptable *causal* proposition only to the extent that there is a probability . . . that the action in question *really* takes the course held to be meaningfully adequate.

Weber relates explaining and understanding in this way in the opening chapter of *Economy and Society*. The italics are his and they point up some troublespots. Broadly, we are invited to contrast a level of meaning with a causal level and then combine them so as to arrive at 'sociological knowledge'. That sounds a very reasonable way to proceed; but it is easier said than done.

Part of the message is loud and clear. Actions cannot be explained by statistics alone. That would leave them 'either not intelligible at all or only imperfectly intelligible'. (M. Rouget's vote cannot be explained just by assigning him to a group of workers whose vote can be predicted with 80% probability.) So we must first traverse the level of meaning and then, to settle what is *really* going on, return to the causal level. But there is a crucial ambiguity. Is Weber saying that actions and their motives exist at the level of meaning but cannot be identified without the reassurance of statistics to deal with the problem of Other Minds? Or is he saying that actions have causes as well as meanings and we need both?

Although we shall not press Weber himself for answers, these questions set an agenda for this chapter. Firstly, at the level of meaning, we have yet to reconcile the two ways of rationally

183

reconstructing action. There is scope for rapprochement between the intelligent rule-followers of the previous chapter and the rational agents of Game Theory, if the latter can be made more flexible. Secondly, at the causal level, we have yet to decide which idea of causality offers most to the social sciences, especially when we are concerned with ideal-type models of real-world events. Thirdly, we are not yet clear how to relate interpretative and causal accounts of the social world, not least because unsure how far to go in suggesting that social life *is* what it *means*.

RULES AND REASONS

We can best set about the task of reconciling the rule-guided and strategic aspects of rational action by drawing some conclusions about the actors' autonomy from the previous two chapters. Although we began Chapter 8 with a picture of agents as automatic rule-followers, we soon shed it in favour of a more fluid one. Obedient rule-followers need not be mechanical rule-followers. Indeed they cannot be, since rules are standardly open-ended, subject to interpretation and, in effect, constructed in the course of applying them. Even rules which are deliberately invented are prone to conflict in unforeseen ways, as are rules which emerge by latent processes. As priorities are established and conflicts settled, rules are given shape. Even a single rule is prone to be indeterminate, because it cannot be scripted for all circumstances and needs a kind of interpretation which involves deciding what it will be taken to mean. Hence obedient rule-followers not only know how to go on but also decide how to go on. They have a power to interpret individually and, still more, collectively, which is a power to construct. The effect is to set actors at a useful distance from rules, which nevertheless remain vital for understanding what is done under their aegis.

For instance, if Jack and Jill are neighbours, they are subject to the rules of this relationship, which range from legal requirements about keeping the fence in repair to social conventions about noise at night. But each has latitude in deciding how these rules apply. If they get on well, they will be tolerant both about what counts as a breach and about whether to put up with one. Even if they get on badly, each separately can still resist the pressure of the rules by contending that the late-night noise is reasonable, the remark made to other neighbours not malicious gossip and the fence not in need of repair. That there is latitude in rule-following becomes palpable, when we note that each of us has many roles to play and can choose, within limits no doubt, how much effort to devote to each and how to resolve conflicts among them. *Homo sociologicus* has emerged, in short, with plenty of room for manoeuvre.

On reflection, however, the space thus provided looks larger than *homo sociologicus* can fill out. There is also room for *homo economicus*, the utility-maximising individual of Chapter 6. Even if rules come complete with reasons for action built into them, these reasons underdetermine rational choices. Normative expectations leave options which depend on the utility which the agent attaches to fulfilling them. Thus the utilities attached to Jill's options when planning a party depend partly on what she herself wants and partly on the normative context. We can think of these elements as successive filters, with the normative context yielding a menu of options and the particular choice being made from the menu by rational calculation. This view is complicated but not sabotaged by the points just made about the interdependence of the filters. What Jill wants depends partly, no doubt, on her aspirations as a socialised, socially situated person; but how exactly she responds to normative expectations and what store she sets by them is partly up to her. That is no more than a complication, provided that the moment of decision remains one where she acts on what she calculates to be the maximising strategy, having identified the utilities involved. The upshot is an offer to combine *homo sociologicus* with *homo economicus* by analysing social action as instrumentally rational choice within social enablements and constraints.

HOMO ECONOMICUS REVISITED

Here we must pause, however, because the previous paragraph relies on the version of *homo economicus* which proved dubious earlier. In the standard, basic version *homo economicus* is a *very* mechanical individual, a mere throughput between given preferences and an automatically computed rational choice. In the ideal-type case, where agents are fully rational and know one another to be so, they have no intervening psychological character at all. If Jack is a misogynist, for instance, or Jill a benevolent Hindu, these characteristics will have influenced their preferences and hence their utilities. But they have no further impact on the choices made and there is no way of inferring the characters of the actors from their utilities in any of the games described in Chapter 6, nor would it make any difference if we could. That the utilities are as they are is all we know and all we need to know, granted only that the agents will seek to maximise them. This is entirely deliberate. Rational Choice theory in its standard basic version treats preferences as given, makes their origin irrelevant and focuses solely on how preferences yield forward-looking choices. The ideal-type case has been deliberately purged of all particular psychology.

There is now an obvious question about how a theory so abstract relates to the messier real world and the messier people who inhabit it. Presumably these inhabitants do have a psychology, one which makes them distinct individuals, as opposed to different illustrative bundles of preferences, and governs their actual processes of decision-making. But, in so far as psychology is thought of as a generalising science, which explains behaviour by reference to psychological laws, the point leads only to an interesting dispute about realism of the kind stirred up by Milton Friedman in Chapter 3 (p.53). It does not lead to crediting Jack and Jill with any autonomy or reflective self-direction. Instead each becomes the point of intersection of a subset of these laws, as applied in the relevant conditions. (Anyone, who compares what John Stuart Mill says about psychological laws in Book VI of *A System of Logic*, as indicated by the quotations in our opening chapter, with what he says about 'Individuality' in *On Liberty*, will wonder how a generalising psychology is supposed to respect our individuality.) Jack and Jill still do not truly qualify as individuals. There is no antidote to a wholly mechanical *homo economicus* here. Were the ideal-type case to need a less mechanically rational agent, a richer psychology would not help, if that psychology were mechanical too.

THE CENTIPEDE

Why want less mechanical agents? Recall the Prisoner's Dilemma (p.123), where individually rational choices sum to a result which is inferior for both players. The game is crucial, if Rational Choice theory, aided by Game Theory, is to succeed in analysing social norms as the outcome of non-cooperative games among rational agents. We noted, without exploring it, a suggestion that the solution which eluded rational agents in the one-shot game might be reached in the repeated game. But this suggestion is a matter of hot dispute and, in any case, a solution for the one-shot game would be a much greater prize. It would offer a master key to the analysis of norms, rules and practices which secure individuals against Pareto-inferior outcomes. I would now like to return to the topic to see what more can be done in the space not occupied by *homo sociologicus*, using a fresh game which seems to me to pose the root question more clearly. As a preface, here is a passage from Hume:

> Your corn is ripe today; mine will be so tomorrow. 'Tis profitable for us both that I shou'd labour with you today, and that you shou'd aid me tomorrow. I have no kindness for you, and know that you have as little for me. I will not, therefore, take any pains on your account; and should I labour with you on my own account, I know I shou'd be disappointed, and that I shou'd in vain depend upon your gratitude. Here then I leave you to labour alone: You treat me in the same manner. The seasons change; and both of us lose our harvests for want of mutual confidence and security. (1739, Book III, Part 2, Section 5)

Translating its implicit assumptions about utilities into game-theoretic form, we get the 'Centipede' shown in Figure 9.1. (Glance ahead to Figure 9.2 to see how it gets its name.) In this Centipede players A and B take it in turns to play either down or across. The game starts at the leftmost node and A has the opening turn. If he plays down, the game ends at once with the payoffs shown at the bottom of the downstroke ((0,0): the first number in each bracket being A's payoff and the second B's). If he plays across, B has a similar choice of whether to play down (−1,2) or to play across, in which case the game ends at the right-hand node with scores of (1,1). Both players do better if the game

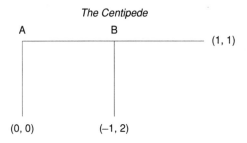

Figure 9.1   The Centipede

proceeds cooperatively to an outcome of (1,1) than if A kills it at
the start by playing down. But this is not what will happen, if A
and B are the rational agents of Chapter 6. A will reason that B
would play down, if allowed a turn, since B would prefer $(-1,2)$ to
(1,1). So A, preferring (0,0) to $(-1,2)$, plays down; and both
players are the losers.

The game in Figure 9.1 is equivalent to a Prisoner's Dilemma,
except that the players do not play at the same moment and the
second player is not guaranteed a move. Its serial character is
shown by using what game theorists call its 'extensive form'.
Why it is called a 'centipede' becomes plain, when we use an
example where many more turns are possible. Suppose that
Jack and Jill have a pile of ten pennies in front of them, a present
from a kind friend. They are to play in turn, each taking one
penny or two. Whenever one penny is taken, the turn passes; as
soon as anyone takes two, the game ends and the remaining
pennies vanish. Each keeps the pennies by then acquired.

This version is shown in Figure 9.2, which looks much more
like a centipede (and would look even more so, if articulated for
one hundred pennies). Sadly, the point is as before. If A and B are
rational agents, A will take two pennies at the opening move,
ending the game at once. This seems ridiculous but the logic is
precise. If the game were to reach the far right node, A would
play down, preferring six pennies to five. So B would play down at
the previous node. A, foreseeing this, would play down at the
node before; and so on. This 'backward induction' works its

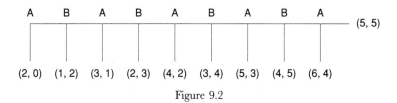

Figure 9.2

way back to the very first node, where A therefore plays down. Ridiculous!

The Centipede seems to me to force the basic issue neatly. One could still shrug one's shoulders and comment that, since the logic clearly tells the first player to open by playing down, there is no more to be said. But, whereas a similar shrugging off of a mutually inferior outcome in the Prisoner's Dilemma might be fair comment on a dismal fact of real life, the Centipede is a scandal for Game Theory.

Moreover, the source of the scandal is easy to spot. A and B would both do better in Figure 9.2 if they were willing and able to make an agreement and to trust one another to keep it. In that case A could open by taking one penny (moving across), thus making B an offer, and B could respond by taking one penny (also moving across), thus accepting it. Similarly Hume's farmers will both get their harvests in, if the rational agents of Figure 9.1 can only make and keep a simple promise. Since all benefit from this profitable and, indeed, commonplace practice, it should surely commend itself to rational agents? If so, the obvious reaction is to amend the apparatus of Game Theory to allow the remedy.

'AN ANIMAL CAPABLE OF PROMISING'

But this turns out to be no minor amendment. As Nietzsche remarks in *The Genealogy of Morals* (II.1), 'To breed an animal capable of promising (*das versprechen darf*) – isn't that just the paradoxical task which nature has set herself with mankind, the peculiar problem of mankind?' The task is paradoxical because '*darf*' ('capable' in a sense implying fit and entitled) carries a

moral charge strange to nature. The binding character of promises is indeed the peculiar element which is eluding us. The snag
remains that game-theoretic reasons for action are always and
only forward-looking, whereas the logic of promises requires
backward-looking reasons. When Jack promises Jill to do something tomorrow, he is binding himself that today's promise will
motivate him tomorrow. This undertaking need not be unconditional. If, having promised to help with her harvest, he sees his
children in mortal danger, she is not entitled to expect him to turn
up regardless. But such implicit conditions do not include overriding a promise just because, when tomorrow comes, it is more
profitable not to keep it.

Yet that is precisely what the standard, unamended, apparatus
implies. For an agent, whose rational choice is governed solely by
comparison of expected utilities, bygones are always bygones.
Anyone who plays across at the right-hand node of a Centipede
is simply not a rational agent, as defined so far. But perhaps this
awkward-looking point calls only for a minor amendment. After
all, Figures 9.1 and 9.2 are unlikely to tell the full story. If Jack is
to have any further dealings with Jill, it may not pay him to leave
her in the lurch. Even if he is not, she will spread word of his
rotten conduct and his reputation may suffer. Even if he can avoid
that, he may still regret the terrible pangs of a bad conscience. All
in all, it can be a mistake to be guided only by what accountants
term 'the bottom line'.

Yes; but we are still where we were at the end of Chapter 6. If
any such factors can make a difference in the Centipedes above,
then the utilities have been misrepresented in Figures 9.1 and 9.2.
Rational Choice theory does not assume selfish agents, still less
stupid ones who cannot see that a good reputation may be useful.
Rational agents can have any preferences, including those
prompted by generosity, friendship and public spirit. But they
then always do whatever maximises the expected satisfaction of
their own preferences. This may not be altogether plain in the
Centipedes above, since Figure 9.2 seems to deal in pennies and
Figure 9.1 in corn. Strictly and crucially, however, utilities are a
common currency which takes each and every element of satisfaction into account. An amendment which let rational agents act

contrary to the logic of a correctly stated utility schedule would therefore cut very deep.

There is a large difference between rewriting utility numbers and switching standpoints. It is one thing to rewrite the scores in Figures 9.1 and 9.2 so that, when all sources of utility are included, the problem does not arise. It is quite another to suggest that truly rational agents can escape the logic of dominance *after* the problem has been set. While concern for others remains instrumental in the precise sense defined, one's own projects will often be best furthered by playing a free-rider strategy. It is then still rational to play it and I see no reason to doubt that the scores in Figures 9.1 and 9.2 represent common enough situations even after *all* consequences have been taken into account.

It remains tantalising that in everyday life much depends on the exact relationship between the players and on how directly each is concerned for the other's welfare. Strangers engaged in cash transactions are different from lovers, friends or neighbours. That clearly affects actual two-person games. It matters also in *n*-person games, although the larger the number of players the less personal their relationship tends to become. But none of this affects the crux, which is that Game Theory works solely in utilities, thus homogenising all varieties of motivating reason. Actual social relationships have only such bearing as can be represented in utilities; and it remains unsurprising if agents whose behaviour is always instrumental at the moment of choice often renege on agreements which have a cost to keeping them.

The Centipedes above mark the crux by pointing up some 'rational' choices as scandalously self-defeating. The scandal results from the use of these all-purpose utilities. Lovers do not have an escape denied to misanthropes or to strangers meeting in a market. Once the utilities are in place, whatever their source and whatever the relationship of the players, the problem is set and rational agents are trapped in it by the logic of dominance. That is why radical revision is needed, if we want 'an animal capable of promising'.

A REMEDY IN THE JUDGEMENT AND
UNDERSTANDING?

So let us turn radical, starting with a suggestive passage from Hume's discussion of 'the origin of justice and property' in the *Treatise*. Hume observes that 'in the original frame of our minds, our strongest affection is confined to ourselves; our next is extended to our relations and acquaintances; and it is only the weakest which reaches to strangers and indifferent persons'. This 'partiality', he continues, is an obstacle to the success of social arrangements intended to remedy the 'inconveniences' of human nature and our 'natural uncultivated ideas of morality', being based on our affections, merely reinforce it. There is a remedy, however, in the emergence of conventions of justice and property, provided that they involve the needed impartiality. Hume describes its source thus:

The remedy, then, is not derived from nature, but from *artifice*; or, more properly speaking, nature provides a remedy, in the judgement and understanding, for what is irregular and incommodious in the affections. (1739, Book III, Part 2, Section 2)

What is suggestive here is not the very idea of a remedy – farmers do, after all, collaborate at harvest time – but its location in the judgement and understanding. What is this new resource and can it be adopted by *homo economicus*? If so, we shall need a more complex moral psychology than hitherto. Harry Frankfurt (1971) proposes one where the agent has two tiers of preferences, one ranging over outcomes, as before, and the other ranging over these first-order preferences. For example, Jack is an alcoholic who prefers gin to water, but is also a reluctant alcoholic who would prefer to prefer water to gin. Perhaps judgement and understanding can lead him to act on the second-order preference. Similarly John Harsanyi (1955) has claimed that we have 'ethical preferences' as well as more ordinary ones. Thus Jill might ordinarily prefer hand-woven Persian rugs to factory imitations but also have a decisive contrary preference due to what she has learnt about child labour in the manufacture of the genuine article. In similar vein, Jack and Jill together might be able to pick their way through the 'Penny' game of Figure 9.2, if their 'judgement and understanding' can prod them into implicitly making and keeping an agreement.

But the remedy is not straightforward. Firstly, two-tiered preferences are not enough of an apparatus. Although a disintegrating alcoholic may do better to act contrary to his first-order preference for gin, a guilt-ridden homosexual may do better to shed his second-order preference for a change of sexual orientation. If so, 'judgement' is not to be equated with always accepting the guidance of the higher tier. Consider the dilemma facing a woman who has hitherto been a contented mother and home-maker but has begun to wonder whether she has, in effect, been conned into a vicarious life of self-denial. Shall she settle for her existing preferences, presumably second- as well as first-order, or shall she radically reorder them? Answers call for judgement at a yet higher order, where there is surely more to it than adjusting a pair of mental scales so as to give a more satisfying balance of utilities.

Indeed the whole image of mental scales is fast becoming an obstacle. It might serve initially, when, for instance, one is weighing a sure prospect of £100 against an uncertain prospect of £500 and there is no worry about the sense in which 'more' is 'better'. But the last two examples raise questions of the agent's identity, where it is far from plain what makes what better for whom. Such questions were held in check earlier by so reducing the specific content of 'utility' that 'preference' could do all the work: anything can apparently be weighed against anything, since the agent is assumed to have consistent preferences. Once we have distanced the woman from her current preferences, however, her rational choice between particular goods or courses of action is suspended, while she decides what sort of person to become. No remedy in the judgement and understanding is yet in sight for such irregularities.

Secondly, how exactly does judgement help with strategic choices? The prospect of cracking the Centipede by reflection on the advantages of making a binding agreement is beguiling. But this artifice will not work while each player remains a utility-maximising individual, who, therefore, still plays down at the last node. The problem remains that reasons for playing across can motivate only if playing across yields better consequences for that player, as measured by what has *already* been included in the utility numbers. It is not hard to identify the sorts of reason which judgement might be hoped to introduce. For instance, the very fact that one has (implicitly) made an agreement is commonly regarded as a reason for keeping it. The fact that an outcome of (5,5) is fair to both parties would often be thought a reason to prefer (5,5) to (6,4). But such facts remain idle, while the theory can comment only that, if they affect the players, then the utilities are misrepresented in Figure 9.2. There is as yet no remedy in the judgement and understanding, which would let rational agents override the numbers for reasons not animated by comparison of consequences.

I am not saying flatly that *homo economicus* cannot be found a moral psychology which allows truly binding agreements and genuinely backward-looking reasons which can nevertheless motivate. We have found at least some scope for making rational agents reflective in responding to conflict between their first- and second-order preferences. To that extent their preferences can be less 'given' and they themselves become less of a mere throughput between input and computed output. But something more radical is still needed, if they are to circumvent dominantly inferior choices by judgement and understanding. Can Rational Choice theory stand the strain of a further amendment or are its resources exhausted? Since scholarly opinion remains deeply divided, I leave it to the ingenuity of readers to decide.

We have found some ways to make *homo economicus* less myopic without destroying the model. Nevertheless the Centipede remains more troublesome for an economically rational agent than it does for a flexible *homo sociologicus*, who can have social norms as reasons for action without thereby becoming their creature. Intelligent rule-followers can negotiate Centipedes with aplomb. That is, after all, how real farmers manage not to lose their harvests for want of mutual confidence and security. Notice, however, that this line does not by-pass the previous questions about the relation of self to roles. They remain packed into the notion of 'intelligent' rule-following and emerge as soon as actors ask not only what a particular rule gives them reason to do but also whether they have sufficient reason to follow that rule. Although philosophers may need to be socially minded when thinking about practical reason or even personal identity, sociologists do not have a by-pass marked 'Social Identity'.

The opening suggestion was that social action is instrumentally rational choice within social enablements and constraints. It has emerged that choices can be individual and reasoned, without necessarily being instrumental. Indeed, if all choices were solely instrumental, the social enterprise would not even be possible. Yet we have not been reworking the notion of choice simply to have it swallowed by the notion of rule-following. The starting image was of two filters, with the normative context creating a menu of options and then the particular choice made by rational calculation. The upshot, I think, is that the filters coalesce. Strategically rational choices depend on normative expectations, which themselves depend on what it is strategically rational for a social agent to choose. Self, roles and reasons cannot be disentangled.

RULES, REASONS AND CAUSES

This messy result makes for untidiness in dealing with the other questions on the chapter's agenda. These concern causality and how the causal level relates to the level of meaning. Since an attempt to leave everything tidy would double the length of the book, I shall be brief.

Are reasons for action causes of action? A first reaction to this vexed philosophical question might be that of course they are: one can hardly doubt that people act *because* they desire and believe what they do. But this response simply turns the question into one of whether 'because' has a different sense when the topic is action from its sense in other explanations. That could be a helpful move, if we were clear by now about the right naturalistic analysis of 'because' in general. But our conclusions have been modest. Chapters 2, 3 and 4 left us pretty sure that there is more to a causal explanation than a citing of empirical correlations holding in relevant conditions. Even if successful predictions were not the touchstone, however, we were not clear what could warrantably be done with notions of 'natural law' or 'natural necessity' and with realist claims about the existence of causal mechanisms with causal powers. So, although we should distrust Weber's indication that an acceptable causal proposition is finally one couched in terms of statistical probability, we have no commanding account of causation by which to judge whether reasons are causes.

We can safely say, however, that for the rational agents of standard Rational Choice theory reasons are indeed causes. If preferences are given and choices are straightforwardly computed, the agents' inner workings are stages in a causal process on any definition of 'causal'. Admittedly the part played by beliefs may complicate the point, if beliefs are supposed to be rationally arrived at, rather than treated simply as further given subjective elements in the process of decision. We should certainly not assume that rational deliberation is to be correctly analysed as a series of psychological causes and effects. Nevertheless there is a strong presumption that an agent conceived as a throughput between external inputs and a computationally generated output is one for whom reasons for action are causes of action.

The analysis of rule-followers is trickier. If institutions and practices were the 'Systems' of the top left box, we could readily think of rule-following as action caused by pressure of the system transmitted through the psychology of the agent. But we were persuaded that the Wittgensteinian notion of a 'game' belongs squarely to Understanding. This led us to think of actions as moves in a game, motivated by their meaning. Whatever quite this comes to as a proposition in the philosophy of mind, it stops us construing action as physical behaviour caused by mental states. On the contrary, by reconstructing the rules followed and thus discovering the meaning of the action, we learn all there is to know about what the agent is doing and why. That almost makes it sound as if the very idea of a mental state drops out as irrelevant.

But it is not so simple, if we also stress the Wittgensteinian theme that the actors construct the rules in the course of interpreting and applying them. Then we become curious about the actors' own understanding of how to go on. Yet an insistence that rule-followers can be intelligent and creative does more to enrich the level of meaning than to suggest that reasons have causes outside it. A conclusion that reasons for action which stem from the actor's understanding of the game do not have causes of any sort is at least defensible.

When thinking about roles, however, we were inclined to invoke a self, distanced from the roles it plays and perhaps even, in principle, from any rules it follows. Equally, further thoughts about *homo economicus* led us to distance rational agents from the preferences which had earlier defined them. That deepens the question further and I have nothing short to say about Kantian ideas of autonomy, rational or moral, except that there is much to be learnt by reading *The Groundwork of the Metaphysic of Morals* (1785) or *The Critique of Practical Reason* (1788).

These comments leave it correspondingly open how to resolve the issues raised by determinism, since we have not settled the sense of the thesis that every event has a cause or causal explanation. If naturalism were to prevail, the crux for free action would still be whether compatibilists can maintain that freedom is not only compatible with determinism but presupposes it. Mill's hope that all is plain sailing once we recognise that causes do not necessitate their effects is by now looking too optimistic. But, even if reasons are causes and have causes in their turn, there is still much to argue about and nothing follows directly about the possibility of free action. Meanwhile, if the relation of reasons and actions is not a causal one at any level, the question of whether determinism remains a threat is open.

RATIONAL EXPECTATIONS AND NORMATIVE EXPECTATIONS

The final question concerns the relation of levels and the concluding relation of Explanation to Understanding. I shall leave the overall reckoning to the closing chapter. To end the present one, I would like to make an ontological suggestion about a social world where choices are strategic and rules are constructed in the course of following them.

In the strategic interplay of rational agents, each has what economists term 'rational expectations'. Much is packed into this phrase, including the proposition that each agent has a model or theory of the economy and knows that the same model or theory is in the heads of the others. One sees the point: Jack needs to know how Jill construes the possibilities inherent in a situation, before he can form rational expectations about what she will do; and she cannot choose her strategy without knowing how he construes the possibilities too. But this means ascribing to both of them an answer to the disputed question of how the economy actually works. The usual move is to sidestep neatly by crediting them with the same economic theory, namely the standard one. Now follows an intriguing line of thought.

Suppose the standard theory were monetarist, implying that, if government boosts public spending in a recession, inflation will result. Recession strikes and the government rashly boosts public spending. Rational agents, expecting the inflation which they know that other rational agents expect, behave rationally. Entrepreneurs cut back production; workers demand higher wages. Inflation therefore occurs, just as the theory predicted. How elegant! Critics, however, especially those who do not subscribe to monetarism, are quick to complain of a circularity. Suppose the standard theory were Keynesian and implied that public spending in a recession results in growth. Recession strikes and government boosts public spending. Foreseeing growth, rational entrepreneurs increase output and rational workers moderate their demands. The sum of these strategic choices is indeed growth, just as the theory said. The tantalising suggestion (more favoured by Keynesians than by monetarists, be it admitted) is that what will in fact occur can depend squarely on which economic theory is in the heads of rational agents. In other words, rational expectations are akin to self-fulfilling prophecies, which generate what they foresee.

This is a startling idea (helpfully expounded in Hahn (1980)). As an economic proposition it is beyond our scope, especially since not even Keynesians suppose that we can have a flourishing economy just by coming to a shared belief that prosperity is round the corner. But we can see its force and interest by shifting the example. Whether a traffic jam occurs often depends on whether motorists believe that one is building up. If they do, and if their only way to avoid it is to try to get there before it occurs, they may well ensure that there is one. On the other hand, if they have alternative routes, their belief may produce a clear road for any driver too stupid – or too clever – to pay attention! Traffic forecasts are thus very different from weather forecasts. If sailors heed the storm warning, the storm still occurs but they are safe from it; if drivers listen, there is no jam to avoid. The suggestion is that, often at any rate, social events are shaped by the shape which social actors expect them to have.

Keynes once compared the economy with a newspaper competition where readers are invited to rank pictures of young women in order of prettiness, with the prize going to the readers who rank them in what proves the most popular order:

each competitor has to pick, not those faces which he himself finds prettiest, but those which he thinks likeliest to catch the fancy of the other competitors, each of whom is looking at the problem from the same point of view. It's not a case of choosing those which, to the best of one's ability, really are the prettiest, nor even those which average opinion genuinely thinks the prettiest. We have reached the third degree where we devote our intelligences to anticipating what average opinion expects average opinion to be. (1936, p.154)

No doubt some initial shared presumptions about prettiness are needed; otherwise the regress destructs at infinity. But that still leaves scope for the suggestion that it is not nature but the competition itself which determines the order of prettiness. Keynes' image thus prompts a radical reading of the game-theoretic idea that what happens next is a sum of strategic choices. If one isolates this idea, then rational expectations about the social world are generative as well as predictive. That then suggests a striking difference from predictions about the natural world.

How deep the difference goes depends on how hard we can work the thought that actors' expectations can furnish and move the social world. But, even without pressing it far, we are led to reflect on the difference between games against nature and games against strategic choosers. Let us think briefly about probability. In speaking of the probability of a natural event, like rain, as less than 100 per cent, we sometimes mean that there is a random element in nature itself, contrary to the claims of a thorough determinism. But usually we mean that, say, 80 per cent is as accurate a forecast as we can manage on our available evidence. We thus distinguish between physical probability and epistemic probability. (After a tossed coin has come down but before we know how it has fallen, the physical probability that it is 'Heads' is either 100 per cent or 0 per cent; since we do not yet know which, the epistemic probability that it is 'Heads' is 50 per cent.) As our evidence changes, we adjust epistemic probabilities, bringing them, we hope, closer to physical probabilities. Does this way of speaking still make sense, if Jack is estimating the probability that Jill will choose a particular move, whose rationale depends on what probability she believes that he is assigning to her choice of it? There is an intriguing case for holding that the relation between epistemic and physical probability is here reversed, in as much as outcomes are sums of choices. Indeed it may be that the notion of physical probability has to drop out altogether. If so, we seem to be in the realm of meaning in distinct, if teasing, contrast to the realm of natural causation.

The challenge sharpens, when we recall what was said about normative expectations. Whereas rational expectations can create a traffic jam, normative expectations are the very stuff of social life. In Chapter 7, we distinguished the constitutive rules of a Wittgensteinian game or practice, without which there would be no such game, from regulative rules for its conduct, once constituted. Both nevertheless depend on how people interpret the normative expectations involved in their social positions. Meanwhile, social positions are themselves secured by their place in a network of normative expectations. Hence it could be claimed that everything distinctively social in the social world depends on how people expect other people to go on.

'Expect' here has both a normative and a predictive sense. They remain different senses, partly because roles are always underscripted and often rendered indeterminate by role conflict, and partly because, in any case, people are prone not to do what is expected of them. The predictive sense therefore needs to be found a separate point of reference. Here lies possible scope for rapprochement with a refined theory of Rational Choice.

CONCLUSION

The idea that expectations not only make the social world go round but are the very stuff of it will not find favour with naturalists. To redress the balance, let us sum up from their point of view.

Ontologically, more has been suggested than has been established. Expectations matter, no doubt, but they veil a real material world of material power over people and resources, of famine and plenty, of blood, toil, tears and laughter. The natural world does not stop at the social boundary. An animal capable of promising is still an animal and rules which enable and constrain are still rules of animal behaviour in a world whose social workings are causal.

Methodologically, therefore, Explanation still claims the last word. But naturalism can concede the first word to hermeneutics, as a useful heuristic device or short cut. Some naturalists are so sternly behavioural that they will concede nothing to our attempts to understand social life from within. But others readily distinguish a spectator's from an agent's perspective and see merit in reconstructing a level of meaning with the aid of the latter. Then, however, there is explanatory work to do. Some do it directly by arguing that hermeneutics yields acceptable causal propositions only in so far as meanings and reasons are causes of action. In that case, even a Wittgensteinian reconstruction is an internal commentary on a set of natural events. Others proceed indirectly by allowing hermeneutics its games and then explaining why this realm of ideas is as it is in external terms.

Epistemologically, the crux is how we know that 'the action in question *really* takes the course held to be meaningfully adequate'. Here, I confess, the score remains obscure. Those naturalists who are realists about underlying mechanisms and structures still owe us their epistemological warrant. Other naturalists who were earlier drawn to pragmatism are still uncomfortably close to turning physical objects into cultural posits and translating the world as we know it into a web of belief. In that case hermeneutics may hold the trumps after all. The chapter therefore leaves unfinished business as usual.

CHAPTER 10

A value-neutral social science?

There are still two stories to tell about the social world and how it works. We are not yet sure how radically they differ. One starts as an insider's or agent's story about what social life means and the other as an outsider's or spectator's story about the causes of social behaviour and events. But both stories, the naturalistic as much as the hermeneutic, have versions where action is rationally reconstructed from an internal point of view. Both can recognise that social life is set in a material world and that variations in circumstance and resources, individual or collective, affect what goes on. It is not as if naturalism dealt only in material conditions and behaviour, and hermeneutics only in action and the fabric of ideas.

The difference has more to do with whether Explanation or Understanding holds the final ace. Even this is complicated by dispute about which cards belong in which hand. Naturalists can argue that, since reasons for action are causes of action, rational reconstruction is an explanatory process similar in principle to any other identification of causal order in nature. Moreover, since the institutional arrangements of a culture influence action only through the beliefs and desires of agents, questions about how precisely to slot human psychology into social contexts are typical of scientific questions at large and do nothing to challenge the scope of naturalism. Conversely, hermeneutics can retort that a psychology which works with meanings and reasons is thereby radically unlike a natural science, not least because the style of analysis needed for rules, norms and roles prevents our regarding the relation of social to psychological elements as one of cause and effect between distinguishable items.

Accompanying this dispute, there is a hard question about objectivity. Naturalists make much of the demands of objectivity, which they see as general for all sciences and as issuing finally in causal explanations with a single form. Hermeneutics, at least in the versions addressed so far, rests with intersubjectivity and a meaningful order which is as it is understood to be from within. This difference goes very deep indeed. It may be muddied by disputes between holists and individualists within each camp, leading to attempts at horizontal alliances in our window diagram. But, believing that vertical alliances are finally stronger, I propose to discuss objectivity as a general bone of contention between Explanation and Understanding.

A common charge against hermeneutics is that it leads to relativism. It is not instantly plain what the charge implies or that relativism is a Bad Thing. But the presumption is that, since the findings of natural science are the objective results of a search for objective truth, the social sciences are in trouble if they cannot be objective too. If Understanding cannot offer more than subjective or intersubjective fruits, the whole hermeneutic approach is condemned to relativism. The topic is one where stakes and tempers are high. But its threads are tangled and discussion will proceed in two stages. This chapter will chiefly discuss the thesis that the social sciences can and should be 'value-neutral', but will also comment on the scope for moral relativism in the later stages. The next will tackle other species of relativism which beset the search for truth throughout the sciences and are the stuff of current debate.

The chapter will open with the original Enlightenment presumption that scientific and moral progress go together. Having noted how the drawing of a 'fact/value' distinction has subverted this optimism, we shall turn to Weber. His line on value-freedom and value-relevance is neat and remains authoritative. But it calls for nuance and leads to deeper questions. These prompt further thought about the peculiarities of social enquiry, the implications of granting that all scientific judgements involve interpretation and the scope for relativism in ethics. Despite the scepticism encountered on the journey, however, we shall conclude that hope of moral progress is not a lost cause.

FACTS AND VALUES

Condorcet declared firmly that 'truth, virtue and happiness are bound together with an indissoluble chain' (1795, Xth Stage). This arresting piece of Enlightenment optimism now rings sadly hollow. Knowledge has burgeoned in two centuries and, with it, the power to shape the world. But this power can be used for good or ill and some of its uses have been appalling. We may well think that there is no indissoluble chain either in theory or in practice. Indeed, many would add, the whole idea relies on a manifest confusion between fact and value: science is neutral between moral theories and leaves open all questions of the uses to which it should be put; it gives power without guidance.

Social scientists are less comfortable with this attitude than are natural scientists. There is a common suspicion that a human subject matter makes a difference, perhaps partly because what people value is an essential component in what they do and partly because social scientists are people. The suspicion is sharpened by distinguishing between explanation and understanding. If social science is an inside story told by insiders, a strict distinction between fact and value is at least less compelling. 'Virtue' may after all be inseparable from social knowledge and power, even if not for Condorcet's reasons and not with his hoped for implications.

Since this line of thought soon becomes very tangled, we shall do better to begin with the place of ethics in the natural sciences and an occasion for concern about it which still reverberates. The dropping of the atom bomb on Hiroshima and Nagasaki ended the 1939–45 war. But rejoicing among the victors was soon tempered by news of what it had done to survivors. Scientists who had developed the bomb were especially affected. It had been all very well to work away in the distant calm of laboratories, committed to the Allied cause and content to accept that what was done with the results was not their decision. But the pictures and reports which soon went round the world made them realise their special part in the Allied victory. In 1947 a group of eminent scientists, including Albert Einstein and Bertrand Russell, convened the 'Pugwash' conference to discuss questions of ethical responsibility.

The conference rejected the cosy view that scientists are merely technicians who discover means to authorised ends. It would be comforting to think that those who provide the tools are simply citizens among other citizens when government comes to decide how to use them. But, the atom bomb being novel, only its makers knew what it could do. Did that not give them special responsibility? To reply that not even the makers in fact knew the effects of so novel a weapon invited the retort that they should have done: ignorance was no excuse. Some thought this was too harsh and simple. The scientists had stressed all along that this was a weapon without precedent, in need of thorough testing and fit for use only far from civilisation as a threat to encourage surrender. Furthermore, official reassurance had been given along these lines. But this defence was also rejected, on the grounds that naivety about the working of political decisions in wartime would not suffice. Scientists, in sum, had a duty to understand not only the power they were wresting from nature but also the hands into which they were putting it. Expertise carries special ethical responsibility.

The atom bomb was not the only new weapon of the war. Biological and chemical research had produced others as deadly and today's governments have an armoury ranging from nerve gases to nuclear missiles. Similar issues are raised, moreover, by less lethal developments, like the power to play god with human lives through medicine or information technology. It would be a mistake to start by supposing that there is something simple to say about the ethics of knowledge in the natural sciences as a guide to the moral responsibilities of social scientists. But the Pugwash conference gives us a clear start and, as it happens, one of its organisers held the view of ethics which is most relevant to our topic in general. Bertrand Russell was an exponent of a fact/value distinction which put the basis of ethics beyond the scope of reason. He held ethics to be ultimately a matter of sheer personal commitment and, being clear-headed, was simply urging scientists, as experts in a special position and as enlightened persons, to share his own commitment. The connection between being enlightened and being committed is intriguing.

Let us introduce the fact/value distinction less abruptly. Condorcet took the standard Enlightenment view that ethics has a rational basis and hence that scientific progress includes the growth of wisdom. This agreed both with older rationalist ambitions and with the newer empiricism. Rationalists had usually likened moral knowledge to mathematics, starting with self-evident axioms about right and wrong, good and evil, from which particular moral truths could be derived. Empiricists were more inclined to rely on empirical truths about human nature and human flourishing, thus clearing the way for an instrumental science of, for instance, happiness and the means to achieve it. Either way, truth, virtue and happiness were indeed bound together by an indissoluble chain.

The view is entirely plausible, if the world has a moral fabric built into it, as ancient philosophy and Christian theology had assumed. If, as Kepler wrote, 'science is thinking God's thoughts after Him', then science enlightens us about God's design for everything including human life. In that case it is an enquiry into the cause, meaning, purpose, function and reason of things, all rolled into one. By the end of the eighteenth century, however, this traditional equation was coming apart. Thinkers were becoming aware that the new scientific methods ushered in by the scientific revolution had fractured it. The search for a rational causal order no longer relied on methods suited to reveal meaning or purpose in the universe. Suspicion was growing that neither sense-experience nor *a priori* reasoning can yield moral knowledge of the traditional sort purveyed by Reason. Experience, aided by scientific method, can tell us how the world (probably) is, was and will be but not how it should be. *A priori* reasoning only spells out the implications of what we already know; but no moral conclusions can be reached by an inference without a moral proposition among its premises; and there are no moral premises to be had by experience or intuition.

This sceptical line could already be heard in the eighteenth century. Hume suggested it in his *Treatise*, especially in the chapter titled 'Moral Distinctions Not Derived From Reason':

Take any action allowed to be vicious; wilful murder for instance. Examine it in all lights, and see if you can find that matter of fact, or real existence, which you call *vice*. In whichever way you take it, you find only certain passions, motives, volitions and thoughts. There is no other matter of fact in the case. The vice entirely escapes you, as long as you consider the object. You never can find it, till you turn your reflection into your own breast, and find a sentiment of disapprobation, which arises in you, towards this action. Here is a matter of fact; but it is the object of feeling, not of reason. It lies in yourself, not in the object. (1739, Book III, Part 1)

This, admittedly, is no knock-down argument, even when supported by the rest of the *Treatise*. But Hume has since become a standard reference point for the origins of the fact/value distinction and, with it, the thesis, often referred to as 'Hume's law', that there is no way to derive an 'ought' from an 'is'.

It would be a great mistake simply to assume that 'value-judgements', as they have come to be called, can be cleanly separated from judgements of other sorts and lack all rational basis. But let us suppose so for the moment, since it is standardly assumed in textbook discussions of the place of ethics in the social sciences. The distinction between scientific judgements and value-judgements can be marked in various ways. One is by subdividing scientific judgements along the lines of the analytic–synthetic distinction (p.51) and arguing that value-judgements are neither analytic nor synthetic. This is the simpler way, congenial to the aims of Positive science, and would come out neatly, if the claims of Positive science had succeeded in Chapter 3. Pragmatism offers another way, provided that theory-dependence is distinct from value-dependence. In that case scientific judgements can be allowed to include irreducible elements of interpretation without thereby becoming infected by ethical commitments. Realists influenced by Marx uphold a theory of ideology, which contrasts ideology sharply with science. That there is a fact/value distinction thus commands general, if variously founded, agreement.

VALUE-FREEDOM AND VALUE-RELEVANCE

With this preamble, the idea that science, properly conducted, is value-neutral comes as no surprise. For the social sciences, the standard reference is Weber's classic treatment of value-neutrality under the headings of 'value-freedom' (*Wertfreiheit*) and 'value-relevance' (*Wertbeziehung*), as presented chiefly in *The Methodology of the Social Sciences* (1904). Weber, in effect, separates the process of enquiry into three phases: what goes in, what comes out and what happens in between. Here is a brief outline.

The initial phase includes the selection of topics for research. The choice is determined by who thinks what worth investigating and why, and values are plainly involved in it. This is perhaps most obvious where the aim is to extend the power of a vested interest, for instance where a dictatorship wants to know whether death squads create more opposition than they stifle. But values are no less involved in opting for more high-minded enquiries, intended to relieve poverty or simply to seek the truth about some aspect of social life. Countless topics could be chosen and the decisive factors are always value-relevant, whether or not the values are the social scientist's own or, for instance, those of the pay-master.

Values are equally endemic in the final phase, what comes out. What significance the research is held to have and what is done with it depends on someone's judgements of value, not always the social scientist's. That goes, whether the motives are base or noble. Truth and the other commitments of scientists *qua* scientists have no peculiar claim to neutrality. Science is no more value-free in this respect than is property development.

In the middle phase, however, the process of investigation itself can and should be uncommitted. Weber presents the role of scientist *qua* scientist as one solely concerned with facts and explanations, regardless of where they lead. Although he makes it clear that scientists have other roles too, and so cannot disclaim their political and human responsibilities, he is definite about the demands of science itself and rejects any suggestion that such value-freedom is impossible. Thus, I suppose, the study of torture, paid for by a dictator wanting to know how to extract information most cheaply and effectively, could be conducted in a wholly detached spirit of enquiry by a scientist seeking the truth of the matter. Whether the investigator ought to take the task on is another question altogether. So, even if more precariously, is the ethics of the conduct of fieldwork.

This is the voice of Positive science, very clear but, we may suspect by now, too simple. Yet Weber was no brute empiricist and, as we saw earlier, regarded 'ideal types' as essential to science. His 'ideal types' are not simply artifices of a filing system predicated on a neat separation of concepts and objects. Besides, we have the independent reasons furnished by Chapter 4 for thinking that interpretation pervades all aspects of scientific enquiry. The allegedly value-free character of the process therefore needs to be stated with some nuance.

Here we might recall Popper's distinction between discovery and validation. Even if values are sure to infiltrate the conceptual process which inspires conjectures, there are still value-free moments of objective truth, when conjectures risk empirical refutation. These critical moments distinguish not only science from pseudo-science but also, more grandly, open societies from closed ones: critical science has its counterpart in liberal democracy (Popper, 1945). Weber is more ambivalent, however. Like Popper, he believes an open society a fragile hope, in need of constant vigilance if we ever attain it. But he is less inclined to think that reason is squarely on the side of progress. Rationality, at least in its modern, rational–legal forms, can be dangerous. Although traditional societies are oppressive, the spread of rational order need not be liberating. This is no doubt partly for the obvious reason that rational order concentrates power and nothing guarantees that power will be used for good. But Weber has doubts about the neutrality of rational order itself.

Postponing these deeper matters, we can now state an official view of value-relevance and value-freedom in the social sciences, predicated on a clean fact/value distinction. Reason can act as a neutral umpire between conflicting scientific hypotheses but cannot decide among competing values. Although enshrined among the values of science itself, it cannot even prove them the correct ones to adopt. What comes before and after any particular piece of research is inherently value-relevant. Yet, despite these nuances, the core of the scientific process can and should remain value-free.

This standard line sounds clear and defensible. Try it out on some thorny problems in the ethics of research. Does science permit the testing of cosmetics, medicines and surgical techniques on animals? Does it allow vivisection for at least some purposes? The line is that science is neutral. Scientists are party to social debate *qua* citizens and are entitled to refuse on personal grounds but have no view *qua* scientists. This sounds tenable.

But the distinction between scientist and citizen is uneasy. Consider the use of placebos in research where it is deemed important to keep a control group in ignorance. Is science neutral about the testing of a new contraceptive pill on a group of poor Mexican women, some of whom receive placebos and become pregnant? Is it neutral about an American government exercise, in which, allegedly, several hundred black men thought that they were receiving treatment for syphilis, when they were in fact being given placebos as part of a forty-year study of the long-term effects of the disease? Is it neutral about Nazi medical experiments on human beings in concentration camps?

Well, perhaps some knowledge is morally tainted and should not be acquired. (Does this imply that data from Auschwitz should not now be used for benign purposes?) We could try agreeing that 'the values of science' do not permit the pursuit of truth by any and every means, without thereby denying that science itself can be conducted in a value-free way. Science itself implies nothing about what moral constraints scientists should accept, apart from one forbidding the distortion of truth. Admittedly this is a stern constraint of debatable scope. Should researchers blow the whistle, when governments commission research into the working of their policies, suppress embarrassing results and announce that the policies are working splendidly? Should they blow the whistle, when a commercial company distorts their findings in order to sell more of its products or to defend a law suit? Even if an underlying fact/value distinction holds, the ethics of research are not straightforward. Scientists often need courage as well as curiosity in their vocation *qua* scientists. But such reflections, and the codes of professional ethics which they have lately been helping to inspire, standardly assume objectivity at the heart of science. Ethical dilemmas are not allowed to cast doubt on the objectivity of scientific method and its results.

DEEPER QUESTIONS

The official view still sounds tenable. But there are deeper questions, three of which are especially relevant. Firstly, does social science have peculiarities which are masked by a discussion of science at large? Secondly, granted what was said about objectivity in earlier chapters, can theory-ladenness be kept sufficiently distinct from value-ladenness? Thirdly, can the social sciences steer clear of arguments for and against relativism in ethics?

(1) Values in social science

If meaning is 'peculiar to life and to the historical world', then values are central to social science. This may seem to imply only that we need to study what people value in order to understand their actions. That Jehovah's Witnesses act in ways guided by the Bible is no more or less a fact than the fact that cats catch mice. The variety of cultures and values may complicate the work of the social sciences; but no threat to value-neutrality seems to follow from taking meanings seriously.

Why might it? Well, let us focus on the kind of judgements involved in understanding actions and practices from within. The social world is presumed to make sense to its inhabitants but they are not infallible guides to it. Perhaps they cannot be radically mistaken about a world constituted by beliefs, relations and rules, of which they are the conscious embodiments. But their own accounts of it are not always complete and correct. Individuals can mistake their own desires, motives and beliefs, for instance when confused or self-deceived. They can hold inconsistent desires and beliefs, so that Jack's report that he believes p does not let one infer that he does not believe q, even though p implies *not-q*. Different individuals may give conflicting accounts of their shared world, for example of what it means to be a Catholic, conservative or social worker. Besides, singly or severally, they may produce deliberately misleading accounts, especially if they regard the

enquiring social scientist as an intruder. Enquirers therefore cannot merely be credulous chroniclers. They have to judge the
accounts offered. The scope for misapprehension widens further
when we turn to Weber's 'explanatory understanding' (p.150).
The problem is not confined to the enquirer. When a political
party campaigns for better public services, encouraged by opinion
polls showing handsome majority support, and loses the election,
it wonders what was truly moving the voters. When a church with
a traditionally male priesthood is contemplating women priests
and trying to decide whether this innovation is progress or be-
trayal, it searches its understanding of its own tradition. Social
actors, no less than social enquirers, wrestle with the complexity of
the individual psyche and of the cultural webs which surround it.
Since this struggle is itself a source of change, they cannot detach
themselves from a scene which is kept moving by their very efforts
to understand it.

Social scientists might like to view the social world with
Olympian detachment. But explanatory understanding sets
them at least some of the actors' problems. The spectator does
not always see more of the game than the player. Economists, for
example, cannot perch so high above business people, accountants, Treasury civil servants, workers and consumers that they
can peer omnisciently down on their stumblings. Yet judge they
must. Which of the actors' beliefs are to be believed? Which
transactions are significant? Which forecasts will be influential?
In judging, they stand partly inside and partly outside the economic game. Since economics is itself an activity conducted in
public, economists are often directly players as well as spectators.
Economics thus differs from physics. Physicists do not judge stories about the world told by atoms. Atoms tell no stories, whereas
economic agents do; and an economist who thinks these stories
significant cannot avoid deciding which to believe.

Since the actors' stories are full of value-judgements, it may
seem that economics must include judgements on these judgements too. But here we need to tread warily, since it is
not obvious that spectators must take sides in this way. As an
example to think about, consider a functionalist analysis of
Victorian values, inspired by a Marxist theory of ideology.

Virtuous Victorians grounded their ideas of duty in contemporary Christianity. The churches offered stern guidance on the living of a Christian life, the acceptance of one's station and its duties and the importance of respectability. They invoked this framework to explain and justify their attitudes towards children, criminals, subject races, the insane, women who conceived out of wedlock and others in need of a paternal hand. From a Marxist point of view, however, Victorian Christianity was an ideology with various functions. By getting people to think of social life in moral terms, it masked the economic basis of society, the economic forces and relations of production and the economic interests of the ruling and working classes. It helped to legitimate government as serving the common good of all, rather than the interests of a ruling class. It consoled those whose life was harsh by assuring them that matters were thus ordained and that humility would be rewarded hereafter.

These perspectives are askance, rather than flatly opposed. The churches were not at all blind to social changes wrought by the industrial revolution or to the evils of mammon. They conducted industrial missions among the poor and reminded the wealthy that riches are no ticket to the kingdom of heaven. But they set all this out in moral terms alien to a functionalist account. Is the functionalist interpretation neutral or does it imply that Victorian value-judgements were false? It sounds neutral. To call a practice 'functional' is to express neither approval nor disapproval. Some functionalists are conservatives, who approve of whatever serves to keep an existing system stable. Some are Marxists on the look out for whatever is functional for the capitalist system, so that revolutionary thought and action can set about subverting it. Functionalism itself seems to allow either attitude.

Yes; but notice that both attitudes presume that what is functional is thereby explanatory. The actors have a different account of why they believe and act as they do. Christians can agree that the prevalence of Christian beliefs has social consequences, but they cannot agree to a social explanation of why they hold them. The inside story is cast in terms of a spiritual ontology and of good reasons for belief. The functional story subverts these self-images. It may seem to leave room for the inside story, but in fact it undercuts it. Christianity serves its social functions only if sincerely believed. Sincerity includes regarding the internal spiritual story as grounded in truth. From within, any social functions of Christianity are not reasons for holding Christian beliefs. That follows from the proposition that sincerity is crucial for social success. Christians can still learn from functionalists, for instance when fashioning a Christian message suited to the situation of an industrial proletariat. But they are bound to reject an account of why they believe what they do, in which social functions do the explanatory work.

Conversely, therefore, to contend that functions do all the work is to deny the truth of some of the actors' beliefs. Where these beliefs spin fact, theory and value together into an integrated account of how one should live, it is to dispute the truth of some moral beliefs. Is it also to counter those beliefs with an alternative world view or merely to suspend judgement? The question brings us to the second deep matter.

(2) Value-ladenness and theory-ladenness

Pragmatism sought to convince us in Chapter 4 that the mind is always active in choosing what to accept, revise or reject; that there are no facts prior to interpretation; and hence that logic and experience cannot dictate what it is rational to believe. Since the 'power of its own' by which the bee transformed its material before laying it up in the understanding was left mysterious, there is a splendid opening for the suggestion that value-judgements are pervasive throughout what passes for knowledge. Interpretation and choice among theories have an irreducibly normative element, stemming from rules and criteria for rational acceptance which are value-laden. This normative element in the web of belief influences how we choose and define the relevant concepts, how we apply them, and how we fit the resulting interpretations together. The suggestion is that all three phases of the exercise are rule-governed in a manner which conflicts with Weber's assurance that the conduct of science itself is (or can be) a value-free pursuit of truth.

For an example, take the running dispute about the extent of poverty in Britain. There have been three alternative conceptions of poverty. B. S. Rowntree's (1901) study defined it in terms of *subsistence* – an income below that 'sufficient to obtain the minimum necessaries for the maintenance of merely physical efficiency' (1901, p.86). The necessaries included clothes, fuel and some other items but had mainly to do with a basic diet. This definition was used by W. H. Beveridge in his (1942) Report, which inspired the post-war welfare state. The resulting rates for national assistance and national insurance presently came to seem too low, however, and a kinder definition of poverty in terms of *basic needs* took shape in the 1970s. The International Labour Office in 1976 specified two components: 'minimum requirements of a family for private consumption' (food, shelter, clothing and some furniture and equipment) and 'essential services provided by and for the community at large, such as safe drinking water, sanitation, public transport and health education and cultural facilities' (1976, pp.24–25). This gesture to community well-being stands in interesting contrast to the individual and physical focus of Rowntree. But it sets problems of what to include, which, some critics argue, can be met only by shifting to a social conception in terms of *relative deprivation* as 'the only way poverty can be defined objectively and applied consistently' (Townsend, 1979). People are 'relatively deprived' if their resources do not let them meet the social demands of membership of their society – expectations which are then translated into an income threshold required for meeting them.

These three conceptions have very different implications for what counts as poverty and so for what is involved in policies to relieve it. If poverty is a matter of relative deprivation, then the nutritional aspect of people's diet is only part of what must be reckoned with. There is more to food than calories, since what one eats, how it is cooked, where and with whom it is eaten are deeply part of oneself and one's social identity. There is more to deprivation than lack of calories, clothing, shelter and other physical necessaries. A social dimension opens up, thus challenging the previous assumption that one can discern poverty just by scrutinising individuals. Relativity also means that, when the rich become richer, the poor thereby become poorer. Thus television sets were too rare in Britain in 1945 for anyone to be deprived for lack of them. But it can be argued nowadays that those too poor to afford one are denied a cultural facility essential to full citizenship: think about old people, who live alone because their families have grown up to be socially and geographically mobile. This line of thought soon becomes more contentious than Townsend's 'defined objectively and applied consistently' might suggest. If it is allowed, there is no prospect of eliminating poverty in an unequal society, whereas Beveridge could suppose that he was tackling a soluble problem. As to that, however, social changes, like longer life (thanks to the National Health Service), structural unemployment and single parenthood, have undermined his insurance-based scheme and increased the distance still to go.

Enough has been said, I hope, to show that everything about poverty is thoroughly contested. Which conception is to be rationally preferred? This theoretical dispute carries over both to the facts of poverty and to the likely effects of policies intended to reduce it. Nor is poverty a rare example. Other concepts with this contested yet action-guiding character are power, freedom, crime or democracy, to pick notorious examples. The list grows swiftly and soon promises to extend to the guiding concepts of science and epistemology. Could it be that our difficulties in settling on the correct analysis of, for instance, causation, explanation, understanding and knowledge stem from failure to realise that an element of value-judgement is always involved?

Crucially, however, the case for holding that what is theory-laden is thereby value-laden is not so easily made and, even if it were to succeed, we would not need to espouse relativism and despair of objectivity without further ado.

Firstly, there may yet be rational grounds for choosing between theories and for preferring one definition of a concept to another. In Plato's dialogues, the definitions of, for instance, courage, knowledge or justice, which are the start of wisdom on these topics, are reached, and can only be reached, after long Socratic discussion. Rationalists in this tradition have always held that there are true definitions of concepts to be had,

meaning definitions which capture the essence of the thing defined. The system-builders of the scientific revolution, like
Descartes, regarded their axioms as a matter for discovery and
none the less *a priori* for that. Kant attempted to identify the
unique basic categories for different realms of conceptual thinking. More recently, John Rawls presented *A Theory of Justice* (1971)
as offering a 'conception' of justice with strong claims to capture
the true 'concept' of justice (although his (1993) book takes a
different line). Such approaches make it an objective question
whether poverty involves relative deprivation; and the need to
argue the question out does not prove otherwise. The belief
that there is a distinct realm of theoretical truth within the mind's
grasp is unfashionable but still defensible.

Secondly, even if theoretical understanding does turn out not to
be fully distinct from ethical understanding, this may be no disaster. After all, we might be glad to find that social science has
ethical implications! It would mean that moral disputes about the
merit of social policies could bear on the truth of the theories
which implied them. But why rule that out? What exactly leads
one to assume that a moral dispute about the scope and limits of
the state's duty to relieve poverty has no implications for a theoretical dispute about the correct analysis of the concept of poverty? Advocates of the familiar fact/value distinction commonly
suppose that, because there is no objectivity in ethics, scientific
judgements cannot both be objective and entail moral conclusions. Yes, but are we forced to accept the familiar distinction
or concede that one difference between science and ethics is that
science is objective and ethics relative?

(3) Relativism in ethics?

When Condorcet wrote that 'truth, virtue and happiness are
bound together with an indissoluble chain', he did not doubt that
virtue was a proper subject for science. He supposed ethics to be a
branch of knowledge directed to improving life both individually
and collectively. Human goals were pretty self-evident, for example health, wealth and happiness; or perhaps happiness was the
only goal, with evident means to it, like health, wealth, liberty and

justice, and the 'moral sciences' poised to discover how to translate them into policies. In any event, the project included moral progress, 'virtue' being a matter of dispositions which we do well to identify and cultivate both for our own benefit and as a source of mutual benefit in our social relations. Ethics is the agriculture of the mind.

In full flush this Enlightenment optimism presumes that human nature is the same everywhere, that goals harmonise, that the means to them are discoverable and that science can be set an agenda accordingly. It thus presents obvious targets. The assumption of harmony looks instantly vulnerable. But it is less essential than the rest. There is also a line of Enlightenment thinking, starting with Hobbes, which builds conflict deep into the analysis of individuals and society and then gives science the task of engineering a harmony, even if it remains fragile. Provided that conflict is always due to ignorance, it can be finally dispelled through the growth of knowledge, so that, as Condorcet proclaimed, 'the sun will one day shine only on free men who own no other light than their reason'.

Threats to the assumption of a universal human nature are more fundamental. Hume, for all his usual scepticism, held that

Ambition, avarice, self-love, vanity, friendship, generosity, public spirit: these passions, mixed in various degrees and distributed through society, have been from the beginning of the world and still are the source of all the actions and enterprises, which have ever been observed among mankind . . . Mankind are so much the same, in all times and places, that history informs us of nothing new or strange in this particular. (1748, Section VIII, Part I, 65)

Few people, I suspect, would still agree. Variety seems the plainest fact of life, amply confirmed by anthropology and, indeed, history, and giving no surprise to anyone who believes that differences in social structure and culture make for differences in passions and actions.

This might not matter for ethics, however, if we still thought in terms of a moral fabric external to human life and believed that science could seek out causes, functions, reasons, purposes and meanings all at once. In that case we could recognise variety, while still holding that there is a single set of moral truths which everyone ought to accept. But we opened the hermeneutic case with Dilthey's remark that 'life has no meaning outside itself'. A thoroughly destructive relativism seems to follow at once.

Ethical relativism is not flatly sceptical about all claims that moral beliefs can be true or false. Some relativists hold that in Rome one should do as the Romans do and in Athens do as the Athenians do; or that you are truly bound by your commitments and I by mine. But they are united in denial that there are any universal moral principles which might allow ethics its traditional claims to objectivity. Any power or right of moral beliefs to guide action can only be of local origin – hence the examples of social and personal origin just given. The plain fact that moral beliefs vary enormously among people, periods and cultures is thus an incitement to relativism, even if it does not entail anything specific. Many relativists do then advance to a full-blooded scepticism. On the social front, a functional explanation of norms, like the Marxist analysis of Victorian religion, makes it easy to account for the power of beliefs to guide action while denying their right to do so. On the personal front, a philosophical theory is more appropriate, for instance the emotivist theory that moral statements are expressions of the speaker's attitude and cannot entitle anyone to act on them, not even the speaker.

Formally, the previous paragraph implies nothing. The mere fact of variety proves nothing in itself. It does not prove that every moral belief is objectively false; nor that every moral belief is true for those who subscribe to it. It does not even prove that there are no underlying moral beliefs, like a duty to care for one's parents, which are universal, if allowance is made for differences in context. Ethical relativism remains disputable in all versions, pending further argument. But the diversity of beliefs, their tendency to vary with social position and personality-type and the general appeal of the fact/value distinction combine to make relativism in ethics a common accompaniment to the standard view about value-neutrality in social science. Yet there remain theories of ethics which attempt to preserve an objective and rational basis without appealing to traditional ideas of an external moral fabric. Two of them are especially relevant to social science.

One is utilitarianism, which maintains that, in Mill's words, 'actions are right in proportion as they tend to promote happiness' (1861, Chapter 2). The basic line is that all human beings desire happiness. To head off the objection about human variety, 'happiness' or 'utility' is standardly so defined that *whatever* anyone wants can be described in utility-seeking terms, as with Rational Choice theory earlier. Although we cannot even try to assess its merits as moral philosophy here, there is no mistaking the influence of Utilitarianism in the social sciences, especially economics. If all action can be analysed universally as motivated by preferences, then one can cheerfully agree that preferences vary as much as you please. If human welfare is next defined in terms of the satisfaction of preferences, then social science has plenty to say about conditions and policies for satisfying preferences, singly or in combination, and can even comment on which preferences to encourage or sanction. Relativism thus fails to subvert objectivity.

The other attempt is Kant's ethic of duty. Here the idea is to achieve objectivity by reflecting on the very notion of a moral reason for action. Kant argued that there is an objective test for any purported ethics: are its maxims universal, impartial and impersonal? Thus it *could not possibly* be right for me to break a promise to you, unless it would also be right for you to break a similar promise to me, since the form of the underlying maxim must be that *all* such promises should be kept. They are to be kept, moreover, not because they are a means to some end which we (or some of us) happen to have – not even the sum of human happiness – but simply because they have been made. In his language, a moral imperative is 'categorical' (unconditional), whereas imperatives of prudence are 'hypothetical' (applying only *if* one wants the consequences of obeying them). Relations between 'autonomous' (truly free) agents are guided by the categorical imperative, since otherwise we would be using others as the means to our own ends and thus failing to apply maxims impartially. To claim autonomy for oneself is to recognise the same claim by others. From this perspective, a moral community is 'a kingdom of ends', where autonomous agents respect one another's autonomy under the impartial aegis of law (the

Kantian *Rechtsstaat).* Reason thus arrives at objective criteria by which to umpire between competing theories of ethics and to filter out at least some inadequate moral codes. Reflection lets us characterise the moral point of view, despite efforts by relativists to deny that there is one.

Utilitarianism thus offers a science of human welfare, grounded in objective properties of human nature. Kant offers an objective analysis of the very idea of morality. Both approaches continue to influence the social sciences. Both, for instance, are deeply involved in theories of democracy and how to improve it. The common ground lies in the broad connections between reason, freedom and morality, which mark out what is loosely called liberalism. Advocates of a standard fact/value distinction will no doubt interrupt here, to complain that liberals have no business trying to mix science and ethics in such ways, especially since there is an evident tension between utilitarian social welfare and Kantian individual freedoms. But, even if liberalism is indeed an 'ideology' and one prone to deep internal disputes, we should beware of simply assuming that it therefore cannot be an exercise in objective science and ethics.

There are other current attempts at objectivity in moral and political philosophy, which try to come to terms with the growing pluralism of modern societies without yielding to relativism. But Kant and utilitarianism retain their importance and give us enough for final thought about value-neutrality. Utilitarians could be said to accept the relativity of values as such but then to recover the high ground by offering a science of preference-satisfaction. Kantians do not concede the relativity of values, only the variety of confusion about them. But they do not go on to prescribe a particular moral code or detailed political constitution. Reason in ethics and politics is content with universal preconditions, which rule some codes and constitutions out but are liberal about others. Both philosophies depend on a view of human nature and make claims in what used to be called 'moral psychology'. These claims lead to different answers about value-neutrality in the social sciences and remind us that there is no single answer to the question.

CONCLUSION

'Truth, virtue and happiness are bound together with an indissoluble chain.' Two centuries later this seems too bold and simple. The current official line is that science describes, interprets and explains but cannot justify. It supplies knowledge and gives power to change the world, but its prescriptions are all of the form 'tell us what you want and we will tell you how to achieve it'. Scientists may have special responsibilities because they conduct the research and foresee how it can be used; but one of these duties is to exclude value-judgements from science itself. That goes for the social sciences too, even though the social world is permeated with values and has social scientists among its inhabitants. Science has nothing categorical to say about virtue.

The wisdom of this line is apparently reinforced by drawing the fact/value distinction and pointing to the huge variety of values among individuals and groups. That almost makes value-judgements relative both as a matter of moral philosophy and as a fact of life. If so, a science with moral implications would forfeit its claim to be a science. But we must take care not to beg the central question. There are ways of disputing the fact/value distinction and what is often done in its name. In the present state of moral philosophy, we are not forced to plead for value-neutrality in order to make the best of a bad job. Besides, we have found some reason to think that social life cannot be understood from within without judging the truth of some of the moral beliefs which the actors hold. Social actors certainly have conflicting theories about themselves, the social world and their place in it. Some of these theories conflict with the enquirer's. The crux is whether to define 'moral' broadly enough to make some of these disagreements into moral ones. To keep the enquiry clean by imposing the fact/value distinction would beg the question.

To return to the beginning, then, we are not yet clear what the hermeneutic imperative implies about relativism. An interpretative social science, which relies on methods for rationally reconstructing subjective and intersubjective meanings from within, seems bound to be caught holding itself up by its own bootstraps. Hence we cannot draw conclusions about

value-neutrality, until we have thought further about the allegedly objective, detached and universal character of a scientific
standpoint. What started as a query about moral progress will
have to be continued in the next chapter.

CHAPTER 11

Rationality and relativism

If there are no facts prior to interpretation, must claims to knowledge of the world always be relative to some set of beliefs held at a particular time and place? That is the problem of knowledge as it emerged in earlier chapters. If action is to be understood by rationally reconstructing its meaning from within, we have a 'double hermeneutic' and a further shove towards relativism. The problem of Other Minds takes on daunting form. Yet, even if daunting in the abstract, it seems easy enough in practice. People often succeed in communicating what is in their minds. Barriers of culture and period make the task harder. But archaeologists perform it, when they reconstruct an ancient city from ash, bone and broken pottery. Historians perform it, when they read the story of feudalism from old parish registers and other archives. Anthropologists perform it, when they penetrate a distant language and culture and discover, for instance, that the Azande believe in witches or that the Nuer classify human twins as birds.

How is it done? Here are two conflicting lines of thought. One is that, since different peoples inhabit intellectual worlds very unlike our own, the key is to be entirely open-minded about what an enquiry may find. The other is that we could not chart these differences, nor justify a claim to have done so correctly, unless we could rely on Other Minds to be basically like us; so the key is to make these similarities our bridgehead. One line leads to some version of relativism, the other to some version of universalism. Which is right or whether they can be combined is a matter of fierce debate and crucial for the proper character of social science.

224

Philosophically, the task is indeed daunting, and not only when the actors studied are distant or dead. Everyday understanding too involves feats of interpretation, even if everyday actors perform them all the time. We shall begin by stating the problem of Other Minds and seeing why it is indeed problematic. Then we shall turn to Other Cultures and explore the general thesis that to understand a culture involves identifying what its members take to be real and rational. This will invite the question 'by their standards or ours?', leading to difficult issues of rationality and relativism. Having discussed various forms of relativism, we shall be faced with a 'hermeneutic circle' and offered four ways of escape. Concluding comments, I should perhaps say now, will reflect my own view about which is most promising.

OTHER MINDS

The problem is usually posed for beginners with the aid of a sharp distinction between the mental and the physical aspects of persons. How does Jack know what Jill is thinking, feeling, perceiving and wanting – in short, what is going on in Jill's mind? He has only her physical behaviour to go by but this includes the sounds she utters and the marks she makes on paper. He presumes, no doubt, that, just as his own physical behaviour is caused by his mental states, so too is hers caused by hers. He has direct access to his own mental states but not to hers. So, it seems, he has to infer them. Yet how can such inferences be justified?

That does not sound too hard. When Jill bangs her elbow and cries out, or looks at a cat and says 'I see a cat', Jack can reason:

(1) When I bang my elbow, I cry out because I am in pain.
(2) Jill has banged her elbow and cried out.
(3) So she is in pain.

or

(1) There is a cat to see.
(2) When I see one, I (often) say so.
(3) So she has seen the cat and is saying so.

This second inference also carries a hint that, if Jill had said '*Ich sehe eine Katze*', Jack would be on his way to learning the German for 'I see a cat'. In general, then, a plausible initial idea is that we understand the mental contents of Other Minds, including what they mean by their words, by analogy with ourselves.

On reflection, however, the analogy is distinctly peculiar. When Jack sees a cuckoo clock, he can infer that there is a cuckoo inside by analogy with other rustic-looking clocks, whose cuckoos he has observed. The conclusion can be empirically tested, for instance by watching for the little doors to open on the next hour. The inference is an inductive one of the form:

(1) Other clocks with properties f, g, h have property i.
(2) This clock has properties f, g, h.
(3) So it (probably) has property i.

But, if this is the model, it does not apply to his knowledge of Jill or serve to justify his beliefs even about what is likely to be in her mind. He has never observed *any* of her mental states, nor will he. The only mental states which could ever be presented to him are his own. It is as if the inference about the cuckoo clock argued for the presence of an unobservable cuckoo on the grounds that there are a lot of unobservable cuckoos about. In other words, the inference by analogy to Jill's state of mind *presupposes* that she is indeed just like him; and that squarely begs the question. Perhaps, when she reports seeing something red, she experiences what he would experience as seeing something green, if he could have her perceptions; but their shared use of language masks this difference. Perhaps, forsooth, she and others are complex machines lacking any mental states like his. How could he possibly know?

Such sceptical doubts will sound absurd. It may be *logically* possible that people differ radically in their perceptions, while talking and acting in ways which factor this out. It may be *formally* coherent to suppose that Jack is the only human subject in a world of robots. But the obvious retort is that it is too far-fetched to bother with: even if it is logically possible, it is utterly improbable. Yet this retort will not do. If probabilities are a matter of inferring from known cases to similar cases, there are no probabilities where there are no known cases. The sceptic is pointing this out and thus objecting to the way in which the problem of Other Minds has been posed. It is as if we had been inveigled into picturing ourselves as captains of one-person submarines who work solely from instruments, never perceive objects on the seabed directly and certainly never see inside another submarine. In that case, no one could previously have compared instrument-readings with things in the sea so as to warrant present claims about what is probable; and still less have compared things in the sea with instrument-readings inside other submarines. The problem of Other Minds is radically insoluble, the sceptic argues, if approached in this manner.

More is at issue here than Other Minds. The common idea that perceptions are mental effects of external physical causes is also being challenged. But that takes us too far afield. So let us concentrate on the point that Jack's inferences from Jill's behaviour to Jill's mental states are unwarranted, if, ultimately, they rely solely on what he knows about his own mental states in relation to his own behaviour. It could perhaps be used to support a stark behaviourism which flatly denied that anyone, finally including even Jack, has mental states distinct from and causing their behaviour. But we need not take this path. So let us continue to suppose that Jill's wink still differs from her blink in that it conveys a message which she intends Jack to understand, but a message which may be meant to mislead him about her true state of mind. Then the problem of Other Minds is one of justifying inferences which can go astray both in particular ways and generally. How can we admit the need for a double hermeneutic without making such inferences baseless?

Weber's move, as we noted earlier, is to fuse behaviour and action at a basic level of 'direct understanding' (pp.147–51). By 'empathy' we *see* that a man with an axe is chopping wood or that a man with a rifle is aiming it at a target. Then we advance to 'explanatory understanding' by various routes, depending on context and what we want to know. The woodcutter turns out to be earning a living in an economic setting where this is his rational way to go about it. The marksman is bent on avenging the murder of a kinsman in a society where the vendetta is an institution. If we ask how such elaborate discoveries can proceed in a justifiable way, Weber's broadest answer is that actions are, for the most part, 'rational' and that explanatory understanding advances by making their rationality explicit. 'Adequacy at the level of meaning' thus rests on a methodological assumption that rationality holds the key to Other Minds.

This line invites an obvious objection. Do we literally 'see' that the marksman is aiming a rifle? The rifle is a compound of wood and metal. To identify it as a rifle, we need to bring a battery of concepts and a wealth of social knowledge to bear. The proverbial visiting Martian, physically equipped to see what we see, would not see a *rifle*. Indeed we too would not have seen a rifle, if the object seen turned out to be, on closer examination, a walking stick or a dummy. Does empathy not therefore involve inference from physical data? Weber could reply, however, that all perception involves concepts and that there is nothing peculiar about applying concepts which ascribe social functions. Perhaps the visiting Martian does not yet recognise wood or metal either. Yet, if an object made of wood and metal is a visible object, so is a rifle. Equally, every perceptual judgement lays a bet. If the rifle turns out to be a plastic fake, it was a mistake to identify it as a rifle; but also wrong to identify it as an object made of wood and metal. The identification of physical objects and physical behaviour involves interpretation. Rifles set no further problem.

That style of reply will suit advocates of naturalism, because it locates actions in the same perceptual frame as other events. Marksmen aiming rifles are no more epistemologically awkward than cats hunting mice. Admittedly the explanatory understanding required to introduce vendettas into the story is more complex. But, even if it requires a social narrative told from the inside, all will finally be cashed out 'at the causal level' in terms acceptable to a unified scientific method. Hence, naturalists can argue, the problem of Other Minds is finally no more than a tricky example of a wider problem of Knowledge.

On the other hand, a Wittgensteinian might retort, it is far from plain that vendettas can be introduced at all into an account grounded so firmly in individual actions whose subjective meaning is directly perceived. We distinguished earlier between the meaning of an action and what the actor meant by it. In Wittgensteinian spirit, we then suggested that the latter might depend on the former, as moves in a game depend on there being rules which constitute the game. In that case subjective meanings cannot be prior to intersubjective meanings; and Weber is mistaken in supposing that empathy is basic to the understanding of social action. Consequently, a Wittgensteinian might continue, there is a distinct and peculiar problem of Other Minds and it does not have an individualistic solution. Granted that, in general, there are no percepts without concepts and no facts without interpretation, there is still a special requirement that the understanding of action involves prior understanding of social practices. Nothing said so far indicates how we can justify claims to identify the practices which hold the key to the problem.

This objection may not sound cogent for personal relations between Jack and Jill. Perhaps he will not understand her bid of two Clubs unless he is a Bridge player and, moreover, familiar with the conventions of the Acol system of bidding. But her yell when she sits on a pin hardly seems to presuppose rules and practices; nor, he hopes, are the emotions displayed in their love letters to one another merely moves in a game of romance. But, even if this were granted, the Wittgensteinian objection still has force when it comes to vendettas, if only because it may not matter for the understanding of moves in the vendetta game whether or not the actors feel the emotions expressed. So let us next turn to the institutional aspects of the problem of Other Minds.

OTHER CULTURES

Here too there is much to be said for Weber's suggestion that rationality holds the key. But the idea now becomes more open-ended. If the ritual suicide of a Samurai is rendered rational by locating it in the context of the Bushido code of honour, then the mind of the actor is thereby made less opaque. That context, or kind of context, does not help in understanding the suicide of a London teenager, however. Reasons for action which stem from institutions are likely to be peculiar to those institutions. Hence this version of the hermeneutic imperative seems to come with an inbuilt relativism. Action is rational relative to context; there is nothing universal about contexts.

Anthropology is a glorious source of examples to illustrate the theme. One in particular has entered philosophical consciousness and, despite many newer ones, it remains markedly enlightening. E. Evans-Pritchard's *Witchcraft, Oracles and Magic among the Azande*, published in 1937, offers a graphic way to focus on the role of rationality in understanding a culture from within and on the scope for relativism in respecting cultural differences. It draws a portrait of a culture whose world differs from ours in its furniture and workings, and it does so from the inside.

In *Witchcraft, Oracles and Magic among the Azande* Evans-Pritchard explored a social world where much of what occurred was deemed to be due to witchcraft and where the malign activities of witches could be diagnosed with the help of oracles and (sometimes) countered by magic. Thus, if a barn collapsed, overtly because of termites, the owner would want to know why *his* barn had been so afflicted. By consulting oracles, he sought to learn the source and character of the curse on his affairs. Then he could engage a witchdoctor to perform vengeance-magic to neutralise it. The whole business was orderly and commonplace, witches being active throughout everyday life and precautions and remedies being woven into the fabric of ordinary living. Indeed Evans-Pritchard reports that he ran his own household in accordance with Zande beliefs and norms for eighteen months and found it entirely satisfactory. (Zande is the singular term, Azande the plural.)

The Azande emerge from his study as subtle and often scientific thinkers, given their presumptions about the prevalence of witches. In particular, there was method in their use of oracles, which formed a hierarchy. The crudest was consulted by use of a rubbing board in a casual way and was held merely to give a rough indication of trouble. Enquiries were then addressed to the more sophisticated poison-oracle in the form of yes-or-no questions. To answer each question, the priest fed drugged grain, called *benge*, to two chickens in turn. In the first trial, the death of the chicken would mean 'yes', and in the second the death of the chicken would mean 'no'. The question would thus receive an incoherent answer, if the *benge* was, for instance, so strong that it killed both chickens or so weak that both survived. A coherent answer was forthcoming only if the same dose produced different results − a duly scientific precaution. All the same, the enquirer could still hesitate, since the ritual of preparing the *benge* could have been wrongly performed or even have been invaded by witchcraft. In that case a final appeal could be made to the King's oracle. In sum:

Witchcraft, oracles and magic form an intellectually coherent system. Each explains and proves the others. Death is a proof of witchcraft. It is avenged by magic. The achievement of vengeance-magic is proved by the poison-oracle. The accuracy of the poison-oracle is determined by the King's oracle, which is above suspicion. (1937, p.388)

Yet Evans-Pritchard did not find the system fully coherent. 'It is an inevitable conclusion from Zande descriptions of witchcraft that it is not an objective condition . . . Witches, as Azande conceive them, cannot exist' (1937, p.63). Among the incoherences was the Zande belief that every descendent of a witch is automatically a witch too. That should have meant that, by the time of Evans-Pritchard's visit, every Zande was a witch; yet the Azande did not regard everyone as a witch.

Azande see the sense of this argument but they do not accept its conclusions, and it would involve the whole notion of witchcraft in contradiction, if they were to do so . . . Azande do not perceive the contradiction as we perceive it because they have no theoretical interest in the subject, and those situations in which they express their belief in witchcraft do not force the problem upon them. (1937, pp.24-25)

Equally, although the oracles were conducted in scientific spirit, they were often wrong in their claims about whether the threat of witchcraft had been lifted, by the test of whether further disagreeable events occurred. But this was never allowed to throw doubt on the basic theory. Failures were accounted for by declaring that further witches were involved or by deciding that there had been a flaw in the rituals or in any other way which upheld the general soundness of the system:

232 The philosophy of social science

Azande see as well as we that the failure of their oracle to prophesy truly calls for explanation, but so entangled are they in mystical notions that they must make use of them to account for the failure. The contradiction between experience and one mystical notion is explained by reference to other mystical notions. (1937, p.338)

Overall, Evans-Pritchard deemed the Azande to be rational after our manner, although within the limits of an intellectual system which rested on false or even contradictory beliefs and whose failures were obscured by appeal to mystical notions. Crucially:

In this web of belief every strand depends on every other strand and a Zande cannot get out of its meshes because it is the only world he knows. The web is not an external structure in which he is enclosed. It is the texture of his thought and he cannot think that his thought is wrong. (1937, p.195)

Evans-Pritchard's approach relies throughout on a distinction between what is scientifically rational and what is mystical. Rationally speaking, the Azande are like us in their attempt to predict and control their world. They reason from premises to conclusions as we do, with the same respect for experiment and scientific method. By contrast, their mystical notions are their own and threaten to encroach on this objective logic, for instance by blocking their critical thinking about experimental evidence. By combining logical and mystical thinking they spin a web which they cannot escape because they cannot think that their thought is wrong.

This may all sound like an empirical answer to an empirical question: what beliefs about the world and how it is ordered do the Azande happen to hold? Answer: they turn out to share our ideas of rationality but to adapt them to the local context. Methodologically, the general strategy seems to be: assume nothing; expect to find beliefs which strike us as irrational; but make sense of them by rendering them rational in their local context. In upshot, other cultures emerge as rational in the main, provided that rationality is suitably tempered with a modest element of relativism.

LIMITS TO EMPIRICISM?

But question and answer become less empirical, when we reflect that Evans-Pritchard had to penetrate the language of the Azande in order to identify their conceptual scheme and then describe their 'web of belief' in English. Reading his book, one notices how much common ground it assumes. For example, he takes it for granted that he, the Azande and his readers all know a tree when they see one and hence that there is a Zande word for a tree, which applies when a visible tree is the topic of conversation, and that, when he translates it as 'tree', his readers will understand. This sounds banal; but it involves not only some empirical hypotheses but also an assumption which, arguably, is not empirical at all. The hypotheses are that he has found the right word for 'tree' and that it marks a significant element in the Zande classification of physical objects. These are hypotheses in the sense that they guide his first steps but could be discarded later, if the balance of interpretation starts to favour a somewhat different scheme of reference and classification. But such adjustments could not be wholesale, since they would need to be made against a background of secure translations. He could be wrong about the word for 'tree' only if he were sure by then of the meaning of many other words. He assumes throughout that, for the most part, the Azande perceive what he perceives and classify perceived objects into kinds in ways and for everyday purposes which he and they share.

Evans-Pritchard certainly makes this assumption; and, since it works out well, he is not led to question it. Indeed, one is inclined to add, it works out so well that it is amply confirmed; and, provided that he could have discarded it if experience had proved recalcitrant, why doubt that it is a general empirical hypothesis? After all, schemes of classification vary enormously and it sounds an empirical question how different cultures in fact classify. On a full-blown relativist view there is no theoretical limit to possible variations. Why think otherwise?

Here is what could be called a 'rationalist' reply. Translation does not go by telepathy. Initial translations can be made only by mapping Zande utterances in the presence of objects and events onto (in this case) English words and sentences which English-speakers would regard as correctly used in the circumstances. The core of 'correct' use is the making of assertions which are true. Hence all translation depends on equating what the speakers of different languages could truly say in describing simple objects and events, which present themselves to all parties in the same way. The success of translation does not show empirically that this is the case, since the first translations inevitably presuppose such shared perceptions. Or, to be exact, while translation does prove empirically that one is dealing with a language, rather than merely complex behaviour as perhaps with apes or bees, it does not prove that the percepts and the basics of the classificatory scheme *happen* to be like ours, since that is an unavoidable pre-supposition. Equally, even if a particular translation can be re-vised later, it can be judged more likely wrong than right only if enough of the local language has been mapped onto this universal scheme to give warrant to the judgement.

Similarly, the 'rationalist' continues, all translation presupposes a basic, universal rationality, whose purely logical elements are negation, non-contradiction and simple inference. Just try suppos-ing otherwise. For instance, try supposing that speakers of lan-guage L so relate sentences P, Q, $P * Q$ and $!Q$ that, given P and $P * Q$ one may infer $!Q$; and try supposing in particular that, with P securely translated as 'it is raining', there is a question whether Q means 'it is not raining' or 'the gods are angry'. Take '*' and '!' to be logical operators (despite a risk of begging the question). The obvious suggestion is that the inference in L translates as:

(1) It is raining.
(2) If it is raining, then the gods are angry.
(3) So the gods are angry.

But now try supposing that the logic of L differs radically from ours. Suppose, for instance, that 'Q' means 'it is not raining', '*' means 'if . . . then not', and '!' means 'So':

(1) It is raining.
(2) If it is raining, then it is not raining.

(3) So it is not raining.

or try 'Q' as 'the gods are angry', '*' as 'if . . . then', and '!' as not:

(1) It is raining.
(2) If it is raining, then the gods are angry.
(3) So the gods are not angry.

We are thus contemplating a logic where, apparently, 'P' implies 'not-P', and hence where anything implies anything, unless, of course, there are theoretical limits to possible variety of interpretation.

Notice, however, that these last two 'inferences' cannot possibly have been correctly translated into English. None of the logical words involved means what 'not' means in English. This is not merely being parochial. We are apparently contemplating a logic where 'P' implies its own negation and so implies whatever one pleases. Since so anarchic a logic is no logic, it cannot be translated into any language where meanings depend on the constraints of negation. Since an anarchic 'language' is not a language, users of such a 'logic' would not have a language. The whole speculation is therefore unintelligible to us and we may fairly ask whether there is any possible sense in which it is possible at all.

The previous two paragraphs, taken together, suggest that translation, and hence understanding, starts by establishing a 'bridgehead' in the unknown language, which it assembles from universal materials. The starting point is *a priori*:

To establish a bridgehead, by which I mean a set of utterances definitive of the standard meanings of words, [the anthropologist] has to assume that he and the natives share the same perceptions and make the same empirical judgements in simple situations. This involves assumptions about empirical truth and reference, which in turn involve crediting the natives with his own skeletal notion of logical reasoning . . . There will be better reason to accept his account than to reject it, only if he makes most native beliefs coherent and rational and most empirical beliefs in addition true. These notions are *a priori* in the sense that they belong to his tools and not to his discoveries, providing the yardsticks by which he accepts or rejects possible interpretations. (Hollis, 1968, p.246)

This bald pronouncement invites a charge of foreclosing on areas of vigorous discussion, especially if one also applies it to understanding ('translation') within a single language or culture. Psychologists are likely to retort that people vary greatly in how they perceive the world, with psycholinguists quick to connect variations in perception to differences in language. Logicians are likely to challenge the claim for a universal logical core by pointing to three-valued and other alternative logics and to disputes about the nature of logic, for instance between classical and intuitionist theories. The bridgehead argument therefore needs to be deployed with care, if it is to carry conviction. The question concerns 'the very idea of a conceptual scheme' (the title of an influential paper by Davidson in Davidson (1984)) and how much diversity there can be. To tackle it, we need next to distinguish various forms of relativism.

FORMS OF RELATIVISM

Return, for a moment, to the initial Positive idea of knowledge, where the world awaited the scientist and provided objective tests of scientific hypotheses. Claims to scientific knowledge had to square with the facts of observation, or, when they went beyond observation, had at least to conform to the laws of logic. There was thus nothing 'relative' about the tests for what was empirically false and for what was logically impossible. But that left obvious scope for relativism on two other fronts, moral and conceptual. Furthermore, the correctives to Positivism put forward by Pragmatists and others in Chapter 4 open the way to relativism about 'facts of observation' and about the objectivity of logic and truth.

(1) Moral relativism

Although not central to this chapter, the case for moral relativism is readily grasped. As we saw earlier, it is easy to argue that there

are no facts, moral or otherwise, to test moral beliefs for truth and
falsity. Nor does the demand that moral beliefs be consistent with
one another do much to restrict them. Hence the plain fact that
they vary enormously among people, periods and cultures is an
invitation to relativism. Since we have already explored the case, I
shall not repeat it here. But two general points are worth under-
lining. One is that moral relativists need not be moral sceptics,
except about absolute and universal principles. It is consistent
with relativism to hold that in Rome one should do as the
Romans do and in Athens do as the Athenians do; or that you
are truly bound by your commitments and I by mine. Relativists
may be objectivists, although they may also not be. The other is
that the mere fact of variety proves nothing in itself. It does not
prove that every moral belief is objectively false; nor that every
moral belief is true for those who subscribe to it. It does not even
prove that there are no underlying moral beliefs, like a duty to
care for one's parents, which are universal, if allowance is made
for differences in context. Hence moral relativism, however familiar and tempting, remains instructively disputable in all versions.

(2) Conceptual relativism

Granted that experience and logic underdetermine what it is
rational to believe about the world, there is plenty of slack for
conceptual schemes to take up in different ways. Cultures vary
hugely in how they classify, conceptualise and order their experience. One scheme furnishes the world with tree spirits and regards thunderstorms as acts of divine displeasure, whereas
another works with subatomic particles and a theory of kinetic
energy. Westerners organise their experience and make sense of it
by means of categories of space, time, causation, number, agency
and persons, for instance, which are plainly not universal, at least
in their details. Other cultures do not have our notion of the self
and some seem to have no notion of personal identity at all. Even
within a single culture deep conceptual divergences are common,
witness the fierce philosophical disputes about self, mind and body
which permeate the philosophy of mind or the radical conflicts
about the ultimate nature of matter in theoretical physics.

That conceptual schemes do vary enormously is undeniable. But, as with moral relativism, we must go carefully. Formally, variety is again no disproof of the idea that there is a single truth to seek about the underlying order of things or about the terms in which the human mind can make coherent sense of experience. Thus Logical Positivists deny all traditional claims to objectivity in ethics and recognise the fact of conceptual variety in science. But they still regard rival claims about the rational order in experience as rival hypotheses open in principle to the test of experience. Conceptual variety does not force one to abandon the idea of an absolute world order, existing as, so to speak, God understands it to be, even if it weakens one's confidence that we yet know much about it.

But our earlier discussion of theory and experience makes for the more challenging thought that conceptual schemes impose order, rather than discover it. Recall Evans-Pritchard's remark that a Zande cannot escape his web of belief, because 'it is the only world he knows' and because 'it is the texture of his thought and he cannot think that his thought is wrong'. If this were precisely true, it would apply equally to every 'web of belief', including the one enclosing Evans-Pritchard and ourselves. Otherwise the Zande could presumably escape by dialogue with Evans-Pritchard, listening to the BBC World Service or travelling abroad. If escape is truly impossible, because a conceptual scheme is not an 'external structure' but 'the texture of his thought', conceptual relativism holds in earnest and all across the board.

(3) Perceptual relativism

The claim that we impose order, rather than discover it, challenges any presumption that perception brings us unvarnished, objective news about the world. The challenge can be starkly put by means of a thesis about language and perception known to anthropologists as the Sapir–Whorf hypothesis:

The 'real world' is to a large extent unconsciously built upon the language habits of the group. The worlds in which different societies live are *distinct* worlds, not merely the same world with different labels attached. We see, hear and otherwise experience very largely as we do because the habits of our community predispose certain choices of interpretation. (Sapir, 1929, p.209, his italics)

We dissect nature along lines laid down by our native languages. The categories and types that we isolate from the world of phenomena we do not find there because they stare every observer in the face; on the contrary, the world is presented in a kaleidoscopic flux of impressions which has to be organised by our minds – and this means largely by the linguistic systems in our minds. (Whorf, 1954, p.213)

We met this theme earlier as a component of Peter Winch's contention that 'reality has no key' (p.156) and of Thomas Kuhn's claim that, when paradigms shift, scientists enter a different world (p.84). If it is right, the 'bridgehead' argument founders because overlapping perceptions of everyday objects cannot be taken for granted.

(4) Relativism of truth

The most radical form of relativism denies that there is anything necessarily universal even about logic. As Winch puts it: 'The criteria of logic are not a direct gift from God but arise out of and are only intelligible in the context of ways of living and modes of social life' (1958, p.100). If the rules of thought which set limits to what it is possible to believe are themselves mutable, then nothing whatever about other cultures can be known *a priori*. Perhaps the Azande did not perceive the contradiction in their thought because, by their own criteria of logic, there was no contradiction.

In that case the task of interpretation includes discovering what the local rules of coherent thought in fact are in any particular culture. If we regard our basic notions of negation, of non-contradiction and of inference from 'P' and 'if P, then Q' to 'Q' as, so to speak, the citadel of coherent thought, then a relativist victory here takes all other logical and quasi-logical relations with it. Believing one proposition would no longer automatically be a reason of any sort for believing another. Whether someone's web of belief had any particular connections between one belief and another would become wholly an empirical question.

LIMITS TO RELATIVISM?

It is rare to find a relativist who embraces all of these forms together. For instance, the Marxist thesis that ideologies are relative to economic structures carries no suggestion that economic structures are anything other than real foundations which an objective social science can discern. Similarly, when Winch remarks that the criteria of logic are not a direct gift from God, he adds that they are nevertheless intelligible in their own mode of social life. This suggests, at first sight, that we have an access to modes of social life and one prior to identifying the local criteria of logic.

Yet Winch also maintains that social worlds make sense only from within and that, in general, 'reality has no key'. This commits him to a wider and indeed full-blooded relativism. 'Forms of life' include rules of classification governing what counts as real and rules of reasoning governing what counts as rational in belief and action. (See also Winch (1964).) Critics can now object, however, that he has landed the understanding of other cultures with a vicious circle. To discover the rules governing thought among the Azande, we need to know that they take witchcraft for real; to discover this, we need to know some of their words for everyday objects; to discover these words, we need to know the rules governing thought among the Azande. Neither perception nor logic can break the circle, because both are internal to the form of life which we are trying to penetrate. To put it simply, we need to know what is locally rational before we can know what is locally real; and we need to know what is locally real before we can know what is locally rational.

This is a version of what is known as 'the hermeneutic circle'. The threat of a circle stems from the hermeneutic imperative itself. In understanding a social world from within, we might be inclined to reject interpretations which would saddle the society with irrational beliefs. But we are aware that beliefs which *we* regard as irrational may be entirely rational from within. So we are also inclined to accept bizarre beliefs and to identify the local criteria of rationality by the test of whether they make otherwise bizarre beliefs rational. That sounds a good way to proceed, even if circular. But it threatens every attempt to justify one interpretation over another. All interpretations become defensible but at the price that none is more justifiable than the rest. If this is indeed the upshot, the circle turns vicious and the hermeneutic imperative to understand from within leads to disaster.

FOUR WAYS OF ESCAPE

If a complete relativism leads to a vicious circle, we might be tempted to reject the hermeneutic imperative itself. But that would be to abandon a search for adequacy at the level of meaning as a first and distinct exercise. So, presumably the trouble has arisen not from the root idea that the world must be understood from within but in the course of applying it. One notices that a 'principle of charity', as it has been called, is at work. This principle bids us assume that other minds and other cultures are rational in their ordering of experience, and seems to imply that we should reject interpretations which would make them out to be irrational.

That sounds like good advice, especially if it stops us being ethnocentric about the superiority of Western rationality. But, if it is leading us to be so charitable that we cannot justify one interpretation over another, something has gone amiss. Here are four possible escapes.

(1) The first, and least constricting for relativism, is to remind ourselves that understanding is piecemeal. The circle which looks so dauntingly vicious when boldly drawn is an abstraction from a series of small advances, each of them made on a balance of advantage. The interpreter must go slowly, always ready to correct a promising translation, if it generates a case for its own amendment. Rough, conjectural interpretation leads piecemeal to more exact interpretation. By all means start with a 'bridgehead'; but realise that it too is only a conjecture and be willing to revise some or all of it as necessary, one small step at a time.

That too is attractive advice. But it seems to me to presuppose what it denies. Can even a small step be taken, if one seriously supposes that the world being explored might turn out in the end to have nothing in common with one's own? Conversely, if amendments depend on a balance of advantage, they also depend on there being enough in common to draw up the balance. Otherwise there would be no warrant for ruling out conjectures so bold that they cancel all previous interpretations. The principle of charity is to be read not as granting that anyone might believe anything but as maintaining that some rational beliefs are held by everyone. Local variation needs to have its limits.

(2) Then what are they? A second escape is to exempt the natural world, and hence the natural sciences, from the attempt to internalise all cognitive activity to forms of life: when it rains, relativists get as wet as anyone else; one cannot keep dry by changing one's vocabulary. This escape limits the scope of perceptual relativism by insisting that there is an external world which stands outside our perceptual constructions. That suggests substituting some form of realism, for instance a causal theory of perception to ground perceptual judgements in facts of the world which cause those judgements. It may be possible to limit perceptual relativism, while still accepting that observation is always theory-laden. Perhaps we can accept that 'percepts without concepts are blind' without thereby making nature internal to culture. Thus, contrary to Sapir, all human beings inhabit the same world with different labels attached.

This too is attractive. But I doubt if it covers enough of the ground to settle arguments about understanding social practices which are not directly addressed to the natural world. It does not touch Evans-Pritchard's problem of relating Zande beliefs about the unseen world of witchcraft to the local ontology of witches, oracles and magical powers. This ontology is internal to the conceptual scheme, even if the Azande would deny it. Yet the practices which go with it are objective social facts, along with the power structure of Zande society. Such facts are no less real for depending on their legitimacy in the minds of those enmeshed in them. Nor are they less real because they would elude a visiting Martian.

(3) A third escape is by way of a two-step sociology of knowledge which bids us understand the web of belief from within and then anchor it in a structure of social institutions external to it. Witchcraft, oracles and magic are social practices. To understand them, we need a coherent set of beliefs about the unseen world; then, to explain them, we need a functional account of the structure of power among the Azande. Presumably the power structure can be described without mentioning beliefs about witches. Thus conceptual relativism is right about the relativity of conceptual schemes, but only in so far as it makes them relative to structures distinct from conceptual schemes.

Here the water becomes too deep for this book. The line has strong attractions for a naturalist who wants to grant social facts a reality distinct both from ideas in minds and from physical forces in the material world. But it needs to be defended on both fronts in ways too complex for present discussion. Let me just say that I am not persuaded by the dissection of social life into beliefs and social structures. Beliefs do not float in thin air and structures are animated by self-conscious actors. Since role-players make the social world go round, it should be a mistake to separate what they contrive to fuse. Meanwhile, this third line does nothing about the arbitrariness introduced by allowing local variation in the most basic criteria for rational belief.

(4) A fourth escape, accordingly, reasserts that there are some universals of coherent thought. In Peter Strawson's words:

there is a massive central core of human thinking which has no history – or none recorded in histories of thought; there are categories and concepts which, in their most fundamental character, change not at all. Obviously these are not the specialities of the most refined thinking. They are the commonplaces of the least refined thinking; and yet are the indispensable core of the conceptual equipment of the most sophisticated human beings. (1959, p.10)

If there is indeed such a 'massive central core', then it can and indeed must be presupposed by any enquirer and putative interpretations can be rejected if they depart from it. What this core actually contains is no doubt a matter for long argument. But its existence would set crucial limits to what falls within the scope of empirical enquiry, thus underwriting the 'bridgehead' argument. The criteria of logic may or may not be a direct gift from God, but, as an indispensable piece of conceptual equipment, they are presupposed by any attempt to make coherent sense of modes of social life.

To take one or more of these escapes is to uphold rationality against relativism. But the four together also serve to emphasise that there is scarcely less room for dispute about the character of rationality as about the varieties of relativism; and this is as far as we can take matters here.

CONCLUSION

In this web of belief every strand depends on every other strand and a Zande cannot get out of its meshes because it is the only world he knows. The web is not an external structure in which he is enclosed. It is the texture of his thought and he cannot think that his thought is wrong.

What have we learnt about adequacy at the level of meaning, how it relates to adequacy at the causal level and whether it can be saved from vicious circularity? To summarise the chapter, here are some final comments on Evans-Pritchard's image of the web. They should be treated with caution, as they reflect my own views on a troubled topic.

(1) The web may be the Zande's only world but he can, in theory at least, escape its meshes. It cannot be true that every culture is utterly enclosed. Otherwise a visiting anthropologist could not have traced the strands and described them in another language. Translation presupposes shared concepts applied in the same way to shared experience. I take this to be a formal condition *a priori* of anyone's knowing that 'x' in $L(1)$ means the same as 'y' in $L(2)$. This leaves plenty of scope for argument about what exactly is presupposed and it certainly allows for rich cultural

diversity. But it usefully denies that the ideal tool of understanding is, so to speak, the one-way mirror (or telescope for historians). Understanding *starts* from within, by assuming a common humanity. That entrances are also exits is an important element in cultural change.

(2) The Zande can, therefore, think that his thought is wrong. Perhaps he, like we, cannot accommodate too abrupt a change; and, if the 'bridgehead' argument is right, some beliefs are immune to revision. But reflection, prompted by discordant experience or conceptual discrepancies, can reweave the web a little at a time. Revisions can even sum to what, with hindsight, may be deemed a paradigm shift. The web is not an external structure; but nor is it static. Adequacy at the level of meaning needs to capture its directions of movement.

(3) Nevertheless, in a different sense, the Zande cannot think that his thought is wrong. 'Reflection can destroy knowledge.' This pleasantly paradoxical remark comes from Bernard Williams' *Ethics and the Limits of Philosophy* (1985, p.148) and makes the point that people's sense of social and moral direction can depend on not asking too many questions. The Homeric hero knew who he was and where he belonged. He knew his way about a world whose roles and norms were sanctioned by the gods and taken largely for granted. When his descendants tried to justify the conceptual and moral foundations of this world, the reasons previously guiding their actions lost their power to guide. By demanding reasons for reasons, reflection can destroy practical knowledge. Similarly among the Azande the King's oracle has to be above suspicion, if their world is to persist. In this sense the Zande cannot think that his thought is wrong. A paradigm shift does not literally usher in a new world but it does require new people and new identities.

(4) Relatedly, there is a question of who 'we' are. The 'bridgehead' argument insists that 'we' are sometimes the whole of humanity. But at other times 'we' are a sub-group. Depending on context, 'we' may be moderns, Westerners, Anglo-Saxons, philosophers, English-speakers and so forth. In opposing

relativism about truth and logic, the argument does not oppose
relativism about what constitutes the identity of different groups.
It does suggest, however, that one should not sunder humanity
into pre-modern, modern and post-modern. Our shared rationality transcends historical context and sets limits to pluralism both
metaphysical and political.

(5) If there is 'a massive central core of human thinking which has
no history', what makes differences of cultural identity possible?
Evans-Pritchard, I think, traces the enclosed identity of the
Azande to their shared possession of 'mystical notions'. That is
a shrewd move, if one wants to maintain the autonomy of meanings and of webs of belief. On the other hand, it creates problems
with the use of rationality as the epistemological key to understanding. If one equates rationality with scientific method and
sound inference, 'mystical notions' are written off as irrational.
Then how are they to be understood from within?

(6) Interestingly, Evans-Pritchard takes a different line in his later
Nuer Religion (1956). Instead of a sharp divide between the scientific and the mystical, he there regards all practices as rational
exercises in making sense of experience. Scientific and religious
thinking remain different in character but both are rational in a
single sense which finally has more to do with attunement with
nature than with mastery and control of it. Thus the Nuer hold a
belief which appears to translate as 'twins are birds'. Evans-
Pritchard treats it, thus translated, not as a piece of mystical
illogicality, nor as an opaque expression of some aspect of social
relations, but as fully intelligible once one knows that twins, like
the birds of the air, are especially favoured by *Kwoth*, the spirit of
the Above.

(7) This might seem to answer the question of how mystical
notions can be understood. But it does so under threat of reinvi-
gorating the hermeneutic circle. Evans-Pritchard blocks the threat
by standing up for truth in religion. *Nuer Religion* ends with these
words:

Though prayer and sacrifice are exterior actions, Nuer religion is ultimately an interior state. The state is externalised in rites which we can

observe, but their meaning depends finally on an awareness of God and that men are dependent on him and must be resigned to his will. At this point the theologian takes over from the anthropologist. (1956, p.322)

The theologian, who has evidently taken over already, is a seeker after truth. But social scientists will hardly grant that one can understand only what, at bottom, one believes to be true. So I offer a less drastic conclusion. The first step towards charting a world from within is to understand what its inhabitants believe. Where one is convinced that a belief is both true and held for good reason, no further step is required. False beliefs which are held for good reason can be understood by relating them to 'bridgehead' beliefs. Bad reasons, however, call for explanation at a causal level, which supplies an external structure to account for them. Rationality thus comes first but relativism then has its turn.

(8) We began with two conflicting lines of thought. One was that, since different peoples inhabit intellectual worlds very unlike our own, the key is to be open-minded. The other was that we could not chart these differences, nor justify a claim to have done so correctly, unless we could rely on Other Minds to be basically as rational as ourselves. I suggest that both lines of thought are right but that the latter takes priority. We can understand why some beliefs which we think irrational are found rational by other people; but only once we have set limits to relativism.

CHAPTER 12

Conclusion: two stories to tell

The problems of structure and action have led us a fine dance. We had hoped for a single key to the problems of structure and action. But the quest for it, as we tried out Systems, Agents, Actors and 'Games' in turn, may have seemed all too like a dance round a maypole erected in the middle of Figure 12.1.

Start the music, as in Chapter 5, by trying the least plausible of the single keys, the claim that social structures are systems which are external and prior to actions and determine them fully. This view is so grossly blind to the scope for human manoeuvre that the dance soon takes us into the bottom left quadrant, where the 'Agents' of Rational Choice theory and Game Theory make the action and perhaps even the structure too. But these agents, with their given preferences and internal computers, are oddly mechanical. Do they not interpret their situation creatively, fashion their preferences and monitor their own performances? If we think so, we are carried on into the bottom right quadrant, where 'Actors' live a more richly textured existence and their

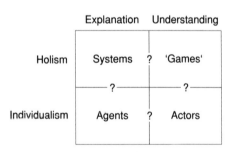

Figure 12.1

248

actions have subjective meaning. But, when we ask how to understand these meanings, we become aware that there are schemes of meaning-rules and normative expectations external to each actor. The dance sweeps on and up into the 'Games' of the top right quadrant, in search of an intersubjective social order. Perhaps this is all we need: an external fabric so thoroughly woven from constitutive rules and regulative rules that it can account for social action in full.

But the dance does not stop there. Even if these 'Games' and 'forms of life' held the key to a social life which *means* nothing beyond itself, they do not exist in a natural vacuum. Are they really self-contained or self-sustaining? They surely vary and evolve in ways affected by natural conditions, material scarcities and the physical state of technology. If these pressures amount to a system which determines the rules, we are back with the 'Systems' of the top left quadrant again, ready for another circuit. Unable to halt with a single factor of the last resort, the dance goes on round again, or, if you prefer, reverses direction. As it progresses round and round the maypole, the ribbons grow shorter and more entwined, each next step becomes easier and we are drawn to a notional central point where everything mediates everything and is mediated by everything in turn.

Some dancers will be exhilarated by this closing in, until Explanation and Understanding, Holism and Individualism have all been embrangled. The result would be an all-embracing social theory where structure is the medium in which action reproduces structure and where this dialectical interplay evolves in a dynamic synthesis. Other dancers, including me, will find the prospect too chaotic to contemplate. Yet all the pure endings, where the dance stops in a single quadrant, have come to seem suspect. Their claims are either merely dogmatic or depend on being so pliant in absorbing recalcitrant elements as to become vacuous. So some combining of elements is wanted, presumably, and the question is what limits to set.

The question marks in Figure 12.1 suggest four plausible combinations. To draw the book together, we shall take them in turn, adding a few suggestive further references, which readers may care to follow up. My own reckoning will be that there is much to be said for trying to mix Individualism with Holism but that Explanation and Understanding do not combine as readily. Hence there will still be two stories to tell at the end. Since not everyone will agree with them, the quick-fire remarks which now follow are to be treated with caution.

We should distinguish adding from blending. It is one thing for two countries to form an alliance and another for them to merge. In general, alliances are easier, provided that the elements do not conflict, but mergers are more exciting. Recall the level-of-analysis problem, with its several layers on which one can ask whether the system determines the units or, on the contrary, the units determine the system. If one rejects both pure alternatives, for instance because where you stand depends partly but not wholly on where you sit, there are two lines. One is to argue that bureaucracies behave as determined both by how they are organised and by who works for them, these being independent factors. The other is to argue that bureaucratic role-play displays an inextricable blend of structure and action. The second line is more exciting, but also trickier, because a freshly blended account of social agency is then needed. Yet the first has its problems too, when we ask what governs the interaction between bureaucracies and persons.

COMBINING INDIVIDUALISM AND HOLISM

(1) Systems and Agents?

The rational agents of Rational Choice theory and Game Theory (Chapter 6) are set within a natural environment. In so far as that means physical geography, it is no threat to their social importance. But in so far as it includes market forces and the laws of supply and demand, and we regard these as social facts, the agents alone are not the whole story. The usual view, I think, is that the agents retain their independence. But, while they remain mechanical calculators with given preferences, their independence is at least threatened by external accounts of how their preferences are determined.

The threat proved awkward for individualism, when we discussed it earlier. Here is another attempt to block it, while keeping structure and action distinct. George Homans' (1964) article 'Bringing Men Back In' was written to counter the fiercely structural sociology which was then in fashion. Homans argued that structural social explanations could get nowhere without the help of psychological propositions like these:

> Men are more likely to perform an activity, the more valuable they perceive that activity to be.
> Men are more likely to perform an activity, the more successful they perceive that activity to be in getting that reward.

So indispensable are they, he added, that 'I now suspect that there are no general sociological propositions, propositions that hold good of all societies or social groups as such, and that the only general propositions of sociology are in fact psychological'. Yes, but the examples offered look uncommonly like tautologies and certainly invite questions about what governs men's perceptions of value and prospective success. The men brought back in must somehow escape being mere links in a social progression from one structural state to the next.

Homans' version of psychology was Rational Choice theory in a strongly behavioural form, where agents' preferences are to be inferred from the pattern of their choices. When we considered this version earlier, we saw no way to resist a straight win for holism, if agents were thus treated as computers plugged into a social system. So we tried to block the threat by making rational agents more reflective and less the victims of their preferences, thus hoping to cast light on the problem of accounting for norms too. But this took us into the realm of Understanding. Yet no general conclusion follows here, because Rational Choice theory is not the only form of explanatory individualism. We could have looked to psychology for other forms or to the philosophy of mind and of language for further analyses of the concept of action. The book has not proved generally that there is no explanatory and independent form of individualism, even if Rational Choice theory is a leading contender and one whose limitations are of particular significance for the social sciences.

Meanwhile, if Systems and Agents make uneasy allies, perhaps there is a way to blend them. An indirect strategy would be to wrest the concept of role-play from the clutches of Understanding by giving it a causal analysis. But that raises ultimate questions about the final relation between explaining and understanding. More immediately, it would be curious if there were no position represented by the question mark in the left-hand column. Indeed David-Hillel Ruben gives a strong argument for such a position in *The Metaphysics of the Social World* (1985). Writing firmly as a naturalist, he argues that the relation between individuals and social groups is not that between parts and wholes. If something is a part of a part of a whole, then it is itself a part of that whole. But human individuals are members of groups; and a member of a member of a social whole need not be a member of that whole. Thus M. Rouget is a member of the French nation and France is a member of the United Nations, but M. Rouget is not a member of the United Nations. Ruben's book is a defence of holism in social philosophy. But, since it does not try to reduce individuals to their social properties, I take it to argue that we are essentially members of groups in a sense which satisfies the question mark. Whether this can be done within a naturalist framework, however, then becomes a further crux.

(2) 'Games' and Actors

When we shift attention to Understanding, it becomes easier to blend individualism with holism than to make them independent allies. Social wholes, being intersubjective, cannot exist without social actors. Conversely, even a pure self needs to show itself in social relations, if the philosophical case for distinguishing personal identity from social identity is accepted. At any rate, the concept of role-play, as treated in Chapter 8, gave us a blend of games and players, and a similar fusion seemed involved in the idea that to follow a rule is, in part, to construct the rule in the course of interpreting it. Normative expectations animate the social world by serving as reasons for action; without such reasons there would be no social world.

I do not pretend that we have plumbed the sense in which Meaning is 'the category which is peculiar to life and to the historical world' at any depth. There remains plenty to perplex us philosophically about meaning and language and, throughout the social sciences, about the implications of a hermeneutic approach. But we have, I hope, found reason to think that, if norms are easier to understand than to explain, it is because hermeneutics makes it easier to see how norms can enable actors to express themselves. The question mark in the Understanding column raises less of a puzzle, except in so far as the Other Minds problem remains as hard as it is fertile.

MIXING EXPLANATION WITH UNDERSTANDING

(3) 'Games' and Systems

Social holists are adamant that there are social facts but, as with Durkheim, are less sure whether to treat them as objective (top left) or intersubjective (top right). We have not tackled this question in earnest, although it can be broached by comparing the idea that 'material productive forces' are the real foundation for 'a legal and political superstructure' (Marx in Chapter 1) with some of the claims made for the dominance of the 'collective consciousness' (Durkheim in Chapter 5). If we have not got further, it may be because we have said so little about power. But it is too late in the book to begin contrasting natural power, which, in Mao's phrase, grows out of the barrel of a gun, with social power, which works by controlling how interests are articulated or even perceived by those over whom it is exercised. So let me simply commend Steven Lukes' (1974) book as a fine start on this major topic.

In general, coexistence between our two ways of conceiving of social facts looks difficult. Earlier we tried negotiating a truce between naturalism and hermeneutics by agreeing that the social world needs to be seen from within as a first step. But the truce did not extend very far. Naturalists wait patiently while hermeneutics reconstructs the social world from within by identifying the rules which constitute and regulate it. They then set about explaining why institutions take whatever form they do at particular historical moments. The hermeneutic camp seems bound to retort that such explanations themselves rely on further social facts of an intersubjective sort; and hence that these explanatory items also belong to the world constructed from within by its inhabitants and so need understanding too. The truce soon collapses.

This dispute can also be conducted at a more abstract level as one about the very possibility of naturalism. We have been thinking of naturalism both as an ontological thesis about the independent and objective character of the world which science investigates, and as a methodological thesis about the unity and objectivity of scientific method. Both theses are vulnerable to hermeneutic attack. If there are no theory-neutral facts, it becomes hard to maintain that the world is independent of the enquirer, at least without adopting a higher-order perspective from which the enquirer can stand back and view a world which includes enquirers at the lower order. But this invites the comment that a God's eye view on a world which includes all of us is beyond our human comprehension. That will not silence naturalists but does make them look to their defences.

The methodological thesis invites the comment that science is a human institution and, like all other institutions, needs to be understood from within. It no doubt includes rules for arriving at objective conclusions; but these rules too are social and the objectivity of the conclusions is internal to the process by which they are reached. This too does not silence naturalists, as we noted in Chapter 11, because it implies so strong a form of relativism that the attack can be met by trying to show that it is self-refuting. I shall not try to take these complexities further now.

On the other hand, we have found one backhanded reason for thinking that the disputants might want to come to terms. They face a common foe. Many institutions have two distinct aspects. For instance, Catholicism can be viewed both as a body of beliefs, which are embodied in its rituals and texts, and as an organised social force in the life of many societies. From the papacy downwards, the offices of the Catholic church have these spiritual and temporal aspects. It might seem that the spiritual aspect operates at the level of meaning and the temporal at the causal level, thus making for dispute among holists about which finally matters more. On reflection, however, and in so far as talk of distinct levels makes sense, both aspects operate at both levels. How? A ready answer is that both come together in the persons of those who occupy the offices. A parish priest, for example, is neither the holder of a powerful social position in his local community, who just happens to subscribe to Catholic beliefs; nor is he a spiritually-minded biped, who just happens to have a particular social flock to care for. His flock have social relations with their father confessor, whose spiritual ministry takes him into the streets and places of temporal power. The social world is the world of social actors in the temple no less than the market.

Holists of both kinds need to unite against this intrusion from below. They retort that the power of the church is not the sum of the abilities of its members. If they can say so with one voice, we shall have a position which satisfies the top question mark. But, as far as I can see, their differences run too deep. The two brands of holism disagree about ontology, methodology and epistemology, with each having more in common with some of the intruders than with the other. I doubt whether more than a temporary alliance is possible, for reasons which will become clearer after a brief comment on the fourth question mark.

(4) Agents and Actors

For philosophers interested in the theory of action, this is likely to be the most tantalising combination. Can we not somehow re-place the 'Rational Fools', as the title of Amartya Sen's challenging (1977) paper dubs them, and populate the social world with persons who judge how to go on by a blend of strategically rational choice, intelligent fulfilling of their roles and an openness to moral concerns? Well, Chapters 8 and 9 did their best to make *homo economicus* human and *homo sociologicus* intelligent. But they also reflected my own reluctant view that a mismatch remains.

There seem still to be two stubborn points of difference, defying hope of a single theory of practical reason.

Firstly, rational agents act in response to their desires and beliefs. They certainly have scope for overhauling their beliefs, so as to remedy logical inconsistencies or lack of evidence. They do it by a process of deliberative rationality, whose importance and character are hidden by the proposition that ideally rational agents have perfect information and a perfect computer. But their desires are what motivate them; and we can do only so much to soften up the idea that rational agents have given preferences. The stubborn core remains that the preferences even of an amended *homo economicus* function ultimately like tastes and must finally be represented by means of forward-looking payoffs. Although the philosophy of mind offers alternative accounts of practical reason which we have not explored, to abandon this core is to discard the model altogether. The price of hanging on to it, however, is that there is no genuine room for reflective self-direction and normative or moral engagement. Role-playing actors fare better on this score. But the theory of practical reason needed for them is incompatible with the previous one. That is stubbornly so, whatever we do about the idea that role-players not only construct their roles while interpreting them but can also stand back, as persons, from all their roles. This idea certainly threatens to drive a wedge between normative and moral engagement, but it does so without letting our 'rational agents' back in either case.

Secondly, therefore, we have two distinct notions of rational reconstruction. One reconstructs action as instrumentally rational choice by a self-contained individual unit, with any normative or expressive elements fed in as influences on the payoffs as perceived by the agent. The other reconstructs action as intelligent obedience to the rules of the game being played, in a sense of 'game' which makes the players no longer self-contained. Relatedly, notice the contrast between the definite singular of 'individual unit' and the uneasy plural of 'players'. The latter, which reflects our inconclusive discussion of whether the intersubjective is prior to the subjective, marks a definite difference between Agents and Actors. But the inconclusiveness again has to do with an unresolved tension between normative and moral engagement to which rational agents are not party.

As with holism, we might wonder whether both sorts of individualist would do well to unite against a threat of intrusion, this time from above. Rational agents are still threatened with structural explanations of their preferences, and rational actors with being absorbed into the practices which they embody. But the two stubborn points of difference seem to me once more to suggest, rather, that each version of individualism has more in common with one sort of holism than with the other sort of individualism.

There remain the two 'diagonal' combinations. Neither appears to me possible. To combine Systems with Actors, we would need to treat social facts both as external, constraining systems and as a sum of subjective meanings which enable the actors' self-definitions. That looks incoherent. There is more scope for trying to combine 'Games' with Agents, for instance so as to solve the problem of norms while leaving Rational Choice theory in good shape. But we tried this earlier without success; and I suggest that it founders for the same reason as that just given for thinking Agents and Actors irreconcilable.

This, if accepted, again puts paid to a grand synthesis at the centre of Figure 12.1, where we planted the maypole at the start of the chapter. Anyone shown Figure 12.1 seems to have an immediate urge to suggest that the truth lies in the very middle, where the dance ends. I do indeed see the attraction. But my view remains that the middle represents a black hole, into which social theories and philosophies vanish without trace.

THEMES AND QUESTIONS

There remain two stories to tell. The stubborn contrast is still that between Explanation and Understanding, with naturalism and hermeneutics still in dispute over ontology, methodology and epistemology. Let us gather in the themes of the book accordingly.

The rival ontological stories concern the social world and its inhabitants. Both stories can agree that it is constructed by a process which shapes social actions or is shaped by them. It is, in some sense, an artifice and the crux is in what sense. Naturalists

will typically have in mind the sort of evolutionary process whereby bees and beehives interact to modify hives and even bees over
time. Humans are, of course, far more complex than bees and,
since even systemic pressures work through the desires and beliefs
of agents, call for a complex psychology. Since this psychology
cannot avoid tangling with questions of the relation between
thought and language, it will need to be very sophisticated indeed, unless there is a neat short cut, like Rational Choice theory.
In the end, however, 'Nature has used only one and the same
dough, in which she has merely varied the leaven'. The final story
is one about how social life belongs to the natural world, viewed
with a spectator's detachment.

An ontology suited to hermeneutics construes the idea that the
social world is an artifice differently. It is an artifice constructed
from meanings. In some versions, these meanings are so commu-
nal that they almost have a life of their own, which takes shape as
the rhythms of history unfold. We have explored nothing so
grand; but we have tried the idea that institutions and practices
are governed by 'forms of life' about which nothing further can be
said. Other versions make us, individually or collectively, our own
sovereign artificers, the makers of our own lives in our own social
world. In that case, nature has not used only one and the same
dough, since human life and the historical world are radically
peculiar.

Methodologically, both stories can open with a chapter on how
to understand action from within. But they soon part company.
At some point naturalists will either introduce an explanatory
causal narrative or insist that this is really what has been offered
all along. Those pressing for a fully hermeneutic story will resist
both moves. There is no easy way to umpire this dispute, not least
because there is no agreed naturalistic account of causal explanation. If our earlier strictures on the methodology of Positive
science are granted, there remain broadly two very different
ways to go. One is to pursue the implications of accepting that
there are no theory-free facts. That leads either into pragmatism
and what was said in Chapter 4 or perhaps into psychological
accounts, which we have not examined, of why we find certain
sorts of causal narrative persuasive. The other is to hold out for

realism and a scientific method which lets us infer from phenomena as we interpret them to hidden causes which would explain them. The umpire can comment only that, faced with such divergence, social scientists are welcome to proceed unencumbered by an established canon.

We used this licence to explore different ideas of rational reconstruction, starting with the clear and competing ideas offered by Rational Choice theory and by an analysis of action as rule-following. But we then spoilt the crispness of the contrast by trying to temper each in turn with reflective, self-monitoring actors. That leaves plenty to think about, philosophically as much as methodologically. In particular, which analysis of conventions and how they relate to reasons for action offers most? What account of practical reason can best connect strategic choice, normative expectations and individual judgement?

Epistemologically, there is still far to go. Positive science can at least call on an empiricist theory of knowledge, resting on foundations laid in direct experience, so that hypotheses can be judged by the test of observation. What happens, if we abandon traditional belief in foundations of knowledge, is unclear. As treated here, realists are so far left looking inexcusably dogmatic and pragmatists alarmingly pliant. Meanwhile, hermeneutic approaches are still struggling to show that rational reconstruction offers an epistemologically defensible way with the problem of Other Minds and an escape from hermeneutic circles.

This may all sound like an open invitation to relativism. We seem left only with narratives, causal or interpretative, which belong to local, historically particular discourses and defy all prospect of finding a meta-narrative to judge them by. But that is not the upshot intended. Chapter 11 was meant to show that this outcome is a disaster resulting from a form of relativism which is self-defeating. In that case, the proper conclusion is that epistemology has to go the long way round, visiting arguments about the historical particularity of all ways of searching into and discovering truth but then returning with renewed determination to transcendental questions of how knowledge is possible.

Meanwhile, here are four summarising questions loosely prompted by the question marks in Figure 12.1:

Can the players of the games of social life be seen consistently
both as followers of rules and as makers of choices?

Shall we adopt a theory of practical reason in which reasons for
action are causes of action?

In making sense of social facts, do we need concepts prior to all
psychology and/or alien to natural science?

Is there a form of determinism which the social sciences do well
to accept?

Finally, I wonder whether Condorcet was right in saying that
'truth, virtue and happiness are bound together with an indissoluble chain'. Some of the links have been made. Naturalists will
comment that knowledge of nature, including the human and
social parts of nature, brings us the power of mastery and control. Although most will add that knowledge is ethically neutral,
there are those who argue for objectivity in ethics and a link
between self-knowledge and virtue. On the other side of the
house, understanding and the power to shape lives are bound
together in the rules which constitute and regulate the life of
societies. Many people will add that normative expectations
have nothing to do with moral duties. But that may be to under-
rate 'the ethics of authenticity', to cite the title of Charles Taylor's
enlightening (1991) book, as a theme for the social sciences, as for
modern life at large; and I do not despair of a notion of autonomy
which links the good life, the free citizen and the norms of a just
society.

If there is such final wisdom to be had, this book has not
achieved it. It has been a much more modest expedition, whose
spirit is well caught by T. S. Eliot in 'Little Gidding':

> We shall not cease from exploration
> And the end of all our exploring
> Will be to arrive where we started
> And know the place for the first time.

Bibliography

Allison, G. 1971. *Essence of Decision.* Boston: Little, Brown.

Ayer, A. J. 1936. *Language, Truth and Logic.* London: Gollancz.

Bacon, F. 1620. *First Book of Aphorisms.* In J. Spedding *et al.*, eds., *The Great Instauration,* London, 1857–59.

Barnes, B. and Bloor, D. 1982. 'Relativism, Rationalism and the Sociology of Knowledge.' In Hollis and Lukes, eds., 1982.

Berger, P. 1963. *Invitation to Sociology.* Harmondsworth: Penguin Books.

Beveridge, W. H. 1942. *Social Insurance and Allied Services.* London: HMSO (Cmnd 6404).

Bloor, D. 1976. *Knowledge and Social Imagery.* London: Routledge and Kegan Paul.

Condorcet, M. de. 1795. *Sketch for a Historical Picture of Progress of the Human Mind.* Trans. J. Barraclough. London: Noonday Press.

Davidson, D. 1984. 'On the Very Idea of a Conceptual Scheme.' In *Inquiries into Truth and Interpretation.* Oxford University Press.

Descartes, R. 1637. *Discourse on the Method.* In E. Haldane and G. Ross, eds., *Philosophical Works of Descartes.* Cambridge University Press, 1911.

  1641. *Meditations on First Philosophy.* In E. Haldane and G. Ross, eds., *Philosophical Works of Descartes.* Cambridge University Press, 1911.

  1644. *The Principles of Philosophy.* In E. Haldane and G. Ross, eds., *Philosophical Works of Descartes.* Cambridge University Press, 1911.

Dilthey, W. 1926. *Gesammelte Werke,* ed. B. Groethuysen. Stuttgart: Teubner Verlag.

Durkheim, E. 1895. *The Rules of Sociological Method.* New York: The Free Press, 1964.

  1897. *Suicide: A Study in Sociology.* London: Routledge and Kegan Paul, 1952.

  1898. 'Individualism and the Intellectuals', trans. S. and J. Lukes. *Political Studies,* vol. 17, pp. 14-30.

261

1912. *The Elementary Forms of the Religious Life*. London: George Allen and Unwin, 1915.

Edgeworth, F. Y. 1881. *Mathematical Psychics*. London: Kegan Paul.

Elster, J. 1989(a). *Nuts and Bolts for the Social Sciences*. Cambridge University Press.

    1989(b). *The Cement of Society: Studies in Rationality and Social Change*. Cambridge University Press.

Evans-Pritchard, E. E. 1937. *Witchcraft, Oracles and Magic among the Azande*. Oxford: Clarendon Press.

    1956. *Nuer Religion*. Oxford University Press.

Feyerabend, P. 1975. *Against Method*. London: New Left Books.

Fontenelle, B. de 1686. *The Plurality of Worlds*, trans. (1688) J. Glanvill. London: Nonsuch Press, 1929.

Frankfurt, H. 1971. 'Freedom of the Will and the Concept of a Person.' *Journal of Philosophy*, vol.68.

Friedman, M. 1953. 'The Methodology of Positive Economics.' In *Essays in Positive Economics*. University of Chicago Press.

Gauthier, D. 1986. *Morals by Agreement*. Oxford University Press.

Giddens, A. 1979. *Central Problems in Social Theory*. London: Macmillan.

Hahn, F. 1980. *Money and Inflation*. Oxford: Basil Blackwell.

Hahn, F. and Hollis, M., eds. 1979. *Philosophy and Economic Theory*. Oxford University Press.

Hargreaves Heap, S. 1989. *Rationality in Economics*. Oxford: Basil Blackwell.

Hargreaves Heap, S., Hollis, M., Lyons, B., Sugden, R., Weale, A. 1992. *The Theory of Choice: A Critical Guide*. Oxford: Basil Blackwell.

Harsanyi, J. 1955. 'Cardinal Welfare, Individualistic Ethics and Interpersonal Comparisons of Utility.' *Journal of Political Economy*, vol.63.

Hobbes, T. 1651. *Leviathan*, ed. J. Plamenatz, London: Fontana, 1962; ed. R. Tuck. Cambridge University Press, 1991.

Hollis, M. 1968. 'Reason and Ritual.' *Philosophy* pp. 231–47. Reprinted in B. Wilson, ed., 1971, and A. Ryan, ed., 1975.

    1988. *The Cunning of Reason*. Cambridge University Press.

Hollis, M. and Lukes, S., eds., 1982. *Rationality and Relativism*. Oxford: Basil Blackwell.

Hollis, M. and Smith, S. 1990. *Explaining and Understanding International Relations*. Oxford: Clarendon Press.

Homans, G. 1964. 'Bringing Men Back In'. *American Sociological Review*, xxix, No. 5, pp. 809–18. Reprinted in A. Ryan, ed. 1975.

Hume, D. 1739. *A Treatise of Human Nature*, ed. L. A. Selby-Bigge. Oxford: Clarendon Press, 1978.

1748. *Enquiries Concerning the Human Understanding*, ed. L. A. Selby-Bigge. Oxford: Clarendon Press, 1975.

James, W. 1890. *The Principles of Psychology*. New York: Dover Books, 1950.

International Labour Office, 1976. *Employment Growth and Basic Needs: a One-World Problem*. Geneva: International Labour Office.

Kant, I. 1781. *The Critique of Pure Reason*, trans. N. Kemp Smith. London: Macmillan, 1929.

1785. *The Groundwork of the Metaphysic of Morals*. Trans. H. J. Paton under the title of *The Moral Law*. London: Hutchinson, 1953.

1788. *The Critique of Practical Reason*. Trans. L. W. Beck. Cambridge University Press, 1949.

Keynes, J. M. 1936. *The General Theory of Employment, Interest and Money*. London: Macmillan.

Kuhn, T. 1970. *The Structure of Scientific Revolutions*, second edition. University of Chicago Press.

Lakatos, I. 1978. *The Methodology of Scientific Research Programmes*. Cambridge University Press.

La Mettrie, J. O. de. 1747. *L'Homme machine*. Trans. G. A. Bussey, under the title of *Man a Machine*. La Salle: Open Court, 1912.

Lewis, D. 1969. *Convention: A Philosophical Study*. Cambridge, Mass.: Harvard University Press.

Lipsey, R. E. 1963. *Introduction to Positive Economics*. London and New York: Harper and Row.

Lukes, S. 1974. *Power: a Radical View*. London: Macmillan.

Marx, K. 1852. *The Eighteenth Brumaire of Louis Napoleon*. In *Karl Marx and Fredrick Engels: Selected Works*, vol. 1. Moscow: Foreign Languages Publishing House, 1962.

1859. Preface to *A Contribution to the Critique of Political Economy*. In T. B. Bottomore and M. Rubel, eds., *Karl Marx: Selected Writings in Sociology and Social Philosophy*. London: Penguin Books, 1963.

Mill, J. S. 1843. *A System of Logic*. London: J. W. Parker. (Book VI, edited by A. J. Ayer, London: Duckworth, 1988).

1859. *On Liberty*, ed. M. Warnock. London: Fontana, 1962.

1863. *Utilitarianism*, ed. M. Warnock. London: Fontana, 1962.

Nietzsche, F. 1887. *The Genealogy of Morals*. New York: Doubleday, 1956.

Parsons, T. 1951. *The Social System*. Chicago: The Free Press.

Popper, K. 1945. *The Open Society and its Enemies*. London: Routledge and Kegan Paul.

1959. *The Logic of Scientific Discovery*. London: Hutchinson.

1960. *The Poverty of Historicism*. London: Routledge and Kegan Paul.

1969. *Conjectures and Refutations*. London: Routledge and Kegan Paul.

1972. *Objective Knowledge*. Oxford University Press.

Przeworski, A. and Teune, H. 1970. *The Logic of Comparative Social Inquiry.* New York: Wiley and Sons.

Quine, W. v. O. 1953. 'Two Dogmas of Empiricism'. In *From a Logical Point of View.* Harvard University Press, 1961.

Rawls, J. 1971. *A Theory of Justice.* Oxford University Press.
    1993. *Political Liberalism.* New York: Columbia University Press.

Robbins, L. 1932. *An Essay on the Nature and Significance of Economic Science.* London: Macmillan.

Rorty, R. 1987. 'Non-Reductive Physicalism.' In K. Cramer, ed., *Theorie der Subjectivität.* Frankfurt: Suhrkamp, pp. 278–96.

Rowntree, B. S. 1901. *Poverty: a Study of Town Life.* London: Macmillan.

Ruben, D-H. 1985. *The Metaphysics of the Social World.* London: Routledge and Kegan Paul.

Ryan, A. ed. 1975. *The Philosophy of Social Explanation.* Oxford University Press.

Samuelson, P. 1963. 'Problems of Methodology – A Discussion.' *American Economic Review*, vol. 52, pp. 232–36.
    1964. 'Theory and Realism – A Reply'. *American Economic Review*, vol. 54, pp. 736–40.

Sapir, E. 1929. 'The Status of Linguistics as a Science.' *Language*, vol. 5.

Schelling, T. C. 1960. *The Strategy of Conflict.* Cambridge, Mass: Harvard University Press.

Sen, A. K. 1977. 'Rational Fools.' *Philosophy and Public Affairs*, 6, pp. 317–44. Reprinted in Hahn, F. and Hollis, M. eds., 1979 and in Sen, 1982.
    1982. *Choice, Welfare and Measurement.* Oxford: Basil Blackwell.

Singer, D. 1961. 'The Level-of-Analysis Problem in International Relations.' In K. Knorr and S. Verba, eds., *The International System: Theoretical Essays.* Princeton University Press, pp. 77-92.

Strawson, P. F. 1959. *Individuals: An Essay in Descriptive Metaphysics.* London: Methuen.

Taylor, C. 1964. *The Explanation of Behaviour.* London: Routledge and Kegan Paul.
    1991. *The Ethics of Authenticity.* Cambridge, Mass.: Harvard University Press.

Townsend, P. 1979. *Poverty in the United Kingdom.* London: Allen Lane.

Wallace, W. ed. 1969. *Sociological Theory.* London: Heinemann.

Weber, M. 1904. *The Methodology of the Social Sciences.* Glencoe: Free Press, 1949.
    1922. *Economy and Society: an Outline of Interpretative Sociology.* Berkeley: University of California Press, 1978.

Whorf, B. L. 1954. *Language, Thought and Reality.* Boston: MIT Press and New York: Wiley.

Williams, B. A. O. 1985. *Ethics and the Limits of Philosophy*. London: Fontana Books.

Wilson, B. ed. 1971. *Rationality*. Oxford: Basil Blackwell.

Winch, P. 1958. *The Idea of a Social Science and its Relation to Philosophy*. London: Routledge and Kegan Paul.

1964. 'Understanding a Primitive Society.' *American Philosophical Quarterly*, vol.1, pp. 307–24.

Wittgenstein, L. 1953. *Philosophical Investigations*. Oxford: Basil Blackwell.

Index

266